To Denis O'Driscoll

From Claude Eggertsen.

January 1983

LIBERAL EDUCATION
for
FREE MEN

LIBERAL EDUCATION

for

FREE MEN

By THOMAS WOODY

Philadelphia

UNIVERSITY OF PENNSYLVANIA PRESS

1951

To
Men and Women
Striving for Freedom

ACKNOWLEDGMENTS

MY THANKS are due to many persons, particularly to Dean Emeritus Christian Gauss, Princeton University, and to Dr. James A. Mulhern, University of Pennsylvania, who read the entire manuscript. Dr. Frederick Luehring and Mr. James House, Jr. did me the favor of reading the last chapter; and Dr. Pincus Schub gave me the benefit of his judgment on certain views pertaining to mathematics. Not a few improvements are due to their questions and suggestions. Errors of omission and commission, failures in respect to fact and of judgment are, of course, mine alone. A heavy debt is also due to a galaxy of scholars, whose translations of classics, Eastern and Western, pagan and Christian, have been drawn upon freely. These and their works are cited individually in the appropriate pages, but a general acknowledgment is gladly made to the Loeb Classical Library, formerly published by William Heinemann, London, and now by Harvard University Press; *The Sacred Books of the East,* edited by Max Müller, *The Works of Aristotle,* translated under the editorship of J. A. Smith and W. D. Ross, *The Dialogues of Plato,* translated by B. Jowett, and *Mulcaster's Elementarie,* translated by E. T. Campagnac, published by The Clarendon Press, Oxford; *The Ante-Nicene Fathers,* edited by Alexander Roberts and James Donaldson, and *A Select Library of the Nicene and Post-Nicene Fathers of the Christian Church,* edited by Philip Schaff and Henry Wace, published by The

Christian Literature Company, Buffalo and New York; *The Aims of Education and Other Essays,* by A. N. Whitehead, published by The Macmillan Company, New York; and *The Educational Theory of Jean Jacques Rousseau,* by Wm. Boyd, published by Longmans, Green and Company, London. I am deeply indebted to Wilhelmine L. Woody and Jeanette C. Weiss for generous aid with the manuscript; and to Sonya S. Stern and Mary C. Wiacek for typing the index. My thanks are extended also to Mr. Phelps Soule and others of the University of Pennsylvania Press for numerous courtesies and expert care throughout the process of production.

T. W.

December 28, 1950

CONTENTS

INTRODUCTION

WHAT is a liberal education? To this question numerous answers are given. Most of them appear to be efforts to recover past ideals: some reflect an early American concept of education; others call to mind Renaissance and Medieval modes. One moment, the worldly gentleman-scholar is on parade; the next, an ascetic monkish ideal is presented as the pattern of liberal learning; again, Greek education is regarded as the master form. Whether Chinese, Hindus, Egyptians, or other Orientals knew aught of liberal education is left unsaid. Is liberal education only a Western concept? Was Macaulay right in imposing an English pattern of education in India, on the ground that she had no liberal culture of her own?

Are all, any, or none of these past patterns valid for today? One varies so much from another that a disinterested observer from Mars might well wonder whether the concept of liberal education has any general validity. If, in his perplexity, he continued his quest by asking for a definition of liberal education, the Martian's confusion would scarcely be diminished. Liberal education, he would discover, has been variously defined, often in conflicting terms: generous, rather than restricted; universal rather than provincial; befitting free men; fit to make men free; an education suitable to men; an education which men and women should share alike; a discipline of the mental faculties; a harmonious development of mind

1

and body; a cultural education; knowledge for its own sake; classical rather than scientific learning; reading a few Great Books rather than many modern ones; education in the arts and sciences; "liberal" arts rather than "illiberal"; education for leisure rather than for occupations; general rather than specialized, professional education.

And yet, certain professions have been called liberal. Were they always so? How did they acquire liberal status? Are the terms incongruous? Was that status attributed to them because their respective bodies of knowledge were reduced to scientific principles, hence generally valid; was it by virtue of the education that was necessary to enter them, or because free men assumed their duties; was it due to their being less lucrative than others, or the fact that those who engaged in them had independent means of maintenance and did not have to charge fees? Advocates in Rome looked askance at fees but did not object to the principle that "one good turn deserves another." Cicero thought medicine an honorable profession for slaves or freedmen. But Varro reckoned medicine among the liberal arts. According to Pliny, few Roman citizens took up medical practice. If Galen had been able to require men to study philosophy before essaying to become doctors, as he himself had done, would he thereby have made medicine a liberal profession and elevated it in public estimation? Do breadth and depth of studies make a profession liberal, or is that a derivative of the social status of its practitioners? If a profession be at first illiberal, due to the unfree status of its practitioners, does increasing comprehensiveness and thoroughness of knowledge at last break down social barriers and confer the title, liberal?

The variant, conflicting patterns and definitions of liberal education, which clearly cannot *all* be valid now, though in some time and place each may have been so, inevitably suggest the desirability of an evolutionary view of the matter, to discover the locus and conditions of its origin or origins, its sociopolitical implications, its modes and purposes, its changing features, its enduring elements, what it borrows from the social scene and what it owes to the aspirations of man. It seems highly important that these and related matters, the changing and the permanent elements, be kept clearly before us, as we seek today for a valid formulation of the pattern of liberal education for free men. The final chapter focuses past experience, with its limitations, and the impact of social change upon this problem.

CHAPTER ONE

CHINESE MODES

OF

LIBERAL LEARNING

WESTERN patterns of liberal education have varied so vastly from time to time that the range scarcely requires any expansion to cover an ancient mode which once flourished in the Celestial Empire. A sketch of it may serve to call attention to the universal preoccupation with ideals of education, in the East as well as in the West, the similarities which tend to unite them, and the differences which set off the Oriental pattern from the Occidental.

Lacking precise knowledge of their early history, the Chinese generalized certain traditions about it, very much as the Greeks and Romans did about their own. Huang Ti (2704-2595 B.C.), according to story, led his people into China from the dry highlands of Central Asia, penetrating the Yellow River valley where, after some centuries, the ancient capital of Yao was established.

In the "highest antiquity," says *Li Ki*, men had no houses but dwelt in nests and caves. Knowing nothing of fire, flax, and oil, they subsisted on vegetation and wild flesh. Later, men learned to use fire, mold metal, and work clay. Agriculture replaced hunting; oxen and horses were yoked to cart and chariot. Bows, arrows, mortar and pestle were invented, and silk culture was initiated. Knotted cords gave way to written characters. Ts'ang Kie, historian under Huang Ti, the story ran, invented more than five hundred hieroglyphs. As early as 2432 B.C., according to certain authors, schools were instituted. These dates may mean little more than those assigned by legend to the sack of Troy and the miraculous founding of Rome. But, though they may not be taken seriously, archaeological evidence shows the existence of writing before the Chou dynasty, 1122 B.C. Then, in any case, an essential step had been taken toward an extension of man's mind.

The ancient economy of China was a feudalism in which agriculture had made considerable progress and acquired respectability. The Son of Heaven, at the head of government, had his "field of a thousand acres," which, says *Li Ki*, he tilled himself—naturally with tenant farmers. The subject princes ruled their states, large or small, in which each had his "hundred acres." In the hierarchy of functional classes, scholars stood above farmers, workers, merchants, and soldiers.

The status of women was one of continuous subjection to father, older brother, husband, or son. "If the wife does not serve her husband, the rules of propriety will be destroyed." A hen "crowing at dawn brings ruin upon the family." Spheres of men and women were ideally sharply defined: "Men should not speak of what belongs to the inside of the house, nor the women of what belongs to the outside."

Three great religions, Buddhism, Taoism, and Confucianism, developed in China. The first two, with their ascetic leaning, were primarily the hope and solace of the masses, though not exclusively. Confucianism, an aristocratic, intellectual, doctrinaire system, laying emphasis on political and social order, came to be favored by the ruling class. Six hundred years after the birth of its founder, the Confucian cult had gained a fixed place in official schools, and its observance became obligatory on scholars and officials. Confucianism consolidated and preserved a cultural tradition already old, running back at least to the Chou dynasty. This ancient mode, embodied in the classical works of Confucius and his disciples, constituted the chief intellectual content of liberal education for China's officialdom for two thousand years.

Central in the doctrines of Confucianism, which aimed preëminently at propriety, morality, and social order, is the principle of relationships and duties—those of sovereign and subject, father and son, husband and wife, brother and brother, friend and friend. When each understands these relationships and performs the duties pertaining to his own situation, human affairs are in good health. Confucianism has been commonly condemned by Westerners because of its unprogressive character. Certainly, its stress was on conformity. But Western progress has over and over demonstrated its capacity for injuring human beings, whose well-being, happiness, and "good life" are, by general agreement, the primary concern of liberal education. The ideal of "do unto others," familiar to Western ears, was embodied in the Confucian social philosophy: "What a man dislikes in his superiors, let him not display in his treatment of his inferiors; and what he dislikes in his inferiors, let him not display in his service of his superiors. . . ."[1]

Education is a means to social order. Governments are destroyed and new ones established by force, but only by

[1] Müller, F. M. (Ed.): *The Sacred Books of the East*, XXVIII, 419. 50 vols. Clarendon Press: Oxford, 1879-1910. Quoted by permission of the publishers.

education of loyal officials can any government long remain. Therefore, let the wise ruler "employ the able and promote the worthy." *Tao* is the way; but *Tao* is not self-applied; men must know *Tao* and be able to apply it. Men are selfish and look to their own profit, even as water runs downhill. They must be educated, just as one must build a dam to stop water. "If you establish education, evil will vanish; while if you abolish education, evil will grow, and even punishments will not prevent it. . . ."[2]

Right education and social order are rooted in a knowledge of things, as it is written in the *Great Learning:*

Things have their root and their branches; affairs have their end and their beginning. To know what is first and what is last will lead near to what is taught in the Great Learning. The ancients who wished to illustrate illustrious virtue throughout the kingdom, first ordered well their states. Wishing to order well their states, they first regulated their families. Wishing to regulate their families, they first cultivated their persons. Wishing to cultivate their persons, they first rectified their hearts. Wishing to rectify their hearts, they first sought to be sincere in their thoughts. Wishing to be sincere in their thoughts, they first extended to the utmost their knowledge. The extension of knowledge is by the investigation of things. Things being investigated, their knowledge became complete. Their knowledge being complete, their thoughts were sincere. Their thoughts being sincere, their hearts were then rectified. Their hearts being rectified, their persons were cultivated. Their persons being cultivated, their families were regulated. Their families being regulated, their states were rightly governed. Their states being rightly governed, the whole kingdom was made tranquil and happy.[3]

The ideal education of the Chou period emphasized six virtues, six good actions, and six arts. Wisdom, benevolence,

---

[2] Shryock, J. K.: *The Origin and Development of the State Cult of Confucius,* 52. Century Company: New York, 1932.

[3] Müller: *op. cit.,* XXVIII, 411 *f.* Quoted by permission of The Clarendon Press, Oxford.

goodness, righteousness, loyalty, and harmony were the highest virtues. In actions, one must honor parents, be friendly to brothers, cordial to relatives by marriage, be neighborly, trustful, and sympathetic. The six arts were rituals, music, archery, charioteering, writing, and mathematics. Of rituals, music, archery, and charioteering there were five types; of writing, six; while mathematics included nine operations.

According to *Nei Zeh,* young gentlemen of good family were to have the ideal education which prepared them for office. The process began as soon as the child could feed himself. He was to speak clearly and boldly. Numbers and the cardinal points were learned at six. At ten, under a master, he was taught the various types of characters, calculation, conduct, polite conversation, and reading the Tablets. Music, odes, and dancing the *ko* were learned at thirteen. Archery, charioteering, and the *hsiang* came when he was grown up. At twenty, he learned to dance the *ta hsia,* performed certain ceremonies and filial and fraternal duties, and was "capped." At thirty, he married; and at forty he was appointed to office.

As in the Western world in Classic and Renaissance times, Chinese girls seldom participated in the liberal education considered desirable for their brothers. There were exceptions, to be sure, but the statement that "a woman without ability is normal" doubtless expressed the common conception of female capacity. This being the case, girls as a rule learned "woman's work," polite speech, and obedience in the bosom of their families, and for three months before marriage were schooled in the virtues, speech, carriage, and work of wives.

Formal education was derived from certain Chinese books: *Trimetrical Classic, Century of Surnames, Millenary Classic, Odes for Children, Canons of Filial Duty, The Juvenile In-*

structor, The Great Learning, Doctrine of the Mean, Confucian *Analects,* works of Mencius, *Book of Changes, Book of
History, Book of Odes, Book of Rites,* and *Spring and Autumn
Annals.* The first task was to memorize, the next to read the
classics with critical understanding. Finally, the student was
schooled in writing themes on classical patterns. Fidelity to
the thoughts and ancient modes of expression was tested in
public examinations, which, if passed successfully, opened
the way to office.

What did the ancient Chinese balance of mental and physical training imply? Music, archery, and charioteering were
among the six arts, and all were closely interrelated. Archery
and charioteering were of practical value in war, obviously,
but the end sought by the combination of music and dancing
with them was aesthetic and moral rather than narrowly or
solely practical. At a later time, shooting from horseback
supplanted the "archery ceremony" of the Chou period.
Legge says of certain descriptions of archery contests that
they sought "to show the attention paid to archery in ancient
times" and its contribution to moral and general education.
Thus, the *She I, Meaning of the Ceremony of Archery* expounds the philosophy of the contest:

> The archers, in advancing, retiring, and all their movements, were
> required to observe the rules. With minds correct, and straight car-
> riage of the body, they were to hold their bows and arrows skilfully
> and firmly; and when they did so, they might be expected to hit the
> mark. In this way (from their archery) their characters could be seen.

> To regulate the discharging of the arrows, there was—in the case
> of the son of Heaven, the playing of the Zau-yu; in the case of the
> feudal lords, that of the Li-shau; in the case of the dignitaries, the
> Great Officers, that of the Zhai-pin; and in the case of officers, that
> of the Zhai-fan.

> The Zau-yu is expressive of joy that every office is rightly filled;

the Li-shau is expressive of the joy at audiences of the court; the Zhai-pin is expressive of the joy in observing the laws (which have been learned) ; and the Zhai-fan is expressive of the joy in being free from all failures in duty. Therefore the son of Heaven regulated his shooting by keeping in his mind the right feeling of all officers; a feudal prince, by keeping in his mind the times of his appearing before the son of Heaven; a dignitary, being a Great Officer, by keeping in his mind the observing of the laws . . . and an officer, by keeping in his mind that he must not fail in the duties of his office.

In this way, when they clearly understood the meaning of those regulating measures, and were thus able to avoid all failure in their services, they were successful in their undertakings, and their character and conduct were established. When their characters were established, no such evils as oppression and disorder occurred; and when their undertakings were successful, the states were tranquil and happy. Hence it is said that "the archery served to show the completeness of the archer's virtue."

Therefore, anciently, the son of Heaven chose the feudal lords, the dignitaries who were Great Officers, and the officers, from their skill in archery. Archery is specially the business of males, and there were added to it the embellishments of ceremonies and music. Hence among the things which may afford the most complete illustration of ceremonies and music, and the frequent performance of which may serve to establish virtue and good conduct, there is nothing equal to archery: and therefore the ancient kings paid much attention to it.

Therefore, anciently, according to the royal institutes, the feudal princes annually presented the officers who had charge of their tribute to the son of Heaven, who made trial of them in the archery-hall. Those of them whose bodily carriage was in conformity with the rules, and whose shooting was in agreement with the music, and who hit the mark most frequently, were allowed to take part at the sacrifices. When his officers had frequently that privilege, their ruler was congratulated; if they frequently failed to obtain it, he was reprimanded. If a prince were frequently so congratulated, he received an increase to his territory; if he were frequently so reprimanded, part of his territory was taken from him. Hence came the saying, "The archers shoot in the interest of their princes." Thus, in the states, the rulers and their officers devoted themselves to archery, and the practice in connexion with it of the ceremonies and music. But when rulers and officers practice ceremonies and music, never has it been known that such practice led to their banishment or ruin.

*   *   *

To shoot means to draw out to the end, and some say to lodge in the exact point. That drawing out to the end means every one unfolding his own idea; hence, with the mind even-balanced and the body correctly poised, the archer holds his bow and arrow skilfully and firmly. When he so holds them, he will hit the mark. Hence it is said, "The father shoots at the father-mark; the son, at the son-mark; the ruler, at the ruler-mark; the subject, at the subject-mark." Thus the archer shoots at the mark of his ideal self; and so the Great archery of the son of Heaven is called shooting at the mark of the feudal prince. "Shooting at the mark of the feudal prince" was shooting to prove himself a prince. He who hit the mark was permitted to . . . retain his rank as a prince; he who did not hit the mark was not permitted to retain his rank as a prince.

When the son of Heaven was about to sacrifice, the rule was that he should celebrate the archery at the pool, which name suggested the idea of selecting the officers by their shooting. After the archery at the pool came that in the archery hall. Those who hit the mark were permitted to take part in the sacrifice; and those who failed were not permitted to do so. The ruler of those who did not receive the permission was reprimanded, and had part of his territory taken from him. The ruler of those who were permitted was congratulated, and received an addition to his territory. The advancement appeared in the rank; the disapprobation, in the loss of territory.

*   *   *

Archery suggests to us the way of benevolence. The archer seeks to be correct in himself, and then discharges his arrow. If it miss the mark, he is not angry with the one who has surpassed himself, but turns round and seeks for the cause of failure in himself. . . .

Confucius said, "How difficult it is to shoot! How difficult it is to listen to the music! To shoot exactly in harmony with the note given by the music, and to shoot without missing the bull's-eye on the target:—it is only the archer of superior virtue who can do this! How shall a man of inferior character be able to hit the mark?"[4]

Dancing, too, was an important element in the old Chinese pattern of liberal education. The *ko, hsiang,* and the *ta hsia* marked the boy's progress from youth to maturity. According to an ancient saying, one judged a king by the condition of dancing in his realm. Six types of dancing, all having religious significance originally and being performed in harmony with music and recitation, were recognized in the Chou period: "split-feather dance," associated with exorcism; "whole-feather dance," worship; "regulating dance," against drought; "tail dance," symbolizing agriculture; "shield dance," portraying defensive action; "battle-axe dance," representing readiness for attack. A seventh, "humanity dance," was later added. With the decline of the old pattern of liberal education and the advent of exclusive emphasis on literary studies, dancing ceased to be part of the scholar's general education.

The ancient philosophy of dancing and of music reveals their interdependence and relation to social order. The steps, postures, rhythmic swaying and whirling of the body, and movements of the arms benefit and give pleasure to the body; the music of instruments and the modulations of the voice are conducive to harmony of soul. One is external, the other internal; each is influenced by the other. Music and ceremonies were established to promote good government. *Yo Ki* explains that kings provided for ". . . ceremonies to direct men's aims aright; music to give harmony to their voices; laws to unify their conduct; and punishments to guard against

4 *Ibid.,* XXVIII, 446-53. Quoted by permission of The Clarendon Press, Oxford.

their tendencies to evil. The end to which ceremonies, music, punishments, and laws conduct is one; they are the instruments by which the minds of the people are assimilated, and good order in government is made to appear."[5]

Where music was of such importance, provision must be made for its study. According to *Yo Ki*, the kings founded schools of music for the various grades of learners, and certain times were set aside for the masters of music to enter the college and direct the pupils' dancing, there being military dances and dances of peace.

Yo Ki expounds, through Yi, a master of music, the relation of music to types of character:

The generous and calm, the mild and correct, should sing the Sung; the magnanimous and calm, and those of wide penetration and sincere, the Ta Ya . . . the courteous and self-restraining, the lovers of the rules of propriety, the Hsiao Ya . . . the correct, upright, and calm, the discriminating and humble, the Fang . . . the determinedly upright, but yet gentle and loving, the Shang; and the mild and honest, but yet capable of decision, the Khi. The object of this singing is for one to make himself right, and then to display his virtue. When he has thus put himself in a condition to act, Heaven and Earth respond to him, the four seasons revolve in harmony with him, the stars and constellations observe their proper laws, and all things are nourished and thrive.[6]

Apart from music, archery, and dancing, which were so intimately linked with the old liberal education, a great array of other sports—hunting, wrestling, jiu-jitsu, boxing, butting, football, polo, shuttlecock, swimming, a variety of golf, pitch-pot (a ceremonial indoor game, involving pitching arrows into a vessel, accompanied by music), health gymnastics, and kite flying—engaged the attention of certain circles in

[5] *Ibid.*, XXVIII, 93.
[6] *Ibid.*, XXVIII, 129 *f*. Quoted by permission of The Clarendon Press, Oxford.

ancient China. Of these, hunting was, in part, a means of securing food, a fitting for war, an act of reverence, and recreation, and thus part of the proper education of rulers. Other sports were largely either for recreation or exhibition.

The origin of hunting was ascribed to great leaders of antiquity, and its practice was enjoined by them upon their followers. According to *Li Ki*, hunting was a duty, but men over fifty might be excused from going on expeditions. When there was nothing to hinder it, three hunts a year were ordained. Not to hunt was an act of impiety; to hunt without obeying the rules was cruelty to Heaven's creatures. According to *Yueh Ling*, a certain month was fixed in which, by means of hunting, the Son of Heaven taught the use of "the five weapons of war, and the rules for the management of horses." Orders were given to charioteers and to grooms to see to the yoking of teams, setting up banners, and assigning carriages according to the rank of the hunters. Then, addressed by the Minister of Instruction, the Son of Heaven proceeded to hunt, being armed with bow and arrows. After the hunt, sacrifices of captured game were made to the "spirits of the four quarters."[7]

In the Chinese philosophy of hunting, the *Doctrine of the Mean* was the rule, just as in other affairs. Not to hunt was evil; hunting to excess was evil likewise. King Wan, distinguished for his avoidance of excess in hunting, ruled his kingdom for fifty years. Others were advised to follow his worthy example. Thai Khang, on the contrary, was idle, dissipated, excessively devoted to the chase, and his unhappy subjects rebelled against him.

Hunting has been called the "image of war." The Chinese, in early feudal days, frequently engaged in warfare and

[7] *Ibid.*, XXVII, 294 *f.*

prepared for it by hunting. So important were war and the skillful use of its instruments, the bow and arrow were symbols of power. A sovereign's present of bows and arrows to a prince symbolized the right to punish in his realm any infringement of royal regulations. Boys were early taught to ride, and to shoot birds, hares, and foxes; when grown, being already excellent archers, they were readily equipped with armor and trained for battle. Sword and spear were used for close fighting; the bow and arrow for distance.

Ultimately, with the passage of primitive conditions, when "every man was trained to fight" in the field, systematic military training was instituted. The *Pi Yung*, credited by certain authors to the Chou period, was a "field of military exercise"—China's *Campus Martius*. Regular military examinations and degrees were added later, to stimulate and reward excellence.

The growth of specialization of military training seems to have paralleled roughly the decline of the all-round, physical-intellectual, liberal education and the development of an exclusively literary training for scholars. Specialization has usually had an inimical effect on general education.

The decline of prestige of physical education in China, and its isolation from the scholarly class, may also have been due, in part, as some believe, to the influence of the great religions, all of which, in varying degree, extolled the studious, reflective life. "Beware of strength," says Lao Tze; "he who in arms is strong will not conquer." According to *Tao Teh King*, "A state may be ruled by measures of correction; weapons of war may be used with crafty dexterity; but the kingdom is made one's own only by freedom from action and purpose. . . . I have three precious things which I prize and hold fast. The first is gentleness. . . . Gentleness is sure to be victorious even in battle, and firmly to maintain its ground. Heaven will save its possessor, by his very gentleness protecting him. . . . A master of the art of war has said, 'I do not dare to be the host to commence the war; I prefer to be the guest [*i.e.*] to act on the defensive. . . .' There is no calamity greater than lightly engaging in war. To do that is near losing the gentleness which is so precious. . . ."[8]

It is commonplace knowledge that the ancient Western concept of liberal education, which in Athens aimed at a balance of physical, intellectual, and aesthetic development, was later metamorphosed into an almost wholly intellectual training, based on certain authors. A somewhat similar development took place in ancient China. In its emphasis on memorization, translating or reading the classics and writing on classical themes, imitating the best models, Chinese practice was similar to that of Western schools during the Renaissance and later periods of Ciceronianism, the chief difference being that China's students imitated their own classics, whereas those of France, Germany, and England gleaned fields their fathers had not sown. This exclusively literary training which marked the last few centuries of old Chinese education, especially pronounced after the Ming dynasty, was quite out of harmony with the pattern of earlier days, when physical training had been joined with mental, moral, and aesthetic education.

The emphasis of Chinese master-molders of personal conduct and public order on adherence to certain fixed modes of demeanor in archery, pitch-pot, music, dancing, hunting, and other exercises, calls to mind Plato's view that music, dancing, games and gymnastic should be kept in "their orig-

8 *Ibid.*, XXXIX, 100 *f.*, 110 *ff.* Quoted by permission of The Clarendon Press, Oxford.

inal form," lest innovations therein should lead to disturbing changes in government.[9] Though some may doubt whether changing games and the rules thereof has such potency in altering states, it is certain that fundamental economic, social, and political changes induce modifications and reinterpretations of music, games, dancing, and other elements of a culture. Early in the present century, breaking at last with the old, exclusively literary tradition, the Chinese called for an up-to-date definition of Confucian teaching. Pointing out that Confucius had included archery and charioteering among the "six arts," the revolutionaries of Ch'ang Sha declared that these were then the arts of war, and that, interpreted for modern times, they mean the inclusion of drilling and physical exercises in education.

The ancient patterns of liberal education in China—both the balanced and the exclusively literary—were clearly selective in function, being designed to prepare an aristocracy of scholarship for the service of government. Admission to the public tests of scholarship was without respect to family or financial status, it is said. Nevertheless, since schools were mostly private, educational preparation depended on the economic circumstances of families, and relatively few could support the long struggle for scholarly excellence and at last attain the reward of official office. Modern China, witnessing the disintegration of feudalism and the old aristocratic patterns of education, is seeking a new mode of liberal education, fit for her free men and women and capable of fitting them for freedom.

[9] *Republic,* IV, 424; *Laws,* VII, 797, 800. *The Dialogues of Plato.* (Trans. by B. Jowett) 5 vols. Oxford University Press: New York, 1892.

CHAPTER TWO

THE ATHENIAN
PATTERN

THOUGH Aristotle says that Egyptian priests first cultivated the mathematical arts,[1] the origin of liberal education is commonly traced to the Greeks. What was the Greek conception? Was there only one Greek pattern of liberal education, fit for free men and designed to fit them to be free? Much depends on the breadth of conceptions of freedom itself. Spartans, having a narrowly circumscribed notion of freedom, designed a training appropriate to their ends. This training was narrow, outsiders thought. Yet Spartans, whose women boasted that they alone brought forth free men, doubtless considered theirs a proper liberal education. Athenians, whose life was less restricted, required a more generous education commensurable with their social pattern. Moreover, out of Athenian practice something new arose. Philosophers at Athens, nourished in that larger freedom which she afforded, set forth ideal patterns of liberal education, in many respects far removed from Athenian practice. In thinking of Greek liberal education, to which Western educators have constantly referred as a model, it is necessary, therefore, to discriminate between the real and the ideal. Let us first sketch the practice.

[1] *Metaphysica*, A, 1. *The Works of Aristotle*. (Trans. under the editorship of J. A. Smith and W. D. Ross) 11 vols. Clarendon Press: Oxford, 1908-31.

Old Athenian education was marked by certain central traits. Foremost was service to the state. Man against the state was a concept foreign to early Athenian practice, as it was to the Greek mind generally. Later, to be sure, economic, social, and political changes altered Athenian life and destroyed the *raison d'être* of education for state service. Even then, however, though everything was "ready to burst with liberty," as Plato wryly remarked, the ideal of service to the state continued to be reflected in philosophical patterns of liberal education.

Early Athenian education was designed for state service, as was that of Sparta, but the modes of preparation differed greatly in the two cities. At Athens, education and other institutions rested on the basis of private property. The family was the first school; beyond that, education was in part private, partly public. While left largely in private hands, the eye of government was on education. Laws, credited to Solon, required fathers to teach their sons a trade,[2] regulated the places of exercise, the hours of opening and closing schools, and the age of boys allowed to enter them.[3] It is also said that Solon's law required boys to learn their letters and swimming. According to Plato,[4] the laws required fathers to have their sons taught music and gymnastic. All will recall Socrates' expression of devotion to the law of his city.

The laws reflect a concern that palaestra and *didascaleum*, though privately supported, should serve the commonweal. Gymnasia, built and operated at state expense and supervised by public officials, carried forward physical training from

[2] Plutarch: *Solon*, 22. *Plutarch's Lives*. (Trans. by B. Perrin) 11 vols. William Heinemann: London, 1914-26.

[3] Aeschines: *Timarchus*, 9-12. *The Speeches of Aeschines*. (Trans. by C. D. Adams) William Heinemann: London, 1919.

[4] *Crito*, 50. *The Dialogues of Plato*. (Trans. by B. Jowett) 5 vols. Oxford University Press: New York, 1892.

about fifteen to eighteen. Military training of young men from
nineteen to twenty completed preparation for service to the
state, the sons of those who had died in battle being educated
at state expense, presented publicly, and sent forth in full
armor, sworn to defend their city, its property, and its gods.
"For," as Pericles said, "where the rewards of virtue are
greatest, there the noblest citizens are enlisted in the service
of the state."[5]

War, a prerogative of the state, frequently exercised,
shaped physical training effectively for its service, and also
influenced mental education. Isocrates[6] was of the opinion
that Homer, often called the educator of Hellas,[7] had been
stressed in education so that his praise of fighting men might
hearten new generations of fighters. Socrates is represented
as pleading for physical exercise as preparation for war.[8]
Xenophon is frankly in favor of an apprenticeship to arms
which enables a people "to live at the expense of much
stronger folk."[9] Lucian[10] depicts Solon explaining that the
state's interest in elaborate gymnastic exercises is to habitu-
ate youth to endurance, make them ready to "meet blows half
way, and never shrink from a wound." It is just "so much
practice against the day of battle."

A second tendency in Athenian education served to correct
the first. Without subscribing to the view that all Athenians

[5] *Thucydides*, II, 46. (Trans. by B. Jowett) 2 vols. Clarendon Press: Oxford,
1900.
[6] *Panegyricus*, 159. *Isocrates*. (Trans. by G. Norlin and L. Van Hook) 3 vols.
William Heinemann: London, 1928-45.
[7] Plato: *Hipparchus*, 228; *Republic*, X, 606.
[8] Xenophon: *Memorabilia*, III, 12, 1-2. *Memorabilia and Oeconomicus*. (Trans.
by E. C. Marchant) William Heinemann: London, 1923.
[9] *The Cavalry Commander*, VIII, 7-8. *Xenophon: Scripta Minora*. (Trans. by
E. C. Marchant) William Heinemann: London, 1925.
[10] *Anacharsis*, 24-25. *The Works of Lucian of Samosata*. (Trans. by H. W.
Fowler and F. G. Fowler) 4 vols. Clarendon Press: Oxford, 1905.

sought the mean and worshiped the beautiful, or that physical training was simply a form of worship of the body beautiful for its own sake, it is certain that the principle of balance between intellectual and physical elements was honored in Athens. To be sure, it was an ideal which must frequently have failed of attainment, but palaestra and *didascaleum,* under optimum conditions, may well have achieved a reasonable measure of success. Ultimately, of course, specialization, whether that of professionalism in athletics or the development of exclusive devotion to intellectual studies, rendered its realization improbable, if not impossible.

The concept of the mean runs throughout Greek thought. Poets and artists recognized the importance of the canon. "Avoid excess; the mean is best," says Theognis. Philosophers expounded this principle's bearing on education. If adhered to, excesses of athleticism would be avoided. Socrates, who is said to have kept in good physical condition himself,[11] thought it a disgrace not to develop the latent strength and grace of the body. That beauty lay essentially in proportion. Some sports develop the legs, others the arms and shoulders. Dancing seemed ideal to Socrates, because it permitted no part of the body to be idle. Since legs, arms, and neck were exercised, the body would be kept healthy and light.[12] Moderate exercises were beneficial, Aristotle[13] taught, but the strenuous training of Olympic victors often ruined the constitution.

The principle of the mean implied a balance and interdependence of mental and physical exercise. In practice, palaestra and music school were means to this end, though

[11] Laërtius: "Socrates," 7. *Diogenes Laërtius: The Lives and Opinions of Eminent Philosophers.* (Trans. by C. D. Yonge) George Bell and Sons: London, 1915.
[12] Xenophon: *Symposium,* II, 17. *Symposium and Apology.* (Trans. by O. J. Todd; with C. L. Brownson's *Anabasis*) William Heinemann: London, 1922.
[13] *Politica,* VIII, 4.

they must often have fallen short of the ideal, for a variety of reasons. Music, alone, would cultivate effeminacy; exclusive attention to gymnastic would lead to hardness, ferocity, even savagery; together, they produce harmony. Thus Plato taught.[14] Socrates held, according to Xenophon,[15] that health of mind was dependent on that of the body. Hence, proper, moderate exercises benefited both. Bad thinking might be caused by ill health. If the body is in bad condition, loss of memory, depression, and even insanity may result. That those who professed to have had "a liberal education" should by their intemperate habits be compelled to run constantly to doctors, seemed disgraceful to Plato.[16]

Attainment of this ideal liberal education was limited by certain factors—particularly, wealth, sex, and the concept of labor. Athenian economy was based on private property. The conflict of rich and poor was already grave in Solon's day, as his efforts at mediation show. The bearing of the differential of wealth on education in later centuries is abundantly clear. Freeborn Athenian youth were entitled to that liberal education which would fit them to live the life of free citizens. Actually, education varied with the wealth of their families. Schooling depended on leisure, which wealth alone could provide. Plato speaks to the point: "This is what is done by those who have the means, and those who have the means are the rich; their children begin to go to school soonest and leave off latest."[17] Some rose to greatness despite the limitations of fortune. Demosthenes[18] boasts that he had an education be-

[14] *Timaeus*, 88; *Republic*, III, 410-11.
[15] *Memorabilia*, III, 12, 5-6.
[16] *Republic*, III, 405.
[17] *Protagoras*, 326. From *The Dialogues of Plato*, translated by B. Jowett. Clarendon Press: Oxford.
[18] *On the Crown*, 257-58. *The Public Orations of Demosthenes*. (Trans. by A. W. Pickard-Cambridge) 2 vols. Clarendon Press: Oxford, 1912.

fitting the station of one who was unhandicapped by poverty. Aeschines, due to indigence, had to perform menial tasks in the poor school of his father. Still, he became a renowned orator and philosopher. Aristophanes' sausage-seller knew nothing but his letters, and them badly.[19] Others of the laborious sort must have fared similarly.

The status of the labor that men do is apt to change as other elements of their society change. The proper, liberal education of citizens, in the days of Athenian grandeur, came to be set apart from manual labor, save for certain exceptions. Yet, in the sixth century, Solon is said to have sought to turn citizens' attention to the "arts of manufacture," and "enacted a law that no son who had not been taught a trade should be compelled to support his father."[20] Agricultural labors had been from early days the lot of the best, the most aristocratic class, the Eupatrid owners of the richest land in the Attic plain. In general, free men dignify whatever labor they perform. Solon seems to have seen no impropriety in having citizens learn industrial arts. It was to be part of the education of free men.

What effected the change in Athenian views of laborious toil? Many factors, doubtless, but among the most important were these: the increase of slaves, which inevitably degraded the kinds of labor to which they were set; increasing wealth, which made it possible for some to live without working. The widening gulf between the rich and the poor, absentee ownership, slave labor, specialization in industry, low wages, and hard conditions of work brought manual labor into contempt, made it ignoble, as philosophers said. Free citizens became

19 *The Knights*, 188-89. *Aristophanes*. (Trans. by B. B. Rogers) 3 vols. William Heinemann: London, 1924.
20 Plutarch: *Solon*, 22.

a minor element in the industries of Athens.[21] Wealth became the measure of a man. "Every friend deserts the impoverished man," says Euripides.[22] No wonder labor was in disrepute, when workers were so hard pressed. Aristophanes pictures them: "As soon as the cock sends forth his morning song, they jump out of bed,—blacksmiths, potters, leather-workers, shoe-makers, bath attendants, flour dealers, lyre-turners, shield makers; all put on their shoes and rush off to work while it is still dark." Was there a labor movement? There was at least a mental bid for it:

> Six hours a day to tiresome tasks are quite enough to give.
> The plain signs following after say distinctly *zethi*,—live![23]

Poets and philosophers—Socrates, Xenophon, Aristotle, and others—continued to speak highly of certain kinds of labor, especially agriculture. Socrates approved the smell of honest toils which all free men love.[24] Hesiod had extolled the labor of plowing, pruning, reaping, building houses, gathering grapes. The rustic bard may well have found a responsive chord in the breasts of early Attic farmers; but his injunction to "strip to sow, and strip to plough, and strip to reap," was probably generally lost on rich absentee owners. Xenophon's ideal citizen, Isochomachus, owns lands as well as his place in town. Agricultural labor, he thinks, is fit for a free man, a gentleman. Crafts are not. Agriculture makes a man valorous, the very best citizen. But when Isochomachus goes to the

21 Laistner, M. L. W.: *A Survey of Ancient History to the Death of Constantine*, 285 *f.* D. C. Heath and Company: Boston, 1929; Whibley, L.: *A Companion to Greek Studies*, 435. University Press: Cambridge, 1905.

22 Lawton, W. C.: *Three Dramas of Euripides*, 133. Houghton Mifflin Company: Boston, 1889.

23 Lawton, W. C.: *The Soul of the Anthology*, 128. Yale University Press: New Haven, 1923.

24 Xenophon: *Symposium*, II, 4.

country, he scrutinizes the work of others, himself taking his horse for a gallop, putting the beast through such paces as are needed in war.

It is noteworthy that in Aristotle's best state citizens would do no ignoble work. Agriculture, though praised in the *Oeconomica* since it does not render the body unserviceable as do illiberal arts, and is even greatly conducive to bravery, making men adventurous against enemies, is not given a place in the *Politica* as a phase of education of the citizens of the best state. Instead, land would be assigned to them and labor provided, so that citizens might have leisure. Slaves, preferably foreign folk, lacking spirit, would be employed to perform all illiberal labor for the free citizen. Aristotle's "good man" might, however, learn a craft of inferiors, but just for his "own occasional use," not as a regular means to self-maintenance or to work for others.[25] Plato, to whom the "useful arts" are mean, assigns labor to an artisan class, who are not citizens, the superior guardian classes being schooled in military arts and higher studies appropriate to their preferred status.[26]

As for "illiberal arts," Xenophon explains that they are incompatible with the life of the citizen, and are "held in utter disdain in our states." Such occupations "spoil the bodies of the workmen," compel them to sit still, live indoors and, in some cases, spend the day by the fire. This softens the body and weakens the mind. Besides, such work leaves no leisure time for friends, and workers are reputedly "bad defenders of their country."[27] Aristotle, likewise, designates as "vulgar" those arts which deform the body; as also those

25 *Politica*, III, 4, 5; VII, 9, 10.
26 *Republic*, VII, 522; *Laws*, I, 644; VIII, 846.
27 *Oeconomicus*, IV, 2-3.

which are "paid employments," for "they absorb and degrade the mind."[28]

The education of that minor citizen element in the industrial life of Athens must have been limited by their financial and occupational handicaps. Some men, engaged in business, may have had "a very fair idea of politics." Poverty may have been no disgrace, no bar to service of the country, as the Periclean eulogy would have us believe; but the artisan's leisure would scarcely suffice for a generous, liberal education. If they learned their letters, even badly, it was well. Was that citizen altogether exceptional, who, wishing to vote for the ostracism of Aristides, had to ask that reputedly "just man" kindly to inscribe his name upon the *ostrakon?* As for the skills by which artisans were to win their maintenance, a natural apprenticeship to their father's trade may have sufficed in early days. Later, a more formal apprenticeship to masters, who took them in for the purpose of training them, seems to have become common.[29] Such a limited training might well enough be considered unworthy of the name of education.

Sex excluded Athenian girls from that liberal education which their brothers might enjoy at school. Custom assigned to them a life at home; for this, training in housewifely arts by the mother sufficed, unless, as Xenophon's description suggests,[30] it was supplemented by the husband at marriage. Athenian women may have been "happy, respectable, and

28 *Politica*, VIII, 2.

29 Plato: *Republic*, IV, 421; V, 467; Xenophon: *On the Art of Horsemanship*, II, 2; Anderson, L. F.: "Some Facts Regarding Vocational Training among the Ancient Greeks and Romans." *Sch. Rev.* (Mar., 1912) XX, 191-201; Glotz, G.: *Ancient Greece at Work*, 277 *f.* (Trans. by M. R. Dobie) Kegan Paul, Trench, Trübner & Co., Ltd.: London, 1926; Westermann, W. L.: "Vocational Training in Antiquity." *Sch. Rev.* (Nov., 1914) XXII, 601-10.

30 *Oeconomicus*, VII, 4-43.

powerful in the sphere of domestic life,"[31] but they had neither
a generous education of the mind nor training of the body.
From the limited household sphere it was hard to escape. In
any case, there was sharp disapproval. "I hate the gadding
woman," says Theognis. A visitor, being informed by a husband that his wife had gone out, exclaims, "Great Zeus! What
has she to do out?" As the old mores decayed, some women
must have grown restive under the restraints of law and
custom. " 'Tis hard, you know," sighs Calonice, "for women
to get out," for one must mind a husband, keep after servants,
bathe and nurse infants and put them to sleep.[32] Medea
laments:

> Of all created things endowed with soul
> And sense, we women are the wretchedest.[33]

Plato might voice belief in women's intellectual capacities,
even admit them to his school; but, in general, thought and
practice continued in the established mode. Few women at
Athens got an enlightening education. Lesbian Sappho, The-
ban Erinna and Corinna, and Aspasia from Miletus contrast
sharply with their Athenian sisters. Pericles might delight in
Aspasia's learning, as Socrates is said to have done, but the
great statesman, faithful to the accepted pattern, praises those
women who are least spoken of among men, whether "for
good or for evil."[34]

Pericles speaks of Athenian education with great pride,
contrasting it with that of the Laconians; for, "whereas they
from early youth are always undergoing laborious exercises

31 Felton, C. C.: *Ancient and Modern Greece*, I, 432 *f*. 2 vols. Ticknor and
Fields: Boston, 1867.
32 Aristophanes: *Lysistrata*, 15-19.
33 Lawton: *Three Dramas of Euripides*, 119.
34 *Thucydides*, II, 45.

which are to make them brave, we live at ease, and yet are equally ready to face the perils which they face."[35]

What did this freer scheme of preparation for life provide for those whose leisure permitted them to profit by it? Plato says that boys were sent to teachers who were to look after manners even more than reading and music, thus preserving and furthering that modesty of demeanor already formed at home. When letters had been learned, the great poets were read, and their admonitions, tales, and encomia on ancient great men were learned by heart, to kindle a desire to emulate their example. Teachers of the lyre, likewise careful of conduct, made them acquainted with lyric poets whom they set to music, intending to teach them to be "more gentle, and harmonious, and rhythmical," and thus prepared for speech and action.[36] The range of authors, liberal but all Greek, included Homer, Hesiod, Theognis, Solon, Alcman, Tyrtaeus, Pindar, Aeschylus, Euripides, and perhaps Aesop's fables. There was no foreign language study. Homer was the foremost and most constant element. Alcibiades is said to have beaten a schoolmaster because there was no copy of Homer in his school.[37] Learning much of an author by heart was common; some, indeed, may have learned all of Homer, as Niceratus says he did at his father's insistence,[38] but such feats were, presumably, rare. Did Athenian prisoners at Syracuse, said to have won their liberty by reciting long passages from Euripides, simply repeat what they had learned in school?

Pericles boasted that Athenians, even those who engaged in business, had a fair notion of political matters, and all were

[35] *Ibid.*, II, 39.
[36] *Protagoras*, 325-26.
[37] Plutarch: *Alcibiades*, 7.
[38] Xenophon: *Symposium*, III, 5.

"sound judges of a policy."[39] A man devoid of interest in public affairs, they regarded as useless. Such understanding and concern in respect to civic matters may have been developed informally rather than by teaching. Plato says that, having finished with the masters of music school and palaestra, the state compelled youth to learn the laws, to guide their conduct, whether as rulers or ruled.[40] To the young men who have been registered as citizens and have learned the laws, the state speaks directly, not through others, says Aeschines.[41]

While attending the school of the Muses—learning letters, writing, literature, music, a little arithmetic, and perhaps something of drawing and painting which, Aristotle says,[42] was added by some, boys also attended the palaestra. These elementary places of exercise, like the music schools, were private, though subject to certain public regulations.[43] Here, the paidotribe, aided by flute players (for many exercises were accompanied by music), directed the sports and exercises of the boys. Some palaestras were widely known and much sought after, while others were mean and obscure. Plato was inclined to think some parents sought a good paidotribe more zealously than they did first-rate teachers.

Since some boys came about the age of seven and might continue to fourteen or fifteen, exercises must have been graded according to age and strength. At least two groups—boys, seven to eleven, and youths, eleven to fifteen—seem to have been recognized. Aristotle regarded it as an "admitted principle" that exercises for the young should be light, avoiding severe training and diet, lest the body be injured,[44] but

[39] *Thucydides*, II, 40.
[40] *Protagoras*, 326.
[41] *Timarchus*, 18.
[42] *Politica*, VIII, 3.
[43] Aeschines: *Timarchus*, 9-11.
[44] *Politica*, VIII, 4.

premature, excessive training was sometimes practiced to prepare youth for contests at the great festivals. "Gesticulation"
—bodily movements, serving as preliminary training for
dancing and other gymnastic contests—leapfrog, rope-climb-
ing, tug of war, ball-play, running, jumping, and perhaps
also scaled-down javelin and discus contests seem to have
been included for "boys." Running, jumping, wrestling, javelin, and discus were of central importance in the palaestra.
Wrestling, boxing, and pancratium constituted the most strenuous phase of its program—at least, for those seeking to
enter public contests.

Swimming was common at Athens, and was regarded as
indispensable to a proper education, if one may judge from
the proverbial description of an uneducated person as one
who neither knew letters nor how to swim; but the manner of
its acquisition is obscure.[45] In early times, the palaestra was
apt to be near a stream; later, there were artificial facilities,
some of them with swimming baths.

Whether dancing was a part of regular elementary schooling has been disputed. If not a usual feature, it became an
important element of education for at least a small select band
of boys who were chosen by the *choregus* to be trained for
certain public festivals. At school festivals, too—Musea and
Hermaea—dancing may well have had a place.

The years from fifteen to eighteen were given to physical
sports, supervised by instructors at gymnasia, built and supported at state expense, and directed by a gymnasiarch—a
wealthy, respected citizen. Here, for a fee, those able to afford
it might have the services of special coaches. One gymnasium,
the Kynosarges, was restricted for a time to sons of Athenian

---

45 Grasberger, L.: *Erziehung und Unterricht im Klassischen Altertum*, I,
376 *ff*. 3 vols. Stahel'schen Buch-und Kunsthandlung: Würzburg, 1864-81.

fathers by foreign mothers.[46] The rule seems, however, to have been abrogated by the fifth century. Training in these public gymnasia continued in a more strenuous fashion the work of the elementary palaestra. To the exercises of earlier years, driving, torch races, running in armor, rowing, swimming, and hunting were added. Riding was taught in special academies. Dancing in public choruses would also be part of the education of at least some youths.

Some training for military purposes took place in the nineteenth and twentieth years at Athens. In early days, it seems, the sons of those who died in war were trained and armed at state expense. Though credited, until recently, with great antiquity, this ephebic training lacked, at first, the elaborate systematic character of later times. It seems not to have been regarded as a compulsory element of a free man's education. Still, there was social approval of a certain preparation for a soldier's duties, undertaken on individual initiative. Xenophon represents Socrates as urging young men to attend to this training voluntarily, even though "military training is not publicly recognised by the state. . . ."[47] Isocrates inveighed against the lack of training for war at Athens. Athenian military decline in the fourth century doubtless alarmed many. Orators condemned her decadence; demands for a reform were heard.

After Chaeronea, Athens took practical steps (c. 334 B.C.) to increase her military strength by two years of compulsory training at state expense. This was soon reduced to one year, however, and ceased to be compulsory. Foreigners were admitted in the second century, and soon outnumbered Atheni-

---

[46] *Pausanias's Description of Greece*, I, 19, 3. (Trans. by J. G. Frazer) 6 vols. Macmillan & Co., Ltd.: London, 1898; Petersen, C.: *Das Gymnasium der Griechen nach Seiner Baulichen Einrichtung*, 16. Perthes-Besser, Mauke: Hamburg, 1858.
[47] *Memorabilia*, III, 12, 5.

ans.[48] Physical and military exercises in this state institution included, at one time and another, fighting in armor, javelin, archery, sling, catapult, *kestrosphendone,* marching, various forms of running, wrestling, boxing, swimming, rowing, riding, chariot driving, and pancratium. Specialization being marked, particular instructors were appointed to teach the intricacies of each.[49]

Intellectual and religious exercises mingled with the physical in the Ephebic College. Letters, geometry, rhetoric, and music, Plutarch[50] says, were studied. Letters, a broad term, would include grammatical study, literature, and philosophy. Various schools of philosophy vied for the attention of youth.

This balance of physical and intellectual activities, more apparent than real, was not destined to endure. Military training could not save Athens. Her decline politically and financially, her falling population, disappearance of the original purpose for which ephebic training had been established, and the increasing proportion of foreign students, all helped undermine military arts in the Ephebic College. In Cicero's day, military training of the ephebi seemed "far from rigorous."[51] As physical training became more perfunctory, intellectual pursuits, for which at first there had been little time, more and more engaged attention. In the last century B.C., ephebi were attending philosophical lectures at the Lyceum, Academy, and the Ptolemaion. Finally, one might pursue literary and philo-

48 Forbes, C. A.: *Greek Physical Education,* 154, 159 *ff.,* 173. Century Company: New York, 1929; Freeman, K. J.: *Schools of Hellas,* 219 *f.* Macmillan & Co., Ltd.: London, 1922.

49 Grasberger: *op. cit.,* III, 92 *ff.; Polybius: The Histories,* XXVII, 11. (Trans. by W. R. Paton) 6 vols. William Heinemann: London, 1922-27; *Livy,* XLII, 65. (Trans. by B. O. Foster *et al.*) 13 vols. Harvard University Press: Cambridge, 1919-.

50 *Symposiacs,* IX, 1. *Plutarch's Lives and Writings.* (Ed. by A. H. Clough and W. W. Goodwin) 10 vols. Little, Brown and Company: Boston, 1909.

51 *De Re Publica,* IV, 4 [and] *De Legibus.* (Trans. by C. W. Keyes) William Heinemann: London, 1928.

sophical studies entirely, without enrolling in the cadet corps at all. In the third century A.D., when last heard of, gymnastic contests still continued, but certain military exercises had disappeared.[52] Ultimately, participation in games and athletic contests became a matter of reproach. Libanius boasted that he never played ball at Athens, and he punished a student who forsook his books to become a runner. Likewise, Himerius sought to discourage ball playing and "practising athletics."[53]

Intellectually, too, Athens began to slip backward, though traditional repute long made her an intellectual Mecca to which all eyes turned. The once-bubbling wellsprings of philosophy seem to have dried up. One senses a lack of pressing motive and important goals. Instead of profound, creative thinking on great problems, which marked the height of Athenian enlightenment, philosophic schools degenerated into wordy, formal institutions, whose dimming light, focused more and more on a glorious past, scarcely sufficed to explore present problems or chart the future. Cicero thought Athens' philosophy "topsy-turvy" in his day.[54] Nevertheless, having a tender spot for Athens and believing all philosophy of some benefit, he hopefully sent his son Marcus thither, urging him not to return "empty," a reproach to his teachers and to Athens. But Marcus leaned to Falerian and frivolity rather than philosophy. Even those who went as serious students imbibed a culture almost wholly literary, concerned with verbal niceties and philosophical subtleties rather than profound study of man, nature, or society. As centuries passed, the gulf between literary and philosophical studies and the

[52] Dumont, A.: *Essai sur l'Éphébie Attique*, I, 236 f. 2 vols. Firmin-Didot: Paris, 1875-76.

[53] Walden, J. W. H.: *The Universities of Ancient Greece*, 319, 325. Charles Scribner's Sons: New York, 1909.

[54] *Letters to Atticus*, V, 10. (Trans. by E. O. Winstedt) 3 vols. William Heinemann: London, 1912-18.

critical, fundamental problems of society became wider. Libanius gave intellectual life at Athens a low mark. Teachers, he sadly observed, were little better than their students.

How, now, shall we answer the question: "What was Athenian liberal education?" It was a vital pattern of human culture, rooted in Athens' life, limited by her biases, exalted by her generous traits; changing as Athens grew, it flowered at her maturity, and withered as she declined to a shadow of her former self. Yet there was a permanent residue, vital to this day. Thanks to a degree of freedom for growth, some could slough off slavish conformity and become, in the most exalted sense, men. They who emerged from the dead level of mediocrity charted the highways of the mind. Due to them, Athens became a University of Mankind.

Truth and error mingle together in every seat of learning. Athens had her share of error. But soundness lay in her early respect for labor, her understanding of the necessity for freedom of inquiry, the importance attached to a knowledge of law and interest in public affairs, as part of a free man's education; her sense of the balance and interdependence of health of mind and body, and appreciation of the beauty both might achieve. Realization of these was partial and momentary. Labor fell into contempt, freedom of inquiry felt restraint, education in politics became a memory; luxury, professionalism in athletics, and one-sided intellectualism reduced balance of mind and body to an empty phrase. Realizations are fleeting; ideals endure. After a thousand years of asceticism and orthodoxy, limiting mind and body, the ancient cult of physical and mental excellence came once again to sovereignty in the Western world, where, thanks to factors unknown to antiquity, it acquired lustrous meanings and applications by them unsurmised.

CHAPTER THREE

THEORETICAL
RECONSTRUCTIONS

1

OLD Athens knew one pattern of liberal education fit for free men: discipline of life's labors, games, and music. Its foundations were primitive; its practices evolved without benefit of theoretical considerations. In the fifth century B.C. this ancient mold of life and education was broken. Economic, social, political, and religious changes, and the Persian and Peloponnesian wars, which first raised Athens to the heights of empire and then plunged her into impotence economically and politically, gave impetus to a new intellectualism which sought, among many other things, to formulate a science of politics and the basic principles of education in harmony therewith. These conscious theoretical reconstructions of education and politics were interdependent; they were ideal roads from a world of chaos, in which old values and patterns had disintegrated, to one of orderliness and the "good life."

Cannot social ills be corrected by a reformed education? The question has been asked by many generations. Certain men at Athens were hopeful. Most of their fellow citizens, however, were skeptical, or did not even understand the question. How should they understand it? The virtues of old, associated with men of might and noble name, had been thought inborn. Now here are new teachers who claim to *teach* virtue. Can virtue be made the possession of the hoi polloi who have come to power in Athens? How can justice, courage, temperance, and holiness be taught? Are they not hardy humbugs who profess to teach virtue? Socrates critically eyes famed Protagoras, who asserts that he can teach men the art of politics, make them good citizens—in short, teach them virtue. Only when it is established that virtue is a unity, and knowledge and virtue are one, is Socrates convinced that it can be taught—for knowledge can be, certainly. There is one good, knowledge; and one evil, ignorance. The way is difficult, but it must be taken. There are no short cuts.

Just as in the *Great Learning* the path to virtue was held to begin in knowledge and continue through the rectification of persons and families up to good order in the kingdom, so it seemed to Socrates sufficient to point the way to knowledge and self-mastery. A blueprint of an ideal curriculum and an ideal city was unnecessary. In fact, Socrates would probably have had difficulty imagining a city fairer than his beloved Athens. The Socratic road to virtue is a method of critical inquiry after knowledge. One citadel must be conquered— one's self, mind, and body. One must seek truth among his fellows, the ordinary and those who are reputed to know. Socrates, himself, is only a midwife, assisting the mind's labor to bring forth truth and to recognize the difference between valid truth and counterfeit.[1] In the end, man is his own physician, spiritually and physically. Socrates is said to have kept in excellent physical condition, avoiding excess; and he recog-

---

[1] *Theaetetus*, 150-52. *The Dialogues of Plato*. (Trans. by B. Jowett) 5 vols. Oxford University Press: New York, 1892.

nized the interdependence of physical and mental health.[2] Both are to be attained by self-knowledge and discipline. "Self control is an exact science, and when discovered the whole world may become virtuous." Beyond reason there is no court of appeal. There is no priest, no potentate, no supreme philosopher to hand down decisions.

2

Plato's remedy for the disintegration of political life and education, which he sensed all around him, was an elaborate, precise, authoritarian proposal for the reconstruction of society, government, and education. The profound, sweeping changes advocated in *The Republic*, and also the very different, yet no less drastic measures in *The Laws*, reflect a conviction that existing evils were so deep-seated that anything short of a radical social and educational reconstruction would be of no avail. Plato pinned no hope on a democratic quest for knowledge, or virtue, such as Socrates had in mind. He rejected the Sophists' claim to teach virtue, as well as the Protagorean doctrine that knowledge is what one perceives.[3] The fundamental source of evils lay deep in the constitution of the state. The businessmen, "stooping as they walk," are sinister figures, a destructive force in society: they reduce other men to drones or paupers. Whether because of his aristocratic background, or for other reasons, Plato is plainly contemptuous of Athenian democracy, its avid pursuit of wealth, liberty to be anything or nothing as one pleases, and

---

[2] Diogenes Laërtius: "Socrates," 7. *Diogenes Laërtius: The Lives and Opinions of Eminent Philosophers.* (Trans. by C. D. Yonge) George Bell and Sons: London, 1915; Xenophon: *Symposium*, II, 17-18. *Symposium and Apology.* (Trans. by O. J. Todd; with C. L. Brownson's *Anabasis*) William Heinemann: London, 1922; *Memorabilia*, III, 12, 5-6; IV, 7, 9. *Memorabilia and Oeconomicus.* (Trans. by E. C. Marchant) William Heinemann: London, 1923.

[3] *Theaetetus*, 152.

a sort of equality accorded "to equals and unequals alike."[4]
One must establish a state on sound principles. Within such
a framework, man may be expected to achieve his highest
perfection.

Measured by Plato's standard in *The Republic*, a liberal
education could not be found in Athens. The old music school,
palaestra, and gymnasium, formed on conventional patterns,
too limited and uncritical, could furnish at best only a foundation. The Sophists, enterprising pedagogical specialists and
technicians of the new day, were raising education to an adult
level, but they were teaching the immediately practical and
particular, not the universal; the seeming, not the real truth.
In a society where all manner of things were for sale and
everyone was anxious to get ahead in every way possible, such
useful wares found many purchasers. Socrates had only begun
the task of leading Athenian citizens to see the value of more
durable goods.

Lacking faith in any universal desire and capacity for true
knowledge, Plato judged it best to fashion a state in which
justice might be established for all. To insure justice, one
must know whence injustice arises. In the simplest society,
organized to provide the barest necessities—food, shelter,
clothing—men labor and rest, produce, consume, live in peace
to old age, and leave a like inheritance to their children. This
state is healthy. Here is no injustice. But, not satisfied with
simple maintenance of life, men seek more—relishes, des-
serts, tables, sofas, perfumes, pictures, embroideries, gold,
ivory, and other pleasing things. To supply these, the state
increases the categories of workers—actors, dancers, musi-
cians, manufacturers, contractors, servants, nurses, tutors,
confectioners, cooks, courtesans, physicians. Getting these, the

4 *Republic*, VIII, 555, 558.

healthy state gives way to a diseased constitution. In such a diseased luxury-society, injustice flourishes, arising from the relations of citizens one to another.[5] The population expanding, the territory, heretofore adequate, becomes too small. Some must be seized from neighbors; this requires an army. Wars arise from this process, their causes being the same as those which give rise to "almost all the evils in States."[6]

This "inflamed," luxury-loving society is badly governed, for the most aggressive men pursue wealth and power with greatest success; and, getting government into their own hands, they use it for their own gain and sell out the commonwealth. Justice cannot be established until disinterested governors are found and educated for their political function. Men think injustice more profitable to them than justice,[7] unless they consider the matter critically; and, if they had Gygian rings, they would commit injustice with impunity for their own advantage. In the myth of Er, the one who had first choice of all the lots at once chose tyranny, for his mind was dark; "he had no philosophy" to serve him as a guide.[8] The principle is clear: only philosophy can enable one to choose wisely. Just government depends on making right decisions. Rulers must study to become philosophers, or philosophers must be made kings. Government is the philosopher's true vocation. Cut off from a vocation, philosophy falls into disrepute; without philosophy, government is heir to endless evil.[9]

Justice will be established in the state when each person performs that, and that alone, for which there is a natural bent, which is to be perfected by appropriate training and

---

5 *Ibid.*, II, 372.
6 *Ibid.*, II, 373.
7 *Ibid.*, II, 360.
8 *Ibid.*, X, 619.
9 *Ibid.*, V, 473; VII, 535.

education. In Plato's myth of creation, natures are classified, as of iron, whose virtue is strength; of silver, whose virtue is courage; and of gold, whose virtue is wisdom. Natures are not precisely or uniformly transmitted to children. Golden parents may get iron offspring. Corresponding to these differing qualities in individuals, there are three classes in society, to each of which is assigned that social function which nature seems to have intended: artisans and husbandmen, to produce all goods; soldiers, to defend the state; and philosopher-guardians, to govern and command.[10]

Plato's conception of the nature and educability of women differed radically from prevailing Athenian practice. Women, he thought, were endowed with strength, courage, or wisdom, as were men. The majority of them were fitted by nature for the labors of artisans; a smaller number would make good physical guardians; while a few would qualify as philosophers. The natural capacities of women should be judged in the same manner as those of men, and they should be trained or educated physically and intellectually, in the same way as the men for the functions to be performed.

The selection and training of its future guardians—soldiers and philosophers—is a most serious business of the state, requiring much careful study and an extended period of time. To the lowest industrial class, readily identifiable, apparently, by its spiritlessness and lack of any mark of intellectual ability, Plato gives little attention. Having neither capacity nor need for a liberal education, the apprenticeship of each artisan to his craft is sufficient. Likewise, since the "useful arts" are mean, in Plato's eyes, they are excluded from the education of soldiers and philosophers.[11]

[10] *Ibid.*, III, 415.
[11] *Ibid.*, VII, 522.

Potential soldiers and philosophers, male and female, share an education from seven to twenty, somewhat similar to the old pattern of Athenian education in that it consists of music and gymnastic, capped by military sports and exercises. Important innovations are introduced, however, which reflect Plato's Laconian bias. It is strictly supervised by the state; all live plainly, eat in common, follow a soldierly regimen, have no property, and are paid just enough for their needs. Their future rôle of service to the state is kept constantly before them.[12] Literary and musical elements are severely censored. Poetry which breathes a martial spirit is approved, but immoral elements, and passages likely to inspire fear, are to be ruthlessly excluded, regardless of the high traditional standing of the poet.[13] No innovations are to be suffered in music; they endanger the state, for when music changes, society changes with it.[14] Dorian and Phrygian harmonies, suitable to war and peace, will be retained; but Lydian and Ionian, being soft and sad, are to be abolished. Flutes and other "curiously-harmonized" instruments are also banned, while the shepherd's pipe, lyre, and harp are approved.[15]

Neither music nor gymnastic are ends in themselves. Both are for the benefit of the soul, as Plato says in the *Timaeus*. Each by itself distorts. Music, alone, results in effeminacy, "a feeble warrior." Gymnastic by itself makes for brutality, fierceness, and savagery.[16] The state cannot depend on those who are mere athletes, for their training endangers health, and they are too much inclined to sleep. The soldier-athletes of the ideal state require "a finer sort of training," to make

[12] *Ibid.*, III, 416-17.
[13] *Ibid.*, II, 376-83; III, 386-87, 389-90.
[14] *Ibid.*, IV, 424.
[15] *Ibid.*, III, 399.
[16] *Ibid.*, III, 410-11.

them like wakeful dogs, keen of sight and hearing, able to
endure changes of food, water, heat and cold, and still keep
in health.[17] Athletic professionalism would injure the state,
as also would health gymnastics. It is a disgrace if those who
have a liberal education are compelled to run for doctors
because of overeating and indolence.[18] As to dancing, hunting,
equestrian contests, and gymnastics, it is unnecessary to go
into minute details, for all follow the same general principles.[19] Though inclined to Spartan military discipline, Plato
would avoid its excesses, keeping to military gymnastic which
is "twin sister" to the simple musical education which he
recommends. Simplicity in music leads to "temperance in the
soul," and the same principle in gymnastic produces "health
in the body."[20] Since they are to make up a military class,
children must not be soft; they must learn of war by observing
and doing, going on expeditions, rendering such aid as they
can to their elders.[21] Like "young hounds," let them taste
blood.[22]

A novel, elaborate pattern of liberal studies (by the standard of *The Republic*, the only liberal education) is reserved
for a select few who will continue after reaching twenty years
of age. The principles for selecting the future philosopher-
kings are simple. Those who have shown during their previous
training those qualities needed by soldiers are henceforth
devoted to a warrior's duties. The small remnant who, while
sharing the soldier's training, have exhibited profound intellectual curiosity, a love of ideas, and a readiness to apprehend
real truth are worthy of an education which will fit them for

17 *Ibid.*, III, 404.
18 *Ibid.*, III, 405-06.
19 *Ibid.*, III, 412.
20 *Ibid.*, III, 404.
21 *Ibid.*, V, 467.
22 *Ibid.*, VII, 537.

the rôle of disinterested governors. These, though disdainful
of the usual political ambitions and not keen to rule, will be
ready to assume the labors of governors, when persuaded that
it is their social obligation.

Basic to the liberal education of the intellectual elite, whose
vocation is to establish justice in the state, is Plato's conception of truth. It is also his reply to the fundamental intellectual
problem of the day, discussed by the Sophists and by Socrates:
What is knowledge? Sophist Protagoras had held it to be
what appears to each man to be true.[23] Such a view, highly
flattering to individual opinion, was in harmony with the
extreme political equalitarianism of democracy. Socrates
showed the unsoundness of such a view of knowledge. Plato's
"real" truth is universal, perfect "patterns fixed in nature,"
which endure throughout all time. This immaterial realm of
perfect truth transcends the material, obscure world of sense
perception and opinion. The senses, themselves limited by
their material dependency, deceive us. The world of perfect
abstract patterns, the source of the shadows which we see
around us and call "real," is not to be apprehended by the
senses, but may be more or less grasped by the mind's eye,
when schooled to deal with pure abstraction. Education is the
toilsome process by which the partial, distorted opinions and
sense perceptions, which Plato likens to shadows cast upon the
walls of a cavern in which men have been enchained, may
come to be recognized for what they truly are—misconcep-
tions—and be replaced by an understanding of true reality,
that is, the world of original, universal forms, whose shadows
once deceived us. This genuine truth, this world of pure abstraction is the realm which philosopher-kings strive to gain.[24]

---

[23] *Theaetetus,* 151-52.
[24] *Republic,* VII, 515 *et seqq.*; X, 596 *et seqq.*; *Cratylus,* 389; *Parmenides,*
132.

Clearly, only the keenest minds can compete successfully in such a trial. Dim wits will take easier roads, be satisfied with appearances rather than reality; but, considering their blindness, they must not be permitted to govern the state.

In the education of the elite who are to continue after military gymnastic has been concluded, Plato assigns unique position and value to arithmetic, geometry, astronomy, and music, which must precede dialectic. Arithmetic has practical value for military and business life, but philosophers will pursue it, not to become shopkeepers, but because, in its theoretical aspects, the study of number leads pure intelligence to the acquisition of abstract truth.[25] Geometry, too, has immediately practical values and is indirectly useful in quickening mental apprehension, but the chief reason for its study depends upon its capacity to lead the mind to a vision of true essence, the eternal forms, rather than changing phenomena.[26] Solid geometry, though little developed, ought to be encouraged by state patronage.[27] Like geometry and arithmetic, astronomy has practical uses, being serviceable to farmers, navigators, and soldiers. But its utility to future philosophers lies in the contemplation of motions of heavenly bodies, which can only be apprehended by reason.[28] Music, the sister of astronomy, is necessary, not that one may be able to torture instruments, but to learn the "natural harmonies of number."[29] All studies of the quadrivium will serve the desired end, if emphasis is placed upon their mutual interrelations, but not otherwise. They will provide effective preparation for dialectic, which alone will lead to absolute truth. The pursuit of these prepara-

[25] *Republic*, VII, 526.
[26] *Ibid.*, VII, 527.
[27] *Ibid.*, VII, 528.
[28] *Ibid.*, VII, 529.
[29] *Ibid.*, VII, 531.

tory studies, Plato says, should be a "sort of amusement"[30] rather than a compulsion. A free man should be free in the pursuit of learning, as in other things. What is forced takes "no hold upon the mind."[31] Dialectic, though rated most highly, must not be begun too early, for then it tends to playful argumentativeness and ends in lawlessness. Taken in proper sequence, its benefit to the serious philosopher is great. Five years, from thirty to thirty-five, will be devoted to philosophy;[32] from then on to fifty the philosopher will serve the state in any needful capacity, returning thereafter to further study, and to such public service as occasion may require.[33]

3

Aristotle's approach to the problem of political and educational reconstruction confronting Athenians was more scientific, less dogmatic than Plato's. His good state is not a perfect blueprint never to be changed. Of fundamental importance is Aristotle's rejection of the Platonic doctrine of universal forms, fixed patterns.[34] The sciences are concerned with universal truths,[35] but the methods of science and idealism differ. We must seek truth in the hard cold facts beneath our feet. Knowledge derived from careful scrutiny of things, particulars, and individuals is most serviceable. Of what benefit is a knowledge of the "good itself" to a doctor, a carpenter, or a weaver? Aristotle left no precise scheme of liberal education such as is found in *The Republic* or in *The Laws*, but the prin-

---

[30] *Ibid.*, VII, 537.
[31] *Ibid.*, VII, 536.
[32] *Ibid.*, VII, 539.
[33] *Ibid.*, VII, 540.
[34] *Ethica Nicomachea*, I, 6; cf. *Metaphysica*, M, 7. *The Works of Aristotle.* (Trans. under the editorship of J. A. Smith and W. D. Ross) 11 vols. Clarendon Press: Oxford, 1908-31.
[35] *Ethica*, X, 9.

ciples which should guide in establishing education for the good of man and the state were critically examined and clearly expounded.

The first problem in seeking to form the good state and right education is to determine their ultimate end. If this be erroneously conceived, the result must be failure. Socrates regarded knowledge as the end. Plato defined the goal as justice. Aristotle's judgment as to the ultimate end of men and government rested upon his analysis of the living world. Happiness, he concluded, is the true final end of man and the state as well. Other goods—knowledge, justice and the like—are means to this ultimate good. Happiness is an end, not a means.[36] All men desire happiness. Actions of individuals and groups are designed, though often mistakenly, to attain it. Politics, the art of government, is the master-art; all other sciences lie within its grand domain, each in its more limited sphere serving the ultimate end of man, individually and collectively.[37]

But happiness is a broad term and implies many different things. It depends on being wellborn, having plenty of friends and wealth, plenty of children, a good old age, health, strength, beauty, generous stature, athletic ability, honor, fame, good luck, and virtue.[38] All think these desirable. But, whether considered individually or collectively, these possessions do not carry us far in the quest for good government and education. Is there not some unifying principle, some general definition of happiness? Aristotle conceived of it as a condition inherent in the proper performance of functions, those activities which naturally belong to anything. There is a hierarchy of functions in nature: some are common to the whole living

36 *Ibid.*, I, 7.
37 *Ibid.*, I, 2.
38 *Rhetorica*, I, 5.

world; others are unique, belonging only to a part. Nutrition and growth are common functions of plant and animal kingdoms. Sensation, activity of the irrational soul, is common to animals and to man. But human beings—a part of them, at least—have a higher function, that of the rational soul whose activity is reason and self-direction.[39] Rational activity is the highest human function, man's greatest good, the key to his true happiness. The "good life" is one of activity ruled by reason. In this marriage of knowledge and action, Aristotle offered at once a counterweight to empty intellectualism and thoughtless activity.

Man's happiness as an individual is dependent on a collective life. Being gregarious, "by nature a political animal,"[40] man creates the state whose rôle is to promote and regulate those functions—growth, sensation, and reason—the exercise of which is indispensable to his happiness. Only through the state can man attain his highest happiness, the "good life." A state may be said to be happy when it promotes these functions of man well, for that is its end. Malfunctioning or nonfunctioning of the state means unhappiness and, ultimately, decay and death for man and for the state.

According to nature's law, the rational soul, if developed and not perverted, rules the body and the irrational soul. As Aristotle observed the human scene, however, it seemed to him that nature's gifts were unevenly distributed. The slave and the free are made by nature. In some, the rational soul either does not exist or but slightly, as in slaves; in others, women and children, it is incomplete, or undeveloped.[41] So, he reasoned, there is a natural aristocracy of those potentially fit to govern; and there is a natural slavery, for some deserve

---

[39] *De Anima*, II, 3.
[40] *Politica*, I, 2.
[41] *Ibid.*, I, 5, 13.

by nature to be slaves.[42] Good order and happiness prevail in families and in states when those endowed with a rational element are masters and governors of those in whom it does not exist or is undeveloped. Those who are "free by nature" fulfill their highest function and thus gain happiness by governing; those in whom the principle of submission is implanted are happiest in submitting to the will of masters. War and slavery are "naturally just," Aristotle thought, for they establish dominion of the superior over the inferior. The master-slave relation is beneficial for both slaves and masters, since it provides each with the peculiar type of activities which are conducive to his happiness.[43] In the household, women should be subject to their husbands, for the virtue of women lies in obeying, and that of men in commanding.[44] The distinction between male and female capacities holds good for all the animal kingdom, but the "differentiation is the most obvious in the case of humankind. . . ."[45] In the best state, slaves, women (though they be free), and artisans (they were once slaves, and many still are) will not participate in government, for to do so would render them and the state itself unhappy.[46] These classes, therefore, have no part in liberal education.

The question of balance between permanence and change and their relation to social stability is of fundamental importance. Ancient states commonly sought permanence by prohibiting change. Few seem to have recognized that change and stability might be compatible. Plato's ideal state was to follow the pattern of prohibition. Aristotle's judgment of human

[42] *Ibid.,* VII, 14.
[43] *Oeconomica,* I, 5.
[44] *Politica,* I, 13.
[45] *Historia Animalium,* IX, 1.
[46] *Politica,* III, 5, 9.

desires as they bear on government was sounder. Unlike the *Republic*, his good state—a constitutional government, for this is the best attainable[47]—will be cautiously progressive. Functioning of a living institution implies growth. The good which men desire will not always be just "what their fathers had." Change is not to be lightly encouraged, however, for law relies on habit for obedience, and frequent changes would weaken law.[48]

Education, if rightly established, provides for happy functioning of citizens, individually and collectively. It is, for this reason, an important branch of political science. Nothing contributes more to stability of governments than education, for even the best laws are of little avail if the young are not brought up in accord with "the spirit of the constitution." The principles of education must be in harmony with the political principles of the state. And, since the state has only one end in view—the good life of its members—it alone is competent to direct the education of all. Stories which children hear, plays, theater, pictures and statues which they see, are matters of concern to the state, no less than other more formal instruction, for what is first seen and heard will probably leave a lasting impression.[49]

The order of educational efforts is dictated by nature: that of the body, the irrational soul, and finally reason.[50] The education of the rational soul, though it is the ultimate end, waits upon and is fundamentally affected for good or ill by that of the physical and irrational nature. Those who are in haste about later education, or give no thought to prenatal care or education of the youngest years, are in serious error.

47 *Ibid.*, IV, 8-9, 11.
48 *Ibid.*, II, 8.
49 *Ibid.*, V, 9; VII, 17; VIII, 1; *Ethica*, X, 1.
50 *Politica*, VII, 15.

The education of free men begins with life itself. As all expectations of a happy life are dependent on good heredity, legislators must look to eugenic mating, the age of marriage, diet and exercise of mothers, the health of fathers and the kinds of physical labor they should not perform. The mean is the rule in these matters.

Excess of children is to be avoided.[51] A deformed child will not be kept. In the earliest years, milk diet, habituation to various forms of exercise or motion, and toughening by gradual exposure to cold are recommended, since they are conducive to healthy, sturdy growth. Crying and screaming, being good natural exercise, are not to be restrained. Moral education requires attention even before seven, for the influence of slaves, lewd stories, indecent actions or pictures are to be avoided. Girls are to be educated only in and for the household since women, though free, have no political function in the state.[52]

In respect to the education of potential citizens from seven to fifteen, and from fifteen to twenty-one, Aristotle stresses two principles, the doctrine of the mean and that of catharsis, which are to regulate the exercises of the body and the irrational soul. Physical regimen requires meticulous attention, for body and soul are interdependent, the physical form, proportion, and movements revealing the nature of the soul, as physiognomists taught.[53] Light exercises—such as dancing, running, jumping, throwing the discus and javelin—should prevail to about fifteen, for it is necessary to avoid "severe diet or painful toil" which might injure physical growth. The

[51] *Ibid.*, VII, 16.
[52] *Ibid.*, I, 13; II, 5.
[53] *Physiognomonica*, 2, 4; *Philostratos: Concerning Gymnastics*, 25 *et seq.* (Trans. by T. Woody) Reprinted from *The Research Quarterly* (May, 1936) VII, no. 2.

mean is the true guide:[54] too much or too little exercise has an ill effect on strength and, like extremes of diet and drink, injures health. Too strict early training of the body had been shown to be bad, Aristotle thought, by the fact that Olympic victors seldom won crowns both in boyhood and manhood, their early excessive training having weakened their constitutions. Nor are extremes of physical training justifiable for the sake of war. Laconia had proved that. The noble, not the brutal, must be given first place, for facing really noble dangers requires brave men, not wild beasts.[55]

Following the light exercises, attention from fifteen to eighteen is centered chiefly on studies and activities other than athletic. In this domain there is disagreement as to what should be taught and the relative weight to be given to intellectual and moral training. Decisions must be made in harmony with the true end of the citizen's life. What occupations are liberal and fit for free men, and what are illiberal? Aristotle lays down this principle: "any occupation, art, or science, which makes the body or soul or mind of the freeman less fit for the practice or exercise of virtue, is vulgar; wherefore we call those arts vulgar which tend to deform the body, and likewise all paid employments, for they absorb and degrade the mind."[56] Even "liberal" arts, proper to a free man, may become illiberal if one strives for "perfection in them." The young may learn the "useful things which are really necessary, but not all useful things. . . . To be always seeking after the useful" is not becoming to "free and exalted souls."[57] A free man may with propriety learn the crafts of inferiors for

[54] *Ethica*, II, 2.
[55] *Ibid.*, III, 6, 7; *Politica*, VIII, 4.
[56] *Politica*, VIII, 2. Quoted from *The Works of Aristotle*, translated under the editorship of J. A. Smith and W. D. Ross, by permission of The Clarendon Press, Oxford.
[57] *Ibid.*, VIII, 3.

his personal "occasional use," but he may not practice them habitually.[58] Agriculture is praised, in the *Oeconomica*,[59] since it makes men "adventurous against the foe" and does not injure the body as do "illiberal arts." In the *Politics* such valuable effects are sacrificed, however, for agricultural labor is assigned to private and public slaves.

In addition to gymnastics, reading, writing, music, and drawing belong to liberal education, the last particularly because it contributes to sound judgment of "beauty of the human form."[60] Music is necessary to the proper intellectual enjoyment of leisure, which is noble and liberal. The very fact that it cheers the hearts of men would justify its place in the education of the young. It is also a useful amusement, a means to an end. Aristotle takes no stock in Plato's suggestion that study be approached as an amusement;[61] on the contrary, it is "accompanied with pain." Music, however, may be a sweetener of toil, may be to youths like a rattle to an infant, for they will not "endure anything" if they can avoid it, unless it is "sweetened by pleasure."[62]

Besides these, however, music has more exalted educational functions. Just as gymnastic forms the body, various rhythms strike kindred chords in the soul and give it a certain character. The right kind of music, that which is ennobling and harmonious, will set the noblest chords of the soul vibrating. Professional perfection must be avoided, naturally. The utility of music in forming the irrational soul is clarified by reference to the doctrine of the *mean*.[63] The happy, virtuous life is midway between extremes. Music's power over the soul

[58] *Ibid.*, III, 4; VII, 9.
[59] Bk. I, 2.
[60] *Politica*, VIII, 3.
[61] *Republic*, VII, 537.
[62] *Politica*, VIII, 5; Diogenes Laërtius: "Aristotle," 11.
[63] *Ethica*, II, 2, 6.

being involuntary, that which is exciting, like the Phrygian, and that which is sad, as the "Mixolydian," produce kindred effects in the soul. Dorian stands between these extremes, is "manliest" and best, and is proper, therefore, for the education of young men. The very young and those of advanced years, however, may benefit from the Lydian.[64] The choice of instruments is also to be referred to this principle.[65]

Apart from this instructional use, music, like dramatics[66] and physical sports, may be employed for the purgation, or catharsis, of the irrational soul. When considered as a means of catharsis, various rhythms and instruments, previously excluded as improper for instruction, may well be introduced. The flute, for example, will relieve passions.[67]

Following this intellectual and moral discipline, three years (eighteen to twenty-one) are devoted to a continuous physical training in which diet and strenuous exercise are stressed. Studies are set aside at this time, for one should not labor mentally and physically at the same time, the two being opposed.[68] The heavier exercises probably would include wrestling, riding, shooting, marching, and other military training. In the *Rhetorica*,[69] Aristotle expresses admiration for the complete athlete—beautiful, swift, strong—who is excellent in running, wrestling, boxing, and combines the last two well as pancratiast. Exercises would continue to play a part in life even for the old.[70] Brutality and professionalism would be avoided, naturally, being incompatible with the character of the good citizen. But Aristotle would employ the knowledge

[64] *Politica*, VIII, 7.
[65] *Ibid.*, VIII, 6.
[66] *De Poetica*, 6.
[67] *Politica*, VIII, 6.
[68] *Ibid.*, VIII, 4.
[69] Bk. I, 5.
[70] *Politica*, VII, 12.

and skill of the ablest gymnasts, whose science considers what is the suitable and best exercise for different individuals and also that which is "adapted to the great majority of men."[71] Such a science, striving for health and harmony of the body, is highly serviceable, for it does not aim simply at freedom from disease, but at such health and strength that one may use his body generously for whatever befits the free man.[72] Health being so important, one must prepare for it in many ways. Early rising and properly located and planned houses will benefit health.[73] A temperate climate is to be preferred for the state, for this contributes to spiritedness and intelligence, both of which are necessary to those who govern.[74] Physical regimen must attend to everything that makes a citizen fit for war, but it must be balanced by all that which fits for peace. For it is especially disgraceful for men to be excellent in war, and in "peace and leisure to be no better than slaves."[75]

Having arrived at twenty-one years of age, the citizen is ready for active duties in the state, first primarily as soldier, later in the making of laws and policies, and in the enjoyment of contemplative leisure, which is fitting for those able to attain highest happiness.[76] What education for the years of maturity and contemplative leisure should be is uncertain, for the *Politics* is incomplete. But certain inferences, based on Aristotle's view of mind, the end of education and the state, and the character of his own studies, seem reasonable. "Mind," in Aristotle's day, had been little explored. "We have no evidence as yet about mind or the power to think. . . ."[77]

[71] *Ibid.*, II, 8; IV, 1; *Philostratos: Concerning Gymnastics*, 14.
[72] *Rhetorica*, I, 5.
[73] *Oeconomica*, I, 6.
[74] *Politica*, VII, 7.
[75] *Ibid.*, VII, 15.
[76] *Ibid.*, VII, 9.
[77] *De Anima*, II, 2.

It seems different from other kinds of soul, however, and can exist in isolation from them. "Mind," he believes, is "that whereby the soul thinks and judges"; "before it thinks," it is "not actually any real thing."[78] The education of mind, therefore, according to the functional concept, logically considered, should be exercise in thinking and judging, which are its unique activities.

Thinking itself, however, is partly imagination, partly judgment.[79] It is of several types: art, which is capable of creation and involves "a true course of reasoning";[80] science, which knows starting points and can demonstrate its truth;[81] practical reason, neither a science nor an art, which is concerned with attainment of the "good life";[82] intuitive reason, which grasps "first principles," knows "first" and "last" terms";[83] and philosophic wisdom, the "most finished" of all, but not practical.[84] This contemplative reason which, though impractical, deals with "things noble and divine" is the best in man, and activity of this sort is the key to "perfect happiness."[85] Though Aristotle says in the *Ethics*[86] that politics, practical wisdom, is not the "best knowledge," for man is not the "best thing," he seems to recognize that, being all-inclusive, it is truly "the master art."[87] In any case, political life being indispensable to man, his education must be shaped by the requirements of its peculiar mode of thinking—the practical. Now, "all practical processes of thinking have limits" and

[78] *Ibid.*, III, 4.
[79] *Ibid.*, III, 3.
[80] *Ethica*, VI, 4.
[81] *Ibid.*, VI, 3.
[82] *Ibid.*, VI, 5.
[83] *Ibid.*, VI, 6, 11.
[84] *Ibid.*, VI, 7.
[85] *Ibid.*, X, 7.
[86] *Ibid.*, VI, 7.
[87] *Ibid.*, I, 2.

"go on for the sake of something outside the process . . ."[88]
i.e., are not ends in themselves. This view of thinking, and the
practical design of the state and all earlier education for the
attainment of happiness through the performance of the functions natural to man, suggest that further education would
have an eye to practical problems of politics, the master-art;
and since the highest thinking, philosophic, involves both
intuitive and scientific knowledge, the complete liberal education of the citizen for highest happiness would include a
thorough study of the sciences and logic.

4

Progressive political and military decline of the Greek
cities and the phenomenon of empire-building by Macedon
and Rome were paralleled by developments in philosophy.
The compass of educational theory had swung freely in the
circle of the city-state. After Plato and Aristotle, philosophy
was less concerned with the *polis* and politics, and more pre-
occupied with the problems of personal life. How can a man
find his own happiness, regardless of earthly fortune? To this
question Cynic, Epicurean, and Stoic sought the answer. This
individualistic trend had important implications. The new
man would find his larger freedom in a less restricted world.
Most significant were the growing signs of contempt for the
petty city community, wherein Greeks had found their happiness, and the dawning thought of allegiance to a cosmopolitan
world-order, based on reason implanted in all mankind. This
conception was theoretically important; its influence was ultimately registered in the works of Cicero, Seneca, Marcus
Aurelius, in Roman law, and in the formulation of Christian
doctrines. In a significant respect, however, the doctrinal

[88] *De Anima*, I, 3.

world-view of Stoics was destined to remain a dream-world, due to their apathy toward social reform.

In harmony with exaltation of the larger community and the atrophy of the city-state appeared a tendency to celebrate personal spiritual struggle and triumph rather than physical. Athletics had been held in high regard in Greek educational practice. Plato and Aristotle assigned gymnastics a role of importance in their formulation of principles of liberal education. With the demise of Greek freedom, however, physical culture lost its former *raison d'être*, service of the state. Henceforth it must serve the individual, one way or another. For some persons athletics became merely recreation or diversion; others found therein the rewards of professional pot-hunters. Joined with medical science, play and exercise were a means to preserve health, or to regain it. Among intellectuals of the new day, Cynic and Stoic, like their Christian kinsmen, gave to the *askesis* of the athletic world a spiritual meaning and acclaimed the superiority of the soul's struggle over the contests of the race-course and palaestra. Diogenes boasted that he had overcome anger, desire, fear, pain, disrepute, exile, poverty, and even pleasure—greater victories than any Greek or barbarian had won. Was he not, therefore, more worthy of a crown than the athlete who had eaten the most meat?[89] Epictetus saw life as an Olympic contest. Christians, contending as "God's athletes" for immortal crowns, conceived of monastic discipline as insurance against failure at the Last Judgment.

[89] Woody, T.: *Life and Education in Early Societies*, 351-62. Macmillan Company: New York, 1949.

CHAPTER FOUR

JANUS VIEWS LIBERAL EDUCATION

"Forward I Look, and Backward."

1

GLANCING up and down the avenue of years that passed his Roman portals, the ancient deity might descry two patterns of education, each called "liberal" for its day: the first, preeminently of life and for action, with little literary content; the second, chiefly of books and for leisure, though at its ideal best it professed to prepare men for public service, and sometimes did. The one paralleled the rise and decline of the Republic; the other flourished in the late Republic and early Empire, but ultimately died of inanition under one-man rule.

The earlier design of education, known but imperfectly through later sources—mythical history and nostalgic utterances of Romans who mourned its passing—was molded by the rude conditions of Rome's beginning and by wars of expansion whereby she gained mastery over other nations. Of all definitions of liberal education ever offered, only one fits the early Roman: the education of a free man, able to win and maintain his freedom. Judged by a later, literary standard, it was not liberal. It was not generous, broad, universal, or profound; it did not seek to fit man for a "larger intellectual life" or distant goals. It was, indeed, eminently immediate and utilitarian, preparing Roman youth for the duties of every day, in particular those of the home, the farm, warfare, and the forum. Cato, himself a man of letters, had made contact with the Greek world of thought which he saw forging ahead all around him; but his ideal education for a good man and worthy citizen was still practical training in agriculture, war, law, oratory, and medicine.[1]

Though the conception of Rome's freedom and destiny, elaborated in maturer years, may not be taken seriously as a determiner of her early life and education, it reveals man's propensity for seeking a "good" reason to explain and justify the majesty of his sway. Romans, even as others have done, viewed their wars of expansion as a struggle for liberty. It was the destiny of a superior people. The "immortal Gods," Cicero wrote,[2] willed that Romans should be free. War gives dominion to the best. Men able to rule themselves cannot justly be enslaved.[3] But, ultimately, Florus says,[4] the struggle for liberty became a war for "glory and empire." When dominion was complete, the Roman prayer was still the same: "Be still in war supreme." Virgil would grant his people endless sway. The superior must conquer, crush the haughty, spare only those who submit. That others were entitled to liberty seems

[1] Sandys, J. E.: *A Companion to Latin Studies*, 229. University Press: Cambridge, 1925.

[2] *Philippic* VI, 7. *Cicero: Philippics.* (Trans. by W. C. A. Ker) William Heinemann: London, 1926.

[3] Cicero: *Republic*, III, 25. *Cicero: De Re Publica* [and] *De Legibus.* (Trans. by C. W. Keyes) William Heinemann: London, 1928.

[4] *Lucius Annaeus Florus: Epitome of Roman History*, I, 3. (Trans. by E. S. Forster) (With J. C. Rolfe's *Cornelius Nepos*) William Heinemann: London, 1929.

not to have occurred to the early Romans. Florus[5] glories in
the tale of submission of those who had once been free and
"impatient of the yoke," the destruction of "the flower of
Spanish manhood" and "a hundred and fifty cities." The
claims of peace were not always left unspoken at Rome. Some
knew that war ultimately engulfed her in all sorts of evils.[6]
But the arguments for war, which promised to preserve the
Romans' own property and win that of others, seem to have
been generally more persuasive.[7] When the great wars of the
era of expansion were over, the *Pax Romana* doubtless impressed many as the commencement of "the ruin of the sons
of Romulus."

The beginning of Roman liberty, commonly assigned to the
expulsion of Etruscan kings,[8] was liberty for a few. Only
patricians could be consuls. For more than two centuries
plebeians struggled to improve their economic, social, and
political status. Rome's wars, which established sway over
Italy, extended the privileges of plebeians, whose military
services were increasingly in demand. When one of them became dictator, as Rutulus did,[9] their standing was greatly
enhanced.

Actually Rome's quest for liberty was mingled with duplic-
ity and a desire for plunder. The most competent historian of
her imperial progress, though kindly disposed, recognized
that she put people under the yoke while "appearing to confer
a benefit" upon them.[10] Quintus Fabius led his soldiers into

---

5 *Ibid.*, I, 33.
6 *Ibid.*, I, 47.
7 *Dio's Roman History*, XIII. (Trans. by E. Cary) 9 vols. William Heinemann:
London, 1914-27.
8 *Livy*, II, 1. (Trans. by B. O. Foster *et al.*) 13 vols. Harvard University Press:
Cambridge, 1919-; Cicero: *Republic*, II, 30-32.
9 *Livy*, II, 18; VII, 17.
10 *Polybius: The Histories*, XXXVI, 2; XXXI, 10. (Trans. by W. R. Paton)
6 vols. William Heinemann: London, 1922-27.

Etruria, hoping to enrich them all.[11] The prospect of gain[12] influenced plebeians to favor the Mamertines and led to war. That Roman officers' "lust for plunder" stirred hatred on the part of provincials, Cicero knew well.[13] A "deep-seated desire for dominion and for riches," Sallust reported, was alleged by Mithridates as the "inveterate motive" for Rome's wars against all nations.[14] Indeed, greed for goods was viewed by Rome's most original poet-philosopher as a universal cause of war.[15]

War's activities alternated with the arts of peace. If Romans learned the arts of war well and built an empire, they also won eminence in agriculture, foremost among man's peaceful conquests. If warlike destiny and mastery of men was decreed by the gods, culture of the earth and many other arts of peace were credited to Numa, who desired to lead his people from war, to subdue and soften them "along with the soil they tilled."[16] Prior to the Punic wars, agriculture was the chief peacetime occupation of men. Even after various factors had combined to debase labor and make it contemptible, agriculture was still thought worthy of "a well-bred man."[17] As

[11] *Livy*, X, 25; Homo, L.: *Primitive Italy and the Beginnings of Roman Imperialism*, 72. (Trans. by V. G. Childe) Kegan Paul, Trench, Trübner & Co., Ltd.: London, 1926.

[12] *Polybius*, I, 11.

[13] *On the Manilian Law*, 22. Cicero: *The Speeches. Pro Lege Manilia, Pro Caecina, Pro Cluentio, Pro Rabirio, Perduellionis.* (Trans. by H. G. Hodge) William Heinemann: London, 1927.

[14] *Letter of Mithridates*, 5. *Sallust.* (Trans. by J. C. Rolfe) William Heinemann: London, 1920.

[15] *Lucretius: De Rerum Natura*, V, 1435. (Trans. by W. H. D. Rouse) William Heinemann: London, 1924.

[16] Plutarch: *Numa*, 16-17. *Plutarch's Lives.* (Trans. by B. Perrin) 11 vols. William Heinemann: London, 1914-26; *Livy*, I, 19.

[17] Cicero: *Offices*, I, 42. *Cicero's Three Books of Offices . . . On Old Age . . . On Friendship; Paradoxes; Scipio's Dream; [and] . . . Duties of a Magistrate.* (Trans. by C. R. Edmonds) George Bell and Sons: London, 1887; *Marcus Terentius Varro: On Agriculture*, III, 1, 4-5; with *Marcus Porcius Cato: On Agriculture.* (Trans. by W. D. Hooper, rev. by H. B. Ash) Harvard University Press: Cambridge, 1934.

Cato[18] said, if Romans wanted to praise a citizen, they called him a "good husbandman," or "good farmer," considering that the highest commendation. Cicero could find no pursuit more worthy for old age than the "pleasures of husbandmen," for they befit "the life of a wise man."[19] Virgil, poetic architect of imperial dominion, is equally or even more convincing in praise of happy—

> Husbandmen, to whom, remote from clashing of armies,
> Earth, repaying her debts, accordeth an easy existence.[20]

In early times, before the point of diminishing returns was reached, Romans saw war and agriculture as mutually profitable supports of their freedom, their "good life." The conquest of Italy added thousands of square miles for pasturage and tillage, while labor on the land was considered the best possible nursery of "the bravest men and the sturdiest soldiers."[21] To the coördinator of the two, the state, which made their "good life" possible, the citizen owed everything. Individually, man "counted for little in the Roman world," as Paul-Louis observes.[22] The law of the state was the law of his life. Education, though not by the state, was for it. The nobility of Cato the Younger was demonstrated, as Plutarch[23] thought, by the fact that "he chose a public career," when many around him were turning to the quest for wealth. Cicero, loyal to the old ideal, despite changes that were taking place, urged the getting of knowledge that would make men "useful to the State," there being nothing higher than one's duty to it.[24] Yet,

---

[18] *On Agriculture*, Introduction, 2.
[19] *On Old Age*, 15.
[20] Lawton, W. C.: *Introduction to Classical Latin Literature*, 160. Charles Scribner's Sons: New York, 1904.
[21] Cato: *On Agriculture*, Introduction, 4.
[22] *Ancient Rome at Work*, 20 f. (Trans. by E. B. F. Wareing) Alfred A. Knopf: New York, 1927.
[23] *Cato the Younger*, 19.
[24] *Republic*, I, 20; VI, 16; *Offices*, I, 6, 17.

faithful to the old practice of family and private schooling, he disapproved of any uniform state "system of education," officially established by law.[25]

Romans, it has been said, were distinguished for their "practical common-sense" and "lack of imagination."[26] Judgments vary. Certainly they were great borrowers and imitators rather than great original creators.[27] Like sheep, Cato thought, they followed easily the lead of others.[28] That Romans suffered in the creative arts by comparison with others, Virgil was ready to grant. As men of action, builders of armies and empire, they were to excel. Preference for action was deep-rooted. As Sallust says, "the best citizen preferred action to words."[29] Cicero turned to letters when a life of public activity was no longer open to him.[30] Concern with practical matters, business success, and material possessions, Horace believed, had been prejudicial to intellectual affairs. Boys learned too well to divide the *as* into a hundred parts. Such preoccupation with material goods could not produce poems worthy of cedar oil and polished cypress.[31] Ultimately, of course, love of wealth bred luxury, which threatened the undoing of Rome. As Cato said, it is hard "to save a city in which a fish sells for more than an ox."[32]

[25] *Republic*, IV, 3.

[26] Homo: *op. cit.*, 255 *f*.

[27] Abbott, F. F.: *Society and Politics in Ancient Rome*, 161 *ff*. Charles Scribner's Sons: New York, 1909.

[28] Plutarch: *Cato*, 8.

[29] *War with Catiline*, 8.

[30] *Letters to His Friends*, IV, 3; V, 15. *Cicero: The Letters to His Friends* [and] *Letters to Quintus*. (Trans. by W. G. Williams) 3 vols. William Heinemann: London, 1927-29; *Letters to Atticus*, IV, 18. (Trans. by E. O. Winstedt) 3 vols. William Heinemann: London, 1912-18.

[31] *The Art of Poetry*, E. C. Wickham's *Horace for English Readers*, 356 *f*. Clarendon Press: Oxford, 1903.

[32] Plutarch: *Cato*, 8, 18.

The education of a freeborn boy in early Rome began at home. By authority of the Twelve Tables, the father's power over him was complete. Neither advancing years nor public office brought release from filial duty. With his sisters, whose life was even more strictly guarded, the boy played the games of childhood. Together, under the eyes of father and mother, they began to learn right conduct by precept and example, and homely tasks and the offices of religion by seeing them performed. Diet was lean; no one ate or slept too much. Education of girls began and ended in domestic life; that of boys included, with advancing years, the activities of the farm, the forum, and the Field of Mars. Obedience, piety to their gods, respect for law, modesty in word and conduct, practical ability, self-confidence, native intelligence, health, strength, good carriage, and belief in Rome's destiny were highly prized in the education of future fathers and citizens of Rome.[33] As Ennius' couplet summed it up—

> The commonwealth of Rome is founded firm
> On ancient customs and on men of might.[34]

This ancient "ancestral discipline" continued in practice to some extent in later days, as Cato's exemplary care of his son's education and Horace's eulogy of his father show. Memory of it was kept green by Tacitus, Pliny, and others, when Roman home life had vastly disintegrated. "The object of this rigorous system," says Tacitus, "was that the natural disposition of every child, while still sound at the core and untainted, not warped as yet by any vicious tendencies, might at once lay hold with heart and soul on virtuous accomplishments, and whether its bent was towards the army, or the law,

---

[33] Marquardt, J.: *Das Privatleben der Römer*, 89 *ff*. Hirzel: Leipzig, 1886.
[34] Cicero: *Republic*, V, 1.

or the pursuit of eloquence, might make that its sole aim and its all-absorbing interest."[35]

Early Roman farms were small and self-sustaining. Food, clothing, housing, and tools were products of the family's hands. Basically, the economy was twofold. In Varro's phrase, the shepherd's life was "the treble," the farmer played "the accompaniment."[36] To these occupations, a boy's training was attuned. Tending small herds and flocks—his earliest chore, soon followed by heavier tasks—learning to drive oxen at the primitive plow, sowing and reaping spelt, barley, and other grain, and kindred labors, were for him the road to sturdy health and solid wealth. Only when small farms gave way to great estates, when slave labor became common, and war's service lengthened its demands on time, was this road to healthy vigor narrowed and finally closed. Then with Virgil might Romans sigh in vain:

> No pious due is to the ploughshare paid,
> Waste lie our fields, their tillers drawn for war. . . .

General physical sturdiness, developed by hard manual labor on the land, provided a solid foundation for that strenuous military training to which the most competent judges credited Rome's successful conquest of power.[37] Far from rebelling against the sacrifice of himself for the sake of the state, the Roman embraced it with evident zest. Personal success in fighting led to power and preferment in civil life. Cicero thought it "glorious to fall when leading an army." Reason is superior to physical strength, indeed, but a young man's chief claim to fame comes from military accomplish-

---

[35] *A Dialogue on Oratory*, 28. *Tacitus: Dialogus, Agricola* [and] *Germania*. (*Dialogus*, trans. by W. Peterson; *Agricola* and *Germania* by M. Hutton) William Heinemann: London, 1925.

[36] *On Agriculture*, I, 2, 16.

[37] *Polybius*, VI, 52.

ment. Philosophers generally "die in their beds."[38] Pompey's leaving "school and the studies of boyhood" to join the army and "study war in a serious campaign" stirred Cicero to generous praise.[39] Others less literarily inclined than Cicero could scarcely be expected to rate military affairs lower than he.

Excellence and devotion to physical, warlike exercises were credited to all great leaders and to mythical characters. Hostilius was said to have instituted all forms of military discipline and marvelously trained his soldiers.[40] Ovid tells of Romulus and Remus "exercising their naked bodies in the sunshine," trying their strength of arms with gloves, javelins, and heavy stones.[41] Corvus, Livy says, got on well with his men, for he was ready to meet all competitors in military sports, conquering and being conquered without losing poise.[42] A "sturdy body," "vigorous arm," and fondness for war, according to Plutarch,[43] gave Marcellus his name. Numidian Jugurtha won instant approval from Roman soldiers by devotion to running, hurling the javelin, and hunting, which made him a great fighter.[44] The constant retelling of heroic military feats, like that of Horatius Cocles, Polybius[45] considered an important factor in stimulating Roman boys to a desire for like achievement.

Discipline in the army was strict, punishment severe. Training to meet its demands began early on the Campus Martius, where men and youths kept themselves fit and developed skills

38 *De Finibus Bonorum et Malorum*, II, 30. (Trans. by H. Rackham) William Heinemann: London, 1914; *Offices*, II, 13.
39 *Manilian Law*, 10.
40 *Florus*, I, 1, 3.
41 *Fasti*, II, 365 *et seqq. Ovid's Fasti*. (Trans. by J. G. Frazer) William Heinemann: London, 1931.
42 *Livy*, VII, 33.
43 *Marcellus*, 1.
44 Sallust: *War with Jugurtha*, 6.
45 Bk. VI, 55.

useful in war by running, jumping, riding, fencing, swimming, wrestling, throwing weights, hurling spears on foot and horseback. Hunting, too, since it served a useful military end, was approved. No hint is heard of exercise for purely personal pleasure, or for development of physical beauty. The ideal of balance, prized in Athenian training at its best, was foreign to the Roman mind. Roman *ludi* (games) were spectacles rather than athletic contests (*agones*).[46] Soldiers trained in Greek gymnastics, Caesar and others said, could never offer serious competition on the field of battle.[47]

Fathers themselves began this military training. Cato instructed his son in the use of javelin, horsemanship, fighting in armor, boxing, swimming, and sought to inure him to heat and cold. Aemilius Paulus, too, gave his sons the old "ancestral discipline."[48] Marius is said to have gone on a campaign, even though old, so that he might provide his son proper military training.[49] Only when conquests had ended, and policing the Empire had become the job of professional soldiers, paid for their service, did this careful attention to military training decline. Pliny noted regretfully that, whereas once youth had been "inured from boyhood to service in camp" and had learned to command by first learning to obey, there was in his day "neither command nor obedience."[50]

In early times, fitting the Roman citizen for freedom required but little attention to literary learning. Letters may have been introduced about the eighth century, at Cumae, but

---

[46] Gardiner, E. N.: *Athletics of the Ancient World*, 119. Clarendon Press: Oxford, 1930.

[47] *Lucan: The Civil War*, VII, 269 *et seqq.* (Trans. by J. D. Duff) William Heinemann: London, 1928.

[48] Plutarch: *Cato*, 20; *Aemilius Paulus*, 6.

[49] Plutarch: *Caius Marius*, 34.

[50] *Pliny: Letters*, VIII, 14. (Trans. by W. Melmoth; rev. by W. M. L. Hutchinson) 2 vols. William Heinemann: London, 1915.

writing was still rare in the sixth. Documents once credited
to the fifth and sixth centuries may have been more recent.
Even the publication of the Twelve Tables, long assigned to
451 B.C., may have occurred much later.[51] Not until the laws
were available, was reading a really important accomplishment, for there was little writing before 290 B.C.[52] Generously
supposing the casual references of Livy and others to schools
and pupils[53] to be reliable history, there was certainly little
to be read in Latin before Livius Andronicus translated the
Odyssey. Cicero says the laws of the Twelve Tables were still
learned in his boyhood as "a required formula." This was,
indeed, the Roman boy's "first" reader; for many years it
was his only one.

Roman law was the beginning and the end of liberal learning in provincial Rome. Even in the generously literate age of
the dying Republic, Cicero regarded it as the intellectual
foundation for all in public affairs. The Twelve Tables were
to him an entire political science, whose "authority" and
"utility" outweighed all the philosophers. Since Rome had
become the "seat of virtue, empire, and dignity," it was of
preëminent importance to study her "spirit, customs, and
discipline." For, Cicero argued, one must assume as much
wisdom in framing her laws as in the building of "so vast and
powerful an empire."[54]

According to the old discipline, getting an acquaintance

[51] *Livy*, III, 31-32, 34; Cicero: *Republic*, II, 36; *The Attic Nights of Aulus Gellius*, XX, 1. (Trans. by J. C. Rolfe) 3 vols. William Heinemann: London, 1927-28; Cary, M.: *A History of Rome Down to the Reign of Constantine*, 41, 46 *f*. Macmillan & Co., Ltd.: London, 1938.

[52] Frank, T.: *Roman Imperialism*, 59 *f*. Macmillan Company: New York, 1929.

[53] *Livy*, III, 44; V, 27; VI, 25; IX, 36; *Florus*, I, 1, 6; Plutarch: *Romulus*, 6; *Camillus*, 10, 38; *Dio*, VI, 24.

[54] *On Oratory*, I, 44. Cicero: *On Oratory and Orators; with His Letters to Quintus and Brutus*. (Trans. by J. S. Watson) George Bell and Sons: London, 1891.

with law was not simply a literary exercise. It was far more an apprenticeship whereby one learned its applications as it functioned in the Senate and elsewhere, "amid the very shock of battle," as Tacitus says,[55] "under conditions in which any stupid or ill-advised statement" brought quick disapproval from judges, opponents, and one's own friends as well. "Thus," Pliny wrote, musing on the changes time had wrought, "they were taught by that surest method of instruction, example, how far the right of proposing any law to the Senate extended; what privileges a senator had in delivering his opinion; the powers of senators who are magistrates, and the independence of the rest; where it is proper to yield, and where to stand firm; how long to speak, and when to be silent; how to distinguish conflicting motions, and how to discuss an amendment. In a word, they learnt by this means the whole conduct of a senator."[56]

According to Sallust, Romans were *religiosissimi mortales,* ever lavish in gifts to their gods. In that opinion Cicero and other competent judges concurred.[57] Rome's zealously cultivated doctrine of her superiority and destiny to rule others was traditionally rooted in supernaturalism, a ubiquitous primitive animism which intermingled with extensive anthropomorphic borrowings from Etruria and elsewhere. This religion, identified by an eminent scholar as "awe, nervousness, scruple"—superstition—and rituals designed to propitiate the spirit world and ease man's fears,[58] had a profound effect on Roman life. Fostering belief in these superstitions by private and public rites was a marked feature of education. Po-

[55] *On Oratory,* 34.
[56] *Letters,* VIII, 14.
[57] Sallust: *Catiline,* 9; *Livy,* V, 54.
[58] Fowler, W. W.: *Social Life at Rome in the Age of Cicero,* 319. Macmillan Company: New York, 1909.

lybius held that this scrupulous fear of the gods, with which their minds were so thoroughly imbued, essentially explained "the cohesion of the Roman State."[59] This asserted advantage was temporary, however; ultimately, it was balanced by disadvantage, for the Roman people, trained to belief in magic practices, were quick to turn to strange new cults when old ones proved impotent. As disintegration grew, the government itself fell into confusion and contradiction, seeking at one time to prohibit popular new cults and then to encourage them. Under such circumstances, it is not strange that many of the ablest, most independent minds exhibited the frankest unbelief and contempt in regard to old practices. Claudius Pulcher threw the holy chickens into the sea, that they might drink since "they would not eat."[60] Caesar, as Suetonius tells us, refused to permit unfavorable auspices to hinder his plans for action. A soothsayer, having reported evil omens, was told: "They will be more favourable when I wish it; it should not be regarded as a portent, if a beast has no heart."[61]

2

When Rome's conquests embraced all Italy and then stretched eastward beyond the sea, the intimate contact thus established with Greek culture began to effect a metamorphosis of her mind which paralleled, and ultimately transcended in importance, the changes of her material life. This transformation of the original design of education thought fitting for a free Roman began in a limited way in the third century. The rise of literary study in the time of Andronicus and Ennius seemed quite "humble" to Suetonius;[62] but with

59 Bk. VI, 56.
60 Suetonius: *Tiberius, 2. Suetonius.* (Trans. by J. C. Rolfe) 2 vols. William Heinemann: London, 1914.
61 Suetonius: *Julius*, 59, 77, 81.
62 *Grammarians*, 1.

Crates (*c.* 169 or 159 B.C.) Greek grammatical and philological studies gained a solid footing. By the mid-first century B.C. the fusion of Graeco-Roman education was complete. The chief instruments of this new liberal education, at first, were Greek teachers (often slaves), books, grammar and rhetoric schools, libraries, and the so-called University of Athens, to which the wealthiest and most enthusiastic Hellenizers sent their sons. Soon Greek prototypes were paralleled by Latin institutions, more or less faithful to the original, though some things Greek were long discountenanced and resisted by Roman society.

The original pattern of Roman education and the new one which emerged present notable contrasts. The old was principally of deeds, the new chiefly of words; one emphasized character, the other knowledge; one centered in life's strenuous labor, the other, depending upon the possession of leisure, tended ultimately to promote the divorce of life and learning. The old education was actually in close harmony with Rome's political constitution; exponents of the new spoke much of political life and promised preparation for service to it, but schools scarcely exhibited that intimacy of relation with politics which their spokesmen advocated. The old education was Latin, first and last; the new placed Greek first, and then Latin.[63] Now for the first time, a foreign language and literature became the essential elements of a liberal education. Provincialism, which marked education of the vigorous Republic, gave way to a cosmopolitanism under the Empire which found ideological kinship in Stoic equalitarianism. In short, judged by the new standard, the old life and its education, though sturdy and self-reliant, were barbarous. Devotion to war and a

---

[63] *The Institutio Oratoria of Quintilian*, I, 1, 12-14; 4, 1; 8, 5. (Trans. by H. E. Butler) 4 vols. Harvard University Press: Cambridge, 1921-36.

general lack of leisure, Suetonius thought, had left little time
for liberal learning.[64] Cicero contrasted the age of barbarism
and that of civilization. Though he frequently disparaged the
Greeks and certainly regretted that Roman law had fallen
into neglect, his devotion to Greek culture was variously expressed and convincingly demonstrated by his zealous pursuit
of it. The Greeks by their culture "have rescued us from barbarism," he said, and we should be "willing exponents" of
that culture.[65]

The new Roman view of liberal education was conditioned
partly by the growth of wealth and leisure, which made re-
munerative employment unnecessary. Romans of earlier, more
strenuous days had been too occupied with practical affairs
to get a liberal education. Cicero looked disdainfully upon
lower occupations and petty business, but regarded great
business ventures and landholding as worthy of a gentleman.[66]
Real freedom depended on leisure: "He does not seem to me
to be a free man, who does not sometimes *do nothing*."[67] Men
of wealth and position readily accepted the view that liberal
studies should not serve money-making. The question of taking fees was resolved by Quintilian, thus: it is noblest if an
orator defends clients regardless of fees; but this does not pre-
clude accepting some gift or reward, for "one good turn deserves another." If economic necessity compel an orator to
take fees, they are justifiable, but they should always be
moderate, just to meet one's needs. And, of course, such a poor
lawyer will not regard this "payment as a fee"![68] Seneca,

---

[64] *Grammarians*, 1.
[65] *Letters to His Brother Quintus*, I, 1, 9; *Academica*, II, 2. *Cicero: De Natura
Deorum* [and] *Academica*. (Trans. by H. Rackham) William Heinemann:
London, 1933; *Republic*, II, 19, 21.
[66] *Offices*, I, 42.
[67] *On Oratory*, II, 6.
[68] *Quintilian*, XII, 7, 8-12.

satiated with all that wealth can buy, and disillusioned, advises self-denial. Poverty means freedom; wealth, slavery.[69] No study is liberal that leads to money-making.[70]

The ideal of the new liberal education was a hybrid in which the old Roman stress on action was joined with literature, philosophy, and oratory. The embodiment of this ideal, the perfect orator, was to be a man of action, not a literary dilettante. Cicero expressed this view on many occasions. "Well-directed action," he said, must depend upon "knowledge and prudence"; knowledge is "solitary and barren," if not turned to the "service of mankind."[71] Those who govern the state ought to be zealous in study, being careful, however, not to allow it to encroach on "public interest," for by so doing they will be enabled to rule more wisely. Cicero distinguished clearly between the orator, who can use learning, and those who seek for knowledge of the arts but do not expect to put it to use.[72]

In the early period of fusion, this ideal combination of learning and action was to a degree attained by some. Cicero says that "when our empire over all nations was established," almost all youths "ambitious of praise" strove to learn the new art of speaking.[73] Aemilius Paulus, Sulla, Brutus, Sallust, Caesar, and Cicero were notably successful in uniting public service and learning. None of them put learning first. Caesar, who had great natural talent for oratory and studied under Apollonius of Rhodes, renounced it for a military career. Even so, Cicero could think of no one to rank above him, even

[69] *Epistle* XVII. *Seneca: ad Lucilium Epistulae Morales.* (Trans. by R. M. Gummere) 3 vols. William Heinemann: London, 1917-25.
[70] *Ibid.,* LXXXVIII, 1-2.
[71] *Offices,* I, 44-45.
[72] *On Oratory,* III, 23.
[73] *Ibid.,* I, 4.

among those who were wholly devoted to oratory.[74] Dio, too, praised Caesar as a happy embodiment of the ideal, for he united "natural force" and "the most liberal education," and thus was able to understand quickly, decide readily, and arrange everything "most prudently."[75] Cicero was content to devote himself wholly to letters only when a life of public activity was no longer possible for him.[76]

What were the new studies which so completely supplanted the Twelve Tables, once learned "as a required formula"?[77] Varro specified the seven liberal arts of the Greeks (grammar, rhetoric, dialectic, arithmetic, music, geometry, astronomy), to which he added architecture and medicine.[78] To be "an orator possessed of every praiseworthy accomplishment," says Cicero, one must know all the "liberal arts."[79] The Greek "cycle" of studies necessary to general education is approved by Quintilian.[80] Seneca, however, casts doubt on the liberal arts; for, though useful in many respects, they do not teach virtue.[81] Philosophies, too, must be studied, Cicero and Quintilian agree. To Seneca, philosophy is the only truly liberal study, for it is concerned with attainment of virtue.[82]

Eloquence, the sum of the new liberal education, Cicero thought a large and difficult domain, for it included more sciences than was generally understood. Due to the "incredible magnitude and difficulty," few mastered it, though many

[74] Suetonius: *Julius,* 55; Cicero: *Brutus,* 261. *Cicero: Brutus.* (Trans. by G. L. Hendrickson) [and] *Orator.* (Trans. by H. M. Hubbell) Harvard University Press: Cambridge, 1939; *Offices,* I, 1; Plutarch: *Cicero,* 2; *Caesar,* 3.

[75] Bk. XLIV, 38.

[76] *To His Friends,* IV, 3, 4; *To Atticus,* IV, 18; Plutarch: *Cicero,* 40.

[77] Cicero: *Laws,* II, 23.

[78] Sandys, J. E.: *A Companion to Latin Studies,* 229. University Press: Cambridge, 1925.

[79] *On Oratory,* I, 6.

[80] *Institutio Oratoria,* I, 10, 1.

[81] *Epistle* LXXXVIII, 32.

[82] *Ibid.,* LXXXVIII, 23.

sought that end. The orator needs a lawyer's memory, the acuteness of a logician, the wisdom of a philosopher, a poetic gift in language, the voice of a tragedian, and the gestures of an actor. Romans, he thought, had been too busy with practical affairs to gain all these accomplishments, but with leisure and more devotion to study they might hope to win true mastery of them.

In oratory, as in everything, "nature and genius" contribute most; nature must provide the lead—native quickness in learning, a good power of retentiveness, acuteness in invention, ability to embellish and explain, good lungs, good voice, a quick tongue, and a pleasing physical harmony. Education can improve these, but it cannot create them. The orator must study how to use voice, breath, tongue, and in fact his whole body. He must be ready to learn from actors as well as orators.[83]

If one is to speak well, he is to write much. Writing is oratory's best teacher. One cannot become a good speaker simply by speaking; in fact, by so doing one may become a bad speaker. By careful consideration, by reduction to writing in the best form, arrangement and language, imitating excellent models, the best delivery of what is to be spoken will be secured.[84]

There are five parts of oratory: knowing the subject, arrangement of material, retention in memory, choice of fitting language, and a suitable, graceful, dignified delivery. Mastery of the first alone involves vast pains, for one must know the works of poets, historians, what has been written on all the liberal arts, law, Senate usage, Roman government, rights of allies, treaties, conventions—in fact, whatever pertains to

[83] Cicero: *On Oratory*, I, 34; II, 87-88; III, 22.
[84] *Ibid.*, I, 33; II, 22.

matters of government and all antiquity. One must understand these matters; and he must be able to present the argument on both sides of every question. But understanding is not enough, for Cicero does not accept the view of Socrates that "all men are sufficiently eloquent in that which they understand." It is plausible, but unsound. To an understanding of the matter, polished expression must be added if one is to be eloquent.[85]

Cicero is profoundly concerned about the relation of learning to life. The studies being so vast, there is a danger that they may lead away from actual practice in speaking in the forum. But learning and language suitable to the "tumults of the city and forum" are desired, not a florid style, fit for "parade" in schools. Danger also lies in another direction: The orator's serious business is to sway men's minds, lead them to a desired end; to do this, he needs a thorough knowledge of human nature, of the emotions and how to play upon them. Philosophers will investigate such matters; what they discover, the orator must learn and put to use. To reach his goal, the orator must understand and always remember the fundamental truth that the arts are treated in one way by those who investigate them, and in another way by those who practice them.[86] If he avoids the first danger successfully, the true orator will be more than a literary prodigy, a glib speechmaker, able "to bawl for hours by the water-clock." Steering clear of the second, he will be more than a philosopher, in Cicero's opinion, for he will have the philosopher's knowledge plus the eloquence which puts it to effective use.

As a matter of fact, Cicero, the alchemist, would mix those elements of education—liberal and practical—which schools so often contrive to hold in immaculate, unfruitful isolation.

[85] *Ibid.*, I, 14.
[86] *Ibid.*, III, 23.

His ideal orator is the embodiment of a "practical, liberal" education—knowledge put to work. Learning, he suggests, had flowed since Socrates in two directions, like waters from a great divide: philosophy, pure learning, found its way to the Ionian Sea; and oratory, practical learning, flowed into barbarian Tuscan waters. But the "grandeur of the sciences" is lessened by the "distribution and separation of their parts" —specialization which knows nothing beyond its own frontiers. The parts need to be reunited. Why quarrel about names? If anyone calls the "philosopher, who instructs us fully in things and words, an *orator*," there is no ground for objection. And if anyone would call the orator, who has "wisdom united with eloquence, a *philosopher*," no one should complain.[87]

Quintilian, a teacher, a bookish man by comparison with Cicero, lived in an age of decadence when unity of action and knowledge was more conspicuous for its failure than for its realization, but he still urged preparation of the orator, a man of action and learning, as the ideal embodiment of liberal education. The purpose of rhetoric is to persuade men to right action. If assemblymen, senators, and judges were all philosophers, eloquence would scarcely be needed.[88] The man who plays his rôle as citizen, meets all demands of public and private life, guides the state by his counsel, and purges it of "its vices," is "the orator of our quest." He must be like Cato's model, "a good man, skilled in speaking."[89] Such a properly educated man will always be ready for action. He is "armed for battle, ever ready for the fray"; speech will not fail him in court or in daily domestic affairs. He will not falter

---

[87] *Ibid.*, III, 19, 33-35.
[88] *Quintilian*, II, 16, 7-8; 17, 25, and 28.
[89] *Ibid.*, XII, 1, 1.

before any particular case, if he only be given time to study it, "for all other knowledge" is at his command.[90]

The ideal of unity of knowledge and action is still the same; but Quintilian knows the reality is quite different. There are many evils in the schools. Grammarians and teachers of rhetoric do not keep to their proper domains. The fundamental studies are too often taken for granted. Bellowing "with uplifted hand" has become common. It appeals to the "dingier" sort, but it ill becomes a good orator, a properly educated man. Pupils act spitefully if teachers do not praise them, and each applauds the work of his fellows effusively. Beating, which is fit only for slaves, is commonly resorted to by schoolmasters.[91]

There is much pedantry about minutiae in current education, which makes a hash of mind. The depressing thought occurs to Quintilian that he, himself, may seem pedantic. His material, heavy and technical, he fears may be an unpleasant dose for readers! Even to him, the labor is burdensome; but he steers straight ahead, under the inspiration of his patron, to complete a book on oratory more thorough than any of its predecessors.[92]

The pedantic tendency to divorce life from liberal learning, which Quintilian deprecated, had begun long before his time. Though many factors contributed to its growth, the demise of responsible self-government and the rise of autocratic one-man rule were of central importance. Cicero found consolation in letters and philosophy when the death of the Republic left no practical arena for his talents, "nothing else in which to find repose."[93] As imperial rule perfected its dominion,

---

90 *Ibid.*, XII, 9, 21.
91 *Ibid.*, I, Preface; 3, 13 *et seqq.*; II, 1, 1-6; 2, 1-5, 9-13; 12, 9-10.
92 *Ibid.*, I, 5, 14; 7, 33; II, 17, 24; III, 1, 5; IV, Preface; XII, Introduction.
93 *To His Friends*, IV, 3 and 4; *To Atticus*, IV, 18; Plutarch: *Cicero*, 40.

absorbing all prerogatives and leaving man a mere shadow of himself, education, literature and philosophy reflected increasingly the emptiness and purposelessness of life. Intellectual arts flourish best under freedom. If, at times, they had met sharp opposition under the Republic, they were to feel a heavier yoke under the Caesars.

The patronage of Augustus, as Ramsay says, "may have done something to arrest the decay of literature; but with . . . the accession of Tiberius the truth could no longer be concealed that the days of liberty were over, and the natural results followed in every department of human life and thought. Deprived of the inspiration of reality, literature and oratory descended from the public to the private stage, and lost alike their meaning and their manliness."[94] As youth in schools dealt more and more with threadbare themes unrelated to life, so too did adult men of letters. Statius is full of extravagant phrases and fancies, but who would expect bold originality of thought in Domitian's reign? Free speech was at an end; "speech of any kind," Slater remarks, "had to be prefaced with extravagant flattery to the throne."[95] It was a matter of prudence to choose colorless, remote subjects which would not be "displeasing even to the most jealous imperial censorship." The *gravitas* of Roman letters ebbed away, "undermined by the loss of freedom and long capricious persecution." The only truly vigorous and refreshing criticism is that of satire. Moral decay has bred rot in Roman letters. No one wants honest criticism, to be sure, but Persius will give it anyway: Everyone has "the ears of an ass."[96] "Books in the libraries

[94] *Juvenal and Persius*, xxvii. (Trans. by G. G. Ramsay) William Heinemann: London, 1928.
[95] Slater, D. A. (Trans.) : *The Silvae of Statius*, Introduction, 16 *f*. Clarendon Press: Oxford, 1908.
[96] Persius: *Satire* I, 13 *et seqq.*, 114 *et seqq.*

rotted" in the age of Diocletian, says Tenney Frank; for that "savior" denied "all the ideas that had made Rome worthy of rule."[97]

Dramatic art, which had hard going at Rome in the days when Terence's *Hecyra* sought in vain to compete with rope dancers and pugilists, reached its height in the tragedies of Attius. Enjoying but a brief popularity, it degenerated into "a mere literary exercise" after the death of the Republic.[98] Pliny praises the "polite" learning of his day, but he admits that audiences are less interested than "in the time of our ancestors," and there is "little disposition" on the part of the public to attend assemblies.[99] If learning was "polite," it had lost the ruggedness of earlier days. "Liberal" education became an end in itself, or merely a means to personal satisfaction. Seneca's phrase, "we learn for school, not for life," sums up the dominant trend of education. Tacitus complains of the "subject-matter . . . so remote from real life," "bombastic style," and "magniloquent phraseology" of the schools.[100] Their hackneyed themes, Juvenal opines, is "the cabbage" that kills the rhetoric master![101] Divorced from vital problems, oratory became a popular means of entertainment, as Pliny's account of the "most eloquent," "most happy" Isaeus' coming performance shows.[102]

If life's problems suffered from this separation of life and letters in the schools, linguistic scholarship and the Latin tongue were gainers. Teachers from the time of Andronicus to

---

[97] *Rome and Italy of the Empire. An Economic Survey of Ancient Rome*, V, 303. Johns Hopkins Press: Baltimore, 1940.

[98] Duff, J. W.: *A Literary History of Rome*, 231 *f*. T. Fisher Unwin: London, 1923; Lawton: *op. cit.*, 38 *f.*, 59.

[99] *Letters*, I, 10, 13; VII, 17.

[100] *On Oratory*, 35.

[101] *Satire* VII, 150 *et seqq.*

[102] *Letters*, II, 3.

that of Fronto were playing an important rôle in fusing the two cultures and in the development of Latin into a world language. Bilingualism became the rule in intellectual circles. Ovid recommends Greek as well as Latin even for love-making! Some of the first teachers were poets. Gnipho, who taught Cicero, wrote "On the Latin Language." Praeconinus, author of a similar work, was Varro's teacher. Palaemon, far famed grammarian of his day, was the teacher of Quintilian, who produced the most complete treatise on oratory and also taught Pliny the Younger. By the second century A.D., the fusion of cultures, well symbolized by Aulus Gellius, was "all but complete." In Fronto, teacher of Marcus Aurelius, the trend to minute scholarship in the nice discrimination of words reached its peak. Fronto, ever carefully attentive to the right syllable, word, and word order, is critical even of Cicero, who best symbolized the union of eloquence and action, because he did not always choose words "with especial care." The fame of the Frontonian "school" long survived, as Sidonius' *Letters*[103] remind us.

Contempt for the verbalistic trend of Roman education reached a high pitch in Seneca. Neither the old pattern nor the new qualifies by his standard as "liberal." Those who are so busy with the minutiae of linguistics and literature fall far short of a liberal education, for it does not consist of scanning poets, pronouncing syllables, nice choice or placing of words, memorization, finding whether Hesiod or Homer was the earlier poet; nor does it depend on those elements of science that make up arithmetic, music, geometry, astronomy, painting, and wrestling. Only one study is liberal—that is, worthy of a freeborn man. It is the pursuit of virtue, which true phi-

103 *The Letters of Sidonius*, I, 1. (Trans. by O. M. Dalton) 2 vols. Clarendon Press: Oxford, 1915

losophy alone can teach. One can get wisdom without the seven arts; for though they may be useful for many things, and may even "prepare the soul" for virtue, they do not teach it. Seneca is surfeited with literature. By reading too many books the mind is distracted. Only "standard authors" should be read and reread.[104]

Philosophy, once profoundly concerned with problems of society and government in the time of Plato and Aristotle, and which had been viewed by Cicero and Quintilian as necessary to the education of a complete orator, fell from its high estate under the Empire and became almost wholly a private road to virtue, a means of personal adjustment to the conditions which life imposed; or, like grammar and oratory, it was reduced to the hair-splitting technicalities of the schoolroom. The latter, Seneca rejected along with all other "liberal" arts as incompetent to provide a liberal education. High-souled Stoic philosophy might touch a slave or a reformer, or satisfy one's personal longing for happiness, but it did not strive actively for a better society or to improve government. Cicero had maintained that his ideal statesman could not be faithful to Stoic conceptions of good, evil, honor, ignominy, punishments, and rewards and carry through public business by his art.[105] Yet the "noblest use" to which virtue could be put was "the government of the State," as he said in the *Republic*.[106] Stoic philosophers were seldom able to serve the state under the Empire. If philosophers aspired to bring arbitrary government to judgment in the time of Helvidius Priscus, that was a rare exception. As a rule, philosophy like other arts took flight from reality. Even Marcus Aurelius, with the

[104] *Epistle* II; LXXXVIII, 1-4, 20, 23, 32.
[105] *On Oratory*, III, 18.
[106] Bk. I, 2.

power of the mightiest empire in his hands, did not find in Stoicism a guide to constructive social improvement. The best that philosophy suggested to him was: "do nothing unsocial"; turn all "efforts to the common interest, and divert them from the contrary." So far, so good; but it did not go far; if it afforded a vision of what should be, it provided no drive toward the realization of it. Indeed, Stoicism was apt to lead men to think it enough to be neither dissatisfied with the present nor afraid of the future. Live according to nature, and no harm can come to thee. One need not seek Plato's *Republic*, "for who can change men's opinions?"[107]

Stoicism was to Marcus a personal religion, apparently, as it was to others of lesser power and station. As Seneca said, philosophy is a guide to the "higher life," a "pedagogue of the human race," to lead it "to the stars." "The gods are not disdainful . . . they lend a hand as you climb."[108] Thus reduced in status, philosophy seems more competent to prepare for dying than for living.

Notwithstanding these disparaging remarks, which reveal the limitations of philosophy as seen by men of prominence in the world of politics and letters, Roman political thought and law owed something of importance to Stoic teaching. Although Cicero doubted whether the statesman could measure up to certain Stoic ideals of virtue, his conception of a world-order evolving from the exercise of virtue, implanted in the human race by nature, was in harmony with Stoic thought. From the *lex naturale*, rooted in man, emerged the *jus naturale* of society, and the *jus gentium*, or law of nations.[109] In place of the citizenship of petty states and the dichotomy of barbarian

---

107 *The Meditations of the Emperor Marcus Aurelius Antoninus*, II, 6; V, 1, 10; IX, 29; X, 6. (Trans. by G. Long) Burt: New York, n.d.
108 *Epistle* LXXIII, 15-16; LXXXIX, 13.
109 *The Republic*, I, 1 *et seq.*

and Greek, Cynics and Stoics conceived of an ideal world-citizenship, based on the principle of natural right and reason inherent in all mankind. To the mind of a practical intellectual like Cicero, this cosmopolitan ideal seemed to be made manifest in the Roman State. Arbitrary one-man rule, in years to come under the Empire, which found its defense in the legal phrase, *quod principi placuit legis habet vigorem* (the prince's pleasure has the power of law), would often deny effectively the most elementary of human rights. Nevertheless, in Ulpian's contradictory formula, *quoad jus naturale omnes homines aequales sunt*, the principle of human equality under natural law was embodied in Roman law, the Empire's ideal bequest to posterity.

While Romans had some knowledge of Greek gymnastic at an early date, it was only after the war with Pyrrhus that contact was common, and some men of prominence began to indulge in the Greek practices. Scipio Africanus frequented the palaestra; Aemilius Paulus trained his sons according to the Greek mode, while not forsaking Roman discipline.[110] "A contest of athletes," according to Livy,[111] was first introduced at Rome in 186 B.C. By Varro's time (116-27 B.C.), Greek "citified gymnasia" had taken a deep hold on Romans. Every villa had its gymnasium, palaestra, and all that pertained to them.[112] Cicero, despite repeated thrusts at Greek physical training, was entranced with his own palaestra and full of admiration for that of his brother.[113] Under the Empire, public Greek gymnasia and baths flourished. Dio says[114] that Agrippa constructed a Laconian sudatorium about 25 B.C.

110 Plutarch: *Aemilius Paulus*, 6, 28.
111 Bk. XXXIX, 22.
112 Varro: *On Agriculture*, II, Introduction.
113 *To Atticus*, I, 6, 8-10; II, 4; *To Quintus*, III, 1 and 9.
114 Bk. LIII, 27.

Nero is said to have built the first permanent gymnasium at Rome (60 A.D.) and provided oil to Senators and *Equites,* according to "the lax fashion of the Greeks."[115]

The new Hellenized Roman pattern of liberal education reflected, in its emphasis on a certain type of intellectual fare, a frank admission of the superior literary and philosophical attainment of the Greeks. In respect to physical education the situation was the reverse. Despite the ultimate popular acceptance of palaestra and gymnasium as private and public places of recreation, gymnastic training and athletic contests did not become a regular part of general education at the new institutions of learning. Quintilian does concede some value to the gymnast's art, for dancing and physical training may improve the orator's poise and carriage, but he is disgusted with the mad devotion "to the cultivation of the body."[116] In fact, Quintilian's goal is professional excellence, rooted in complete knowledge of the liberal arts; and if music, the actor's and the gymnast's arts will promote that end, one should study them. Seneca strictly excludes from "liberal studies wrestling and all knowledge . . . compounded of oil and mud. . . ."[117] One should "limit the flesh as much as possible." Only a few exercises are approved—walking, running, jumping, swinging weights, vociferation, and riding in a litter. Like a true Roman, Seneca values them because they are "short and simple," tire one rapidly, "and so save our time."[118]

In its exclusion of gymnastics, Roman education rejected the ideal of balance of mind and body which Athens had sought to achieve—save as it might be repeated in an attrac-

115 *Annals of Tacitus,* XIV, 47. (Trans. by A. J. Church and W. J. Brodribb) Macmillan & Co., Ltd.: London, 1921; Suetonius: *Nero,* 12.
116 Bk. I, 11, 15-19; II, 8, 7 and 13-15; XII, 11, 18.
117 *Epistle* LXXXVIII, 18.
118 *Ibid.,* XV, 2-8.

tive phrase, *mens sana in corpore sano*, or recommended by
writers—and revealed the Romans' conviction that their military sports and training were superior to anything the Greeks
had to offer. So far as foreign practices were concerned, the
Spartan system, which bent physical training wholly to military ends, was more nearly in harmony with Roman ideals
and habit. Cicero specifically approved rigorous, Spartan
military training, but deprecated so much attention to athletic
contests, which "the Greeks think glorious."[119] As preparation
for the burdens of war, he thought the Greek training in the
gymnasium ridiculous.[120] Provision is made in the *Laws*[121]
for contests "of body with body," but they are exhibitions
designed for "public pleasure" rather than a phase of general
education.

[119] *Cicero: Tusculan Disputations*, I, 46. (Trans. by J. E. King) William
Heinemann: London, 1927.
[120] *Republic*, IV, 4.
[121] Bk. II, 9, 22; 15, 38; III, 3, 7.

CHAPTER FIVE

LIBERAL LEARNING
IN
EXTREMIS

1

CHINESE, Greek, and Roman conceptions of liberal education had their center of gravity in secular society. It was fit
for free men; it was to fit men for freedom, enable them to
perform the offices of that freedom. Early Athenian practice
and later theoretical reconstructions were meaningless apart
from the city. Of the education of early Rome's citizen-soldier
and the learned orator of the Republic, the same may be said.
The bonds of community were tight. Education to serve the
small city was a relatively simple matter. When the ancient
polis was swallowed up in the Empire, citizen-centered education gradually atrophied. Mental and physical culture began
increasingly to serve purely personal, even otherworldly
ends. Philosophy is a pedagogue leading us "to the stars,"
said Seneca. The city of Cecrops gave way to the city of Zeus.
Still, while the Empire stood intact, Rome was a symbol of
universal power and permanence which hovered in the minds
of men.

At the sack of Rome by Alaric, dismay penetrated even

monastic walls. "The City which had taken the whole world was itself taken. . . ."[1] "If Rome falls, what is there that still stands?" asks Jerome, seeking for relief by turning to his books, as Cicero had done at the death of the Republic. Augustine comes to judgment and gives the answer: both rulers and ruled in old Rome sought suzerainty and conquest rather than justice.[2] Her calamity is the judgment of God. Piety must purge what impiety has contaminated. The true empire is spiritual, perfect, universal. The eternal city is the City of God. It transcends all frontiers; it will not crumble. The aim of life is to avoid evil and attain eternity. The just live by faith.[3] Faith and Eternity become the prime determiners of formal education from the sixth century to the thirteenth.

This seven-century interval is marked by a relatively low ebb of culture. It is the childhood and youth of modern Western peoples. Slowly, painfully, at times grudgingly, they put themselves to the School of Antiquity, much as Romans had once gone to their Greek teachers. Intellectually, this crude, boisterous age of youth suffers by comparison with the Greek enlightenment, the age of Cicero or of Quintilian—the mental maturity of antiquity—but it is not without promise. If the curve of culture falls low from the sixth century to the eighth, it rises in the ninth; if it declines in the tenth, it ascends again from the eleventh. With the rise of trade, the growth of cities, and the emergence of strong secular governments, liberal education reflects less and less concern about eternity, faith, and

---

[1] *Letters of St. Jerome*, LX, 16-17; CXXVII, 12. *A Select Library of Nicene and Post-Nicene Fathers of the Christian Church*, ser. 2, VI, 129-30, 257. (Ed. by P. Schaff and H. Wace) 12 vols. The Christian Literature Company: New York, 1890-95.

[2] *The City of God*, II, 17. *A Select Library of the Nicene and Post-Nicene Fathers of the Christian Church*, ser. 1, II, 32. (Ed. by P. Schaff) 14 vols. The Christian Literature Company: Buffalo, 1886-90.

[3] *Ibid.*, XIX, 4. *Loc. cit.*, ser. 1, II, 401 *ff*.

authority, and frankly reveals anew the old preoccupation with man's earthly *Tun und Streben.*

2

Diverse factors combined to bring the Graeco-Roman pattern of liberal education near to death in the Age of Faith and Eternity. Chief among them were Christian renunciation of the world, invasions from without, and decadence within. Long before Christians came to power, the vitality of liberal studies had been reduced by empty formalism in the schools, and by divorce of life and learning in the literary world.[4] Loss of freedom, one-man rule, lack of reality and of purpose brought a blight on letters. Seneca found little which qualified as truly liberal education.[5] Nevertheless, literary schooling continued and produced imposing results. Fronto's verbal learning is impeccable. Ausonius is a clever versifier, at times truly poetical. Symmachus is a meticulous, scholarly writer of letters. The foliage and flower are colorful, but there is little fruit. Sidonius in the fifth century and Fortunatus in the sixth, like beacons, mark the stream of Latinity, flowing still despite crosscurrents.

To internal decadence were added the increasing dislocations and uncertainties incident to invasions, a declining economy, and petty localism which gradually permeated all phases of life, supplanting the once strong, highly integrated community. The catastrophic character of barbarian inroads, imperial collapse, and their effect on cultural life were once highly exaggerated.[6] It is easy to credit a visible blow, while

---

[4] *Supra,* 80 *ff.*

[5] *Epistle* LXXXVIII, 1-4, 20, 23, 32. *Seneca: ad Lucilium Epistulae Morales.* (Trans. by R. M. Gummere) 3 vols. William Heinemann: London, 1917-25.

[6] Muller, H. F.: *A Chronology of Vulgar Latin,* 8 *ff.* Max Niemeyer Verlag: Halle, 1929.

forgetting the silent, invisible forces. Actually, infiltration
was relatively slow and sporadic.[7] Many tribes had settled
peacefully within Roman borders in the centuries since
Caesar's conquests. The tide rose steadily in many quarters
from the late fourth century. Visigoths entered Roman territory by permission in 376.[8] Foreign soldiers were taken into
Rome's army until it was more barbarian than Roman. A rage
arose for German fashions.[9] Frequently the imperial government found barbarian tribes the firmest aid against its
enemies. Aetius led Burgundians, Franks, and Visigoths to
victory against Attila at Chalôns, in 451. For three decades
Ostragoth Theodoric gave Italy her best government since
Theodosius, a hundred years before. By some, doubtless, the
advent of the barbarians was regarded as liberation from
Roman tyranny.[10] Neverthelss, Vandal power in Africa, Visigoths in Spain, Franks beyond the Loire, and Burgundians,
Alemanni, Angles, Saxons, Jutes, stretching from the Alps
to the North Sea, with Ostragoths in Italy and on the Danube,
tell a tale of political localism that gives the lie to Rome's
former, far-flung power. Justinian's nearly half a century of
effort, from 527 to 565, gave more the appearance and promise than the reality of rehabilitated unity.

The bearing of the invasions on life and learning doubtless
varied with each event. The whole land given to the sword
and going up in one vast funeral pyre, priests enslaved, along
with men, women, and children—such is the portrayal of

[7] Dill, S.: *Roman Society in the Last Century of the Western Empire*, 286 *f*.
Macmillan & Co., Ltd.: London, 1906.

[8] Ogg, F. A. (Ed.) : *A Source Book of Medieval History*, 32 *ff*. American Book
Company: New York, 1907.

[9] Dill: *op. cit.*, 292 *f.*, 297.

[10] Montalembert, The Count De: *The Monks of the West, from St. Benedict
to St. Bernard*, I, 441. 2 vols. Thomas B. Noonan & Co.: Boston, 1860; Thorndike, L.: *The History of Medieval Europe*, 91. Houghton Mifflin Company:
Boston, 1928.

invasions of Vandals and Suevi in *Ad Uxorem, De Providentia Divina,* and the *Commonitorium*—may well be highly distorted pictures. At least, they are relieved by divergent reports. The easy life of Paulinus Pellaeus is disturbed by the "public calamity" of invasions; but, under Gothic rule, he seems to have enjoyed comfort, even luxury, on his estate, and in old age is rescued from narrowed circumstances by receipt of payment from an unknown Goth who has come into possession of his Marseilles estate.[11] Namatianus notes the ruined bridges and houses on the Via Aurelia, the desolated towns. His lands in Gaul have been laid waste; but Rome's temples, her circus crowds, her moral and material splendor still inspire him, and Alaric's deeds stir in him no such pessimism and horror as they do in the breasts of Christians.[12]

The age was one of double-edged fear. It sprang naturally from the external decay of man's once fair, secure, familiar world. It stemmed, likewise, and perhaps with even more benumbing effect, from an *inner* source—that spirit of Christian asceticism which, as Namatianus observed, made men "as much afraid to enjoy the gifts of fortune as to face its reverses."[13] Far from consoling and comforting his misery, the doleful pages of the prophets and preachers of the Last Doom constantly augmented man's distress of mind. Ruined cities, wasted fields, the dying groan, the thinning ranks of citizens—none were made easier to bear by being called, in Gregory's phrase, "plagues of divine justice."[14] If one be-

[11] *The Eucharisticus of Paulinus Pellaeus,* 226 *et seqq.,* 280 *et seqq.,* 575. (With *Ausonius,* trans. by H. G. Evelyn White) 2 vols. William Heinemann: London, 1919-21; Burns, C. D.: *The First Europe,* 62 *ff.* George Allen and Unwin, Ltd.: London, 1947.

[12] Dill: *op. cit.,* 310 *f.; cf.* Fell, R. A. L.: *Etruria and Rome,* 174. University Press: Cambridge, 1924.

[13] Dill: *op. cit.,* 310.

[14] Coulton, G. G.: *Social Life in Britain from the Conquest to the Reformation,* 187 *f.* University Press: Cambridge, 1919.

lieved God's fury at man's sins had sent barbarians to defeat Roman arms, as Jerome argued,[15] the burden was made doubly heavy.

The spirit of Christian asceticism opposed four central features of Greek thought on liberal education: the cult of the body, intellectual and aesthetic culture, the political concept of education for service to the state, and the disparagement of manual labor. The influence of that spirit was profound; nevertheless, its weight varied with persons, periods, and regions. Being fundamentally at war with human nature, it was, in the long run, destined to defeat. Asceticism, in itself, was no novelty to the pre-Christian world. There was a strain of it in Greek philosophy. Pythagoreans had practiced it. Stoics extolled it. "Life, in reality, is an Olympic contest," said Epictetus. Athletes, by severe discipline, strove to win a wreath. Early Christians, however, rebelling against Graeco-Roman life and espousing an otherworldly ideal, gave to *askesis* new interpretations and applications. In sum, they aimed, by discipline, to keep themselves unspotted from the world. Moral training was to be a conspicuous feature of education in the Age of Faith.

"We are God's athletes" was a familiar phrase in the mouths of those Christians who had grown up in the atmosphere of an athletic-minded world. Christian discipline was for a moral wrestling match, a race to be run. The home, the church and monastery were purveyors of that discipline. As the church became more worldly, with its acquisition of preferred status when Constantine professed the Faith, the monastery's discipline was enhanced in value. "Let us not be distressed . . . if our sons must pass ten or twenty years in a monastery. For the longer the training is in the gymnasium,

15 *Letters*, LX, 17. *Nicene and Post-Nicene Fathers*, ser. 2, VI, 130.

so much greater will be the strength which they will acquire."[16] Stagirius reflects how he had first been made strong by monastic training before he was called into the stadium to wrestle with the demon. One must be ready for death and the Judgment. To many, the monastery was the best guarantee of readiness, as a sick boy's plea to his father suggests:

> Oh, my father! help, I pray!
> Death is near my soul to-day;
> With your blessing let me be
> Made a monk right speedily![17]

In no way was Christian asceticism more at odds with Graeco-Roman life than in its denial of physical culture. Instead of striving for harmony of mind and body—the Greek ideal—Christian spokesmen called, with varying degrees of emphasis and dogmatism, for perpetual warfare of mind against body, that the soul might live. One of the more moderate expositions of the matter, which did not gain dominion, however, was set forth by Clement of Alexandria.

Clement was near to the spirit of the Greeks. Unlike many of his colleagues, his view of physical exercise reflected the golden mean: "We must always aim at moderation." Walking may suffice for some persons; but Christians must walk with a grave, leisurely, "not a lingering step." Men and boys may exercise at gymnastic contests—they are good for bodily health, and also conducive to courage of soul—provided men are not thereby kept from better employments. Wrestling and a ball game are named; but such contests are not to serve vainglorious ends. Wrestling standing is preferred, for it is graceful, manly, and serviceable to health. "Illiberal pos-

---

[16] Sawhill, J. A.: *The Use of Athletic Metaphors in the Biblical Homilies of St. John Chrysostom*, 10. Princeton University Press: Princeton, 1928.

[17] Symonds, J. A.: *Wine, Women and Song*, 152. Chatto & Windus: London, 1925.

tures in gymnastics," "cunning and showiness" are disapproved. Dice and gambling are prohibited. Spectacles are the "seat of plagues."[18]

More complete caveats against physical culture and hygiene abounded. Origen's *De Principiis*[19] quotes Paul: "The flesh lusteth against the Spirit, and the Spirit against the flesh: and these are contrary the one to the other." In this spiritual struggle, the arts of the wrestling school avail nought. Cyprian follows Paul, saying, "they that are Christ's have crucified the flesh. . . ."[20] St. Anthony, according to Athanasius,[21] was "ashamed" of the "necessities of the body"—eating, sleeping—"when he thought of the soul's intelligence." The conflict between body and soul is so sharp, Jerome says, that, in some cases, spiritual sickness followed restoration to bodily health. He prefers pallid faces and lean bodies.[22] Neoplatonists and Christians join in the ascetic chorus. Porphory, speaking on abstinence from animal food, declares: "By no means, therefore, ought we to follow the laws of the body, which are violent and adverse to the laws of intellect, and to the paths which lead to salvation." Let us "divest ourselves" of "every thing material and mortal."[23] Plotinus regarded the body as a mere shadow, nothing. Why be concerned about it? Accordingly, he "abstained from baths," and refused med-

---

[18] *The Instructor*, III, 10-11. *The Ante-Nicene Fathers*, II, 283 *f.*, 288 *f.* (Ed. by A. C. Coxe, J. Donaldson, A. Menzies, and A. Roberts) 10 vols. The Christian Literature Company: Buffalo, 1885-87.

[19] III, ii, 3. *Ante-Nicene Fathers*, IV, 330 *f.*

[20] *The Treatises of S. Caecilius Cyprian*, IV, 5. *A Library of Fathers of the Holy Catholic Church*, III, 120. 40 vols. John Henry Parker: Oxford, 1838-61.

[21] "Life of St. Anthony," T. W. Allies, *The Monastic Life*, 26. Kegan Paul, Trench, Trübner & Co., Ltd.: London, 1896.

[22] *Letters*, XLV, 5; LII, 5. *Nicene and Post-Nicene Fathers*, ser. 2, VI, 59 *f.*, 91 *f.*

[23] *Select Works of Porphory*, 22 *f.*, 43. (Trans. by T. Taylor) Thomas Rodd: London, 1823.

ical aid when sick unto death.[24] Monks must first win battles over the flesh, says Cassian. A true athlete of Christ says: "I chastise my body and bring it into subjection," that I who preach to others may not be lost.[25] Christian ascetic discipline is likened to the art of a rope-dancer: At any moment a misstep means disaster.[26] Augustine's *City of God*[27] states that "The corruptible body weigheth down the soul, and the earthly tabernacle presseth down the mind that museth upon many things."

This philosophy did not soon lapse. Prudentius' *Psychomachia* gave a portrayal of this cosmic Battle of the Soul against the flesh that left its imprint on medieval literature.[28] Isidore repeated the familiar theme: "It is advantageous," he said, "for those who are well and strong to become infirm, lest through the vigor of their health they be defiled. . . ."[29] The "Ancren Riwle," six centuries later, runs, in part: "The other rule is all outward, and ruleth the body. . . . And this is bodily exercise, which, according to the Apostle, profiteth little. . . . The external rule . . . is of man's contrivance; nor is it instituted for anything else but to serve the internal law. It ordains fasting, watching, enduring cold, wearing haircloth, and such other hardships as the flesh of many can bear and many cannot. . . ." The anchoress is to tame her

[24] Kingsley, C.: *Alexandria and Her Schools*, 109. Macmillan and Co.: Cambridge, 1854.

[25] *The Twelve Books of John Cassian on the Institutes of the Coenobia, and the Remedies for the Eight Principal Faults*, V, 16-17. *Nicene and Post-Nicene Fathers*, ser. 2, XI, 239.

[26] *The Third Conference of Abbot Theonas on Sinlessness*, 9. *Nicene and Post-Nicene Fathers*, ser. 2, XI, 524 f.

[27] Bk. XIX, 4. *Nicene and Post-Nicene Fathers*, ser. 1, II, 401.

[28] Thackeray, F. St. J.: *Translations from Prudentius*, lxxi-lxxii. George Bell and Sons: London, 1890; Waddell, H.: *The Wandering Scholars*, 20. Constable & Co. Ltd.: London, 1927.

[29] Brehaut, E.: *An Encyclopedist of the Dark Ages, Isidore of Seville*, 70. Columbia University: New York, 1912,

flesh, but not destroy it. "Ye shall sleep in a garment and girt. Wear no iron, nor haircloth, nor hedgehog-skins; and do not beat yourselves therewith, nor with a scourge of leather thongs, nor leaded; and do not with holly nor with briars cause yourselves to bleed without leave of your confessor; and do not, at one time, use too many flagellations."[30] Extremists, like the Flagellants (c. 1259), remind us that the harshest punishments of the body, so common among the earliest Christian ascetics, still found minds willing to administer them a thousand years after Christianity had come to power in Western Europe.[31]

Mere stress on personal mortification of the flesh did not suffice. Particular exercises, sports, and pastimes, Graeco-Roman and medieval, were attacked. Wrestling, Tertullian says, is Satan's own art. The gymnasium is a place of vanity. Kicks and blows, the athlete's stock in trade, disfigure the face, God's image. No Christian can approve of vain prowess in running, throwing, jumping.[32] Jerome warns against the dangers of dancing;[33] and, pale with fasting and numb with cold, which he courted through "fear of hell," he is beset with visions of dancing girls.[34] Augustine confesses that, in youth, he was fond of play, wanted to be leader in all sports, and hated to lose a ball game.[35]

Cleanliness, long since associated with godliness, was dep-

30 *The Ancren Riwle*, 5, 7, 139, 419 *ff.* (Ed. and trans. by J. Morton) Vol. 57, The Camden Society: London, 1853.

31 Coulton, G. G.: *From St. Francis to Dante*, 192. David Nutt: London, 1906; Froissart, J.: *Les Chroniques*, Livre I, Partie II, chap. 5. 3 vols. Société du Panthéon Littéraire: Paris, 1840.

32 *The Shows, or De Spectaculis*, 18; *Apology*, 38. *Ante-Nicene Fathers*, III, 87, 45 *f.*

33 *Letters*, CVII, 6. *Nicene and Post-Nicene Fathers*, ser. 2, VI, 192.

34 *Ibid.*, XXII, 7. *Loc. cit.*, ser. 2, VI, 24 *f.*

35 *The Thirteen Books of the Confessions of St. Aur. Augustin*, I, 9-10. *Nicene and Post-Nicene Fathers*, ser. 1, I, 49 *f.*

recated by Christian ascetics. Bathing, which had become so thoroughly a part of the Graeco-Roman world of sports, and a matter of personal pride, pleasure and comfort to many, was to be discouraged as a snare and weakness, rarely, if ever, to be indulged. Plotinus abstained from bathing.[36] Silvia reproved Jubinus, who in illness had bathed with cold water, saying that, though near sixty, water had not touched her body, save the finger tips, at communion, despite the many sicknesses she had endured.[37] Clement of Alexandria, most urbane of the Fathers, condemned bathing for pleasure, but allowed it to men for health, and to women for health and cleanliness. Nevertheless, he called "the best bath" that which removes the soul's pollution.[38] St. Jerome advised a young monk, "Let your garments be squalid to shew that your mind is white."[39] The Apostolic Constitutions warned men and women against promiscuous bathing. Even in separate baths, women should "not bathe without occasion, nor much, nor often. . . ."[40] The Benedictine Rule allowed baths to the sick, but seldom to others, "especially to youths."[41]

Besides practicing mortification and condemning participation in sports, the Christian ascetic denounced pleasure in witnessing them. The true Christian's pleasure is contempt for pleasure, says Tertullian. Renunciation, at baptism, of all idolatry requires avoidance of all spectacles, for they begin and they end in idolatry pure and simple. Certainly, Scripture does not say specifically, "Thou shalt not enter

[36] Kingsley: *op. cit.*, 109.
[37] Abbott, F. F.: *Society and Politics in Ancient Rome*, 94. Charles Scribner's Sons: New York, 1909.
[38] *Instructor*, III, 9. *Ante-Nicene Fathers*, II, 282 *f*.
[39] *Letters*, CXXV. *Nicene and Post-Nicene Fathers*, ser. 2, VI, 244-52.
[40] *Constitutions of the Holy Apostles*, I, 6, 9. *Ante-Nicene Fathers*, VII, 393, 395.
[41] *Rule 36. Select Historical Documents of the Middle Ages*, 291. (Trans. and ed. by E. F. Henderson) George Bell and Sons: London, 1905.

[the] circus . . ." but David judges him happy who avoids the meetings of the impious, the path of sinners, the "seat of scorners." Even the horse, God's gift, has been perverted to the service of demons.[42] Augustine[43] is at some pains to keep Alypius from the pestilential pastime of circus games. They who prize morals and modesty, says Minucius Felix, justly hold aloof from vicious spectacles.[44] Shun all spectacles, urges Lactantius, that no "indulgence of any pleasure" may captivate and turn you from God and "good works."[45] More authoritatively, the Apostolic Constitutions[46] charged Christians to avoid all public sports and "shows belonging to demons."

Though Christian opposition and the persuasion of St. Ambrose particularly, in the time of Theodosius I, were influential in bringing an end to pagan games, that end was not swift. Olympic games were abolished in 393; gladiatorial contests at Rome ended in 404; the *venatio* we hear of last in 523.[47] Pronouncements and injunctions continue, however, in Isidore of Seville,[48] and are prominent throughout the Age of Faith. From tourneys, the sports of the medieval worldly set, and more plebeian entertainments, one should keep away. Says the Good Wife:

> Go not to the wrestling, nor to shooting at the cock . . .
> Stay at home, daughter.[49]

---

42 *De Spectaculis*, 3, 9. *Ante-Nicene Fathers*, III, 80 *f.*, 83.
43 *Confessions*, VI, 7, 8. *Nicene and Post-Nicene Fathers*, ser. 1, I, 94 *ff.*
44 *The Octavius of Minucius Felix*, 37. *Ante-Nicene Fathers*, IV, 196.
45 *The Divine Institutes*, VI, 20. *Ante-Nicene Fathers*, VII, 186 *ff.*
46 Bk. II, 62. *Ante-Nicene Fathers*, VII, 424.
47 Showerman, G.: *Rome and the Romans,* 349. Macmillan Company: New York, 1931; Wright, F. A.: *Greek Athletics*, 14. Jonathan Cape, Ltd.: London, 1925.
48 Brehaut: *op. cit.*, 259 *ff.*
49 Coulton, G. G.: *Chaucer and His England*, 109. G. P. Putnam's Sons: New York, 1908.

The greatest friend and the greatest foe of learning is man. By choice he promotes it; by choice he rejects it. Grave opposition to liberal education, as the Greeks and Romans had conceived and developed it, arose in Christian circles. If pagans had occasionally criticized the arts as incapable of conferring a liberal education, as did Seneca, many Christian spokesmen saw pagan poetry, philosophy, music, and dramatic arts as enemies of the soul's salvation. Fortunately, they were never wholly united in this belief. Essentially, the conflict was between faith and reason, orthodoxy and humanism. Could they be reconciled? Eastern Fathers, closer in spirit to the Greek tradition of learning, were inclined to seek a synthesis of pagan and Christian thought. Western churchmen, in contrast, often denied vigorously the possibility of reconciliation. If, ultimately, humanism and reason triumphed over fanaticism and dogmatism, it was in the face of discouragement of official pronouncements and in spite of the personal influence of many who carried weight by virtue of their position at the very fountainhead of ecclesiastical authority.

Although Paul had said that few of the wise would be "called," the first few centuries saw many philosophers in the ranks of churchmen. Justin Martyr, Clement of Alexandria, Origen, Basil, Gregory of Nazianzen, Tertullian, Jerome, Augustine, and others like them, well-schooled in the pagan arts, were at once faced with the problem of reconciling their studies with their new faith. For Justin, Clement, Basil, Origen, and other Eastern leaders, this was no difficult task. The poets, of course, were unfit teachers of religion. But philosophy and Christianity, they held, aimed at the same mark. Socrates and Plato were Christians in philosophers' cloaks. True, the philosophers were often involved in error and contradiction. But the wisdom of Moses and the prophets had been known to, and guardedly taught by, Plato, who even foretold the crucifixion of Christ.[50] Clement, seeking to reconcile faith and reason, considered philosophy a pedagogue to bring the world to Christ. The Christian gospels were to perfect Platonism. Christians needed learning of all kinds, to be able to answer those who had studied Greek disciplines.[51] Origen taught the sciences, logic, ethics, and all poets and philosophers, save atheists, as Gregory Thaumaturgus says,[52] and urged on others the study of geometry, astronomy, and all philosophies which might serve as a preparation for interpreting the Scriptures.[53]

The fourth century saw this friendliness toward pagan letters marred by growing doubt. Basil, educated at Caesarea, Byzantium, and Athens, his panegyrist tells us, "was laden with all the learning attainable" by man. Yet to Libanius, once his teacher, he wrote later, "If ever I learned anything from you, I have forgotten it in the course of time."[54] Elsewhere, he asked: "Are we then to give up literature? I do not say that, but I do say that we must not kill souls. . . . The choice lies between two alternatives: a liberal education which you may get by sending your children to the public schools, or the salvation of their souls which you secure by

50 Clement: *The Stromata, or Miscellanies*, I, 25; V, 1, 14. *Ante-Nicene Fathers*, II, 338, 446, 466, 470; *Justin's Hortatory Address to the Greeks*, 20-32. *Ante-Nicene Fathers*, I, 281-87.

51 Neander, A.: *General History of the Christian Religion and Church*, I, 528. (Trans. by J. Torrey) 3 vols. Crocker & Brewster: Boston, 1849-51.

52 *The Oration and Panegyric Addressed to Origen*, 7-13. *Ante-Nicene Fathers*, VI, 29-34.

53 *Letter of Origen to Gregory*, I. *Ante-Nicene Fathers*, IX, 295.

54 *Letters*, 339. *Nicene and Post-Nicene Fathers*, ser. 2, VIII, 322; Gregory of Nazianzen: *The Panegyric on S. Basil*, 24. *Nicene and Post-Nicene Fathers*, ser. 2, VII, 403.

sending them to the monks. Which is to gain the day, science, or the soul? If you can unite both advantages, do so by all means; but, if not, choose the most precious."

Gregory of Nazianzen rated education the first of all advantages, not only the Christian form of it, which discounts "rhetorical ornaments and glory, and holds to salvation," but also "that external culture which many Christians ill-judgingly abhor, as treacherous and dangerous, and keeping us afar from God."[55] Against the Apostate Julian's edict prohibiting Christians from teaching letters and philosophy, he protested vigorously, and expressed the hope that all who loved learning would share his indignation. Science and learning, he maintained, were to be preferred to all other earthly goods, indeed "next to the joys of heaven and the hopes of eternity."[56] Chrysostom was less generous in his judgment of literary values. Striking a note akin to Basil's, he declared he had long "laid aside such follies" as Greek letters, "for one cannot spend all one's life in child's play." And Gregory of Nyssa wrote to a student of the classics: "your eager pursuit of profane literature proved incontestably to us that you did not care about sacred."[57]

Hostility to pagan letters and philosophy appeared early in the West. Expressed first by individual leaders, official pronunciamentos followed in the course of time. Tertullian's "Prescription against Heretics"[58] bitterly denounced pagan philosophy as the source of deviations from Christian faith:

The same subject-matter is discussed over and over again by the heretics and the philosophers; the same arguments are involved.

---

[55] *Panegyric on S. Basil*, 11. *Nicene and Post-Nicene Fathers*, ser. 2, VII, 398.
[56] Hodgson, G.: *Primitive Christian Education*, 222. T. & T. Clark: Edinburgh, 1906.
[57] *Letters*, 8. *Nicene and Post-Nicene Fathers*, ser. 2, V, 531.
[58] Chap. 7. *Ante-Nicene Fathers*, III, 246.

Whence comes evil? Why is it permitted? What is the origin of man? . . . Whence comes God? . . . Unhappy Aristotle! who invented for these men dialectics, the art of building up and pulling down; an art so evasive in its propositions, so far-fetched in its conjectures, so harsh in its arguments, so productive of contentions— embarrassing even to itself, retracting everything, and really treating of nothing! . . . From all these, when the apostle would restrain us, he expressly names *philosophy* as that which he would have us be on our guard against. . . . What indeed has Athens to do with Jerusalem? What concord is there between the Academy and the Church? what between heretics and Christians? . . . Away with all attempts to produce a mottled Christianity of Stoic, Platonic, and dialectic composition! . . . With our faith, we desire no further belief.

The dream of St. Jerome[59] reveals the agitation of men's minds over the mingling of pagan letters and Christian faith. Eustochium is advised to avoid over-eloquence. "How can Horace go with the psalter, Virgil with the gospels, Cicero with the apostle?" One should not drink Christ's cup and the devil's at the same time. He relates his experience: Though on his way to Jerusalem, he had been loath to leave certain choice books at Rome. So, after fasting, he would read Cicero; after a night's vigil, he would turn to Plautus. Compared with these, the prophets seemed uncouth, barbarous. At length, falling ill, he dreamed himself at the Seat of Judgment. Asked to declare himself, he answered that he was a Christian. But the Judge declared: "Thou liest," thou art a Ciceronian, not a Christian. "For 'where thy treasure is, there will thy heart be also.' " Being beaten at the Judge's command, Jerome cried for mercy. Pardon was finally granted, with the understanding that heavier punishment would befall, if ever he read again the works of Gentile authors.

Authoritarianism grew apace in the fourth century. Opin-

[59] *Letters*, XXII, 29-31. *Nicene and Post-Nicene Fathers,* ser. 2, VI, 34 *ff.*

ions, which once had merely contended against other opinions, gained the sanctity of orthodoxy, and were clothed with the voice of power. The Apostolic Constitutions, considered either "a manual of instruction, worship, polity, and usage" for laity and clergy, or a means to support the authority and unity of the ecclesiastical hierarchy, prescribed complete avoidance of pagan literature:

> Abstain from all the heathen books. For what hast thou to do with such foreign discourses, or laws, or false prophets, which subvert the faith of the unstable? For what defect dost thou find in the law of God, that thou shouldest have recourse to those heathenish fables? For if thou hast a mind to read history, thou hast the books of the Kings; if books of wisdom or poetry, thou hast those of the Prophets, of Job, and the Proverbs, in which thou wilt find greater depth of sagacity than in all the heathen poets and sophisters, because these are the words of the Lord, the only wise God. If thou desirest something to sing, thou hast the Psalms; if the origin of things, thou hast Genesis; if laws and statutes, thou hast the glorious law of the Lord God. Do thou therefore utterly abstain from all strange and diabolical books.[60]

Distinguished for the great learning which he brought to bear on church doctrines, Augustine's intellectual authority in medieval times was superior to all others. His attitude toward pagan letters, therefore, was particularly important. In *Christian Doctrine*[61] he recognized the necessity for Christians to acquire "liberal instruction" from the "heathen learning," that they might put it to the service of truth. Even some truth regarding the one God might be found therein. Eloquence, the art of rhetoric, may be a means to good, as it has been to bad, ends; but the words and wisdom of Scripture

---

[60] *Constitutions of the Holy Apostles*, I, 6. *Ante-Nicene Fathers*, VII, 388, 393.
[61] Bk. II, chaps. 40, 42; IV, chap. 6. *Nicene and Post-Nicene Fathers*, ser. 1, II, 554 *f.*, 577.

must ever take precedence over the rules of eloquence, and
the study of that art should be limited to the young and be
done with as soon as possible. Moreover, Augustine goes on
to say, Scriptures and the Fathers are the source both of wisdom and eloquence; and time will not suffice for the studious
to read more than these writers of the church.[62] Augustine's
influence is believed to have shown itself in the Council of
Carthage (398) which declared: "The bishop shall not read
pagan books, nor those of heretics save in case of necessity."[63]
In his *Retractions,* shortly before death, Augustine discountenanced his earlier stress on the liberal arts.[64]

Sulpicius Severus, a man "excelling in learning and wisdom," Augustine tells us, and sometimes called the "Christian
Sallust," was at unity with the spirit of his day in his attitude
toward pagan letters. What, he asks, did "pagan writers
themselves gain by a literary glory that was to perish with
their generation? Of what profit was it to posterity to read of
Hector's battles or Socrates' philosophy?"[65] Priscillian, an
able man, "ruined an excellent intellect by wicked studies,"
says Sulpicius.[66] Isidore, Bishop of Seville, whose influential
Etymologies provided an outline of priestly education in the
early Middle Ages, shows the widening chasm between pagan
and Christian study. His order of studies is designed to lead
the mind from earthly affairs to "things on high." "Grammarians," he says, "are better than heretics, for heretics per-

---

[62] *Ibid.,* IV, chaps. 2-3, 5-6. *Loc. cit.,* ser. 1, II, 575-77.

[63] Art. 16. Hefele, C. J., *Histoire des Conciles D'Après Les Documents
Originaux,* II, Pt. I, 114. 10 vols. Letouzey et Ané: Paris, 1907-38; *cf.* Landon,
E. H., *A Manual of Councils of the Holy Catholic Church,* I, 122. 2 vols. John
Grant: Edinburgh, 1909.

[64] *Retractationum S. Augustini,* I, 3. *Corpus Scriptorum Ecclesiasticorum
Latinorum,* XXXVI.

[65] Kandel, I. L.: *History of Secondary Education,* 43. Houghton Mifflin Company: Boston, 1930.

[66] *The Sacred History,* II, 46. *Nicene and Post-Nicene Fathers,* ser. 2, XI, 119.

suade men to drink a deadly draught, while the learning of grammarians can avail for life, if only it is turned to better uses." But philosophers and heretics use the same materials over and over and repeat the same errors.[67] So, "a monk should eschew reading gentile works or the writings of heretics; for it is better to remain in ignorance of their pernicious teachings than by trying thus to run the risk of flying into the snare of error."[68]

Gregory of Tours testifies to the actuality of learning's low estate in late sixth-century Gaul. The "practice of letters declines, nay, rather perishes in the cities," and there is "no scholar trained in the art of ordered composition" to relate the events of our day in verse or prose.[69] In this there is some exaggeration. But even against those who could teach and were of a mind to promote learning, a voice of great authority was now raised. Pope Gregory the Great, expressing the philosophy that had been growing for centuries, condemned as unworthy the keeping of "Divine Oracles in subjection to the rules of Donatus." To Desiderius, Bishop of Vienne, he wrote: "A report has reached me, a report which I cannot mention without a blush, that you are lecturing on profane literature to certain friends; whereat I am filled with such grief and vehement disgust that my former opinion of you has been turned to mourning and sorrow. For the same mouth cannot sing the praises of Jupiter and the praises of Christ. Consider yourself how offensive, how abominable a thing it is for a bishop to recite verses which are unfit to be recited even by a religious layman. . . . If, hereafter, it shall be clearly established that the information I received was false,

[67] Brehaut: *op. cit.*, 74, 85 *f.*
[68] Kandel: *op. cit.*, 43.
[69] Preface, *The History of the Franks.* (Trans. by O. M. Dalton) 2 vols. Clarendon Press: Oxford, 1927.

and that you are not applying yourself to the idle vanities of secular literature, I shall render thanks to God, who has not allowed your heart to be polluted by the blasphemous praises of unspeakable men."[70]

The doom of pagan letters, foreshadowed in utterances of Christian spokesmen from Tertullian to Gregory the Great, came near to fulfillment only with the fusion of imperial and ecclesiastical power. State control over education, which philosophers on occasion had reason to regret, despite generous imperial encouragement at other times, had been growing since the first century. Constantine's assumption of Christianity diverted imperial favor to Christians, but recently hated and persecuted. Julian (361) used the same power to deliver literature and rhetoric from the hands of Christians. Universal governmental control over schools was formulated as a policy by the decree of Theodosius and Valentinian (425) which forbade, under penalty, any one to open schools without imperial authorization. Justinian's edict (529) drove teachers of philosophy from their most cherished ground, by forbidding the teaching of philosophy at Athens.[71]

Aesthetically, too, Christians were in revolt. Worldly music, developed to the patter of dancing feet, and dramatic arts, associated in origin with pagan mythology and religion, fell before the wave of Christian asceticism, as did profane literature and physical culture. From early times, condemnation of theatricals was consistent and thorough. Clement of Alexandria called for prohibition of plays, "full of scurrility and

---

[70] Dudden, F. H.: *Gregory the Great*, I, 287. 2 vols. Longmans, Green and Co.: London, 1905.

[71] Procopius: *The Anecdota or Secret History*, XXVI, 1-7. *Procopius*. (Trans. by H. B. Dewing, with collaboration of G. Downey) 7 vols. Harvard University Press: Cambridge, 1914-40; Grasberger, L.: *Erziehung und Unterricht im Klassischen Altertum*, III, 461. 3 vols. Stahel'schen Buch- und Kunsthandlung: Würzburg, 1864-81.

of abundant gossip." What base acts and shameless sayings
are not exhibited in theaters?[72] Comedians, by song and gesture, set forth in plays "the defilement of maidens and the
love affairs of harlots," says Isidore of Seville. Christians,
therefore, should have nothing to do "with the shamelessness
of the theatre."[73]

In place of worldly music, Christians developed the solemn,
antiphonal chant, more in harmony with their experience
and philosophy of life.[74] Jerome charged strictly that Paula
should not dance or know the "world's songs," but learn the
sweet music of psalms. She should not even know the origin
of lyre, flute or harp.[75] Queen Radegund, having taken the
veil, was astonished that one of her sisters in seclusion could
take pleasure in hearing some of the familiar songs of the
world. As for herself, she professed not to have "heard a
single note of that profane music."[76]

In figurative arts, Christians broke with the Greek ideal of
natural imitation, and substituted for it a mystical art, "absorbed in the idea of God," and rooted philosophically in the
Neoplatonism of Plotinus and Augustine.[77] The individual
was debased; the universal and abstract exalted. Augustine's
aversion to sculpture and painting, and his inclination toward
architecture and music, the most abstract and far-removed
from nature, seem to have left a deep impression on artistic
tendencies for centuries to come. But the love of natural
beauty, so near to the heart of man, could not be subjected

[72] *Instructor*, III, 11. *Ante-Nicene Fathers*, II, 289 *f*.

[73] Brehaut: *op. cit.*, 261.

[74] Dickinson, E.: *Music in the History of the Western Church*, 65 *ff*. Charles
Scribner's Sons: New York, 1925; Rowbotham, J. F.: *A History of Music*, III,
89 *ff*. 3 vols. Kegan Paul, Trench, Trübner & Co., Ltd.: London, 1885-87.

[75] *Letters*, CVII, 4, 6, 8. *Nicene and Post-Nicene Fathers*, ser. 2, VI, 191 *ff*.

[76] Montalembert: *op. cit.*, I, 491.

[77] Venturi, L.: *History of Art Criticism*, 64 *ff*. (Trans. by C. Marriott) E. P.
Dutton & Company: New York, 1936.

entirely to ascetic reasonings. Leaving the city and its artificial beauties, some found happiness in returning to a communion with nature long forgot. The loveliest natural solitudes became the seats of monasteries, adorned with lovely
names.[78] Yet, so persuasive was the ascetic warning against
externals, even the beauties of nature, which so subtly beguile
man, took on, at times, a sinister implication and association
for many in the age of Faith and Eternity; for beauty might
be deceptive gilding, hiding evil and darkness. A note in
Walter von der Vogelweide rings true to his age:

> The world is fair to gaze on, white and green and red,
> But inly foul and black of hue, and dismal as the dead.

In the Master of Oxford's Catechism is a mixture of meteor-
ology and theology:

> Wherefore is the sun red at even? For he goeth toward hell.[79]

Pagan gods and the city-state were at unity with each other.
Into the life of the *polis*, Christianity introduced a division of
loyalty. It was easy to say—render this to God, and that to
Casear. But what is Caesar's? What if Caesar claim universal
empire? The prophets declare "these are the last times."
Christ is the stone that will "reduce to nothing" earthly kingdoms.[80] The Christians' battle against pagan cults, especially
the worship of Augustus, was in pagan eyes subversive of the
state's integrity. The worldly, reprobate society suffers by
contrast with the Community of Saints. There is no true justice, says Augustine, save in Christ's commonwealth. The
philosophy of the Prince of Peace could not but mock, or

---

[78] Montalembert: *op. cit.*, I, 38 *ff*.

[79] Coulton: *Chaucer and His England*, 104, 106.

[80] Sulpicius Severus: *Sacred History*, II, 3. *Nicene and Post-Nicene Fathers*,
ser. 2, XI, 98.

threaten, empires built on blood.[81] The conflict, in a sense, and for some, was reconciled when the state became nominally Christian, or Christians became secularized. Churchmen from Augustine to Aquinas sought to rationalize the problem, with what success one can readily see. Many men and women fled, not only from the vanities and vulgarities of pagan society, but from the church which had increasingly taken the world to herself since the middle of the third century,[82] and was soon to seal the union officially.

By flight from the world, ascetic extremists did all in their power to negate and weaken the sanctions of existing society. The soul's salvation was of paramount importance. The call to a decision was clear-cut. Scripture spoke with the tone of awful authority: "Ye cannot serve two masters." Will anyone dare make God a liar, asks Jerome, by serving both?[83] "It is a great offence," says Cassian, for a monk to mention "my book," "my pen," "my coat," "my shoes."[84] Heliodorus is reminded that, when taking vows, he swore to "spare neither father nor mother."[85] It is a "divine thing," says Sulpicius Severus, to ". . . live in opposition to the practice of the human race; to despise the comforts of wedlock."[86]

By the vow of chastity, ties of family were broken. Renunciation of property (and thus, also, taxes) struck a blow at the system of private property and the state's support—a blow which was indeed of grave significance when, under the in-

[81] Augustine: *City of God*, II, 21; IV, 4, 6, 15. *Nicene and Post-Nicene Fathers*, ser. 1, II, 35 *f.*, 66 *f.*, 72; Figgis, J. N.: *The Political Aspects of S. Augustine's City of God*, 51 *ff.* Longmans, Green and Co.: London, 1921.
[82] Harnack, A.: *Monasticism: Its Ideals and Its History*, 19. (Trans. by C. R. Gillett) The Christian Literature Company: New York, 1895.
[83] *Letters*, XIV, 6. *Nicene and Post-Nicene Fathers*, ser. 2, VI, 16.
[84] *Institutes*, IV, 13. *Nicene and Post-Nicene Fathers*, ser. 2, XI, 222.
[85] Jerome: *Letters*, XIV, 2. *Nicene and Post-Nicene Fathers*, ser. 2, VI, 14.
[86] *The Doubtful Letters of Sulpitius Severus*, II, 2. *Nicene and Post-Nicene Fathers*, ser. 2, XI, 58.

fluence of "this divine philosophy," cities became solitudes and deserts filled with people.[87] Millions of monks could not but represent a significant depletion of military potential. But if Christian principles, as some interpreted them, wrought devastation in the existing state, human nature led the way to another. Anchorites achieved the greatest degree of perfection in social denial. When, however, two brethren, then small groups, and finally larger communities came together, new proof of Aristotle's dictum as to man's political nature was at hand. The rule of Pachomius, those of Basil, Benedict and others were all testimony to man's readiness to form communities on the basis of submission to some law. By virtue of the largely autonomous character of monasteries, whose constitutions were inviolable, even though they were under the general jurisdiction of the bishop in whose diocese they found themselves, they became for all practical purposes states within states, forming an economy, a social pattern, an art and architecture, and an education peculiarly their own.

3

Several influences, collectively more powerful than the disintegrative forces, operated to avert the extinction of the ancient mode of liberal education. Of fundamental importance was the extensive and profound Romanization which, carried on for centuries, left a residue that neither invasion, change of government, nor hostile otherworldly philosophy was to destroy.[88] Latin continued to be the instrument of religion and of learning. In making an end of the Empire, it has been said, barbarians conquered a shadow only; the sub-

87 Hase, C.: *A History of the Christian Church*, 150. (Trans. by C. E. Blumenthal and C. P. Wing) D. Appleton and Company: New York, 1880.
88 Chapot, V.: *The Roman World*, 424. (Trans. by E. A. Parker) Alfred A. Knopf: New York, 1928.

stance of Romania remained. Social life, communications, and commerce did not suddenly disintegrate. Private ownership of land and legal usages continued in the Merovingian Age.[89]

Schools of grammarians and rhetoric masters continued to function in Africa under Vandal rule, and Vandal youth attended them.[90] In Italy, Ostrogoth kings learned to speak, if not to read and write Latin; and even under the Lombards, who were less friendly to Roman culture, some schools still throve in the seventh century.[91] Toward the end of the fifth century, though Visigoth, Burgundian, and Frank had long been masters in Gaul, life of the nobility, as revealed in the letters of Sidonius, was easy, even luxurious; and pleasures of mind and body—a good library, reading, writing, correspondence, hunting, hawking, fishing, riding, bathing, games, both active and sedentary, visiting, dining, observing the labors on the land, if one had a mind for it—were enjoyed, much as in earlier days of Roman rule.[92] A century later, Gregory of Tours lamented that letters were perishing in the cities of Gaul. Nevertheless, Merovingian laity still had access to some knowledge of grammar, rhetoric, and legal learning in the early seventh century, through lay schools, which Pirenne considers "pale but authentic survivals of the schools

[89] Muller: *op. cit.*, 9 *f.*; Pirenne, H.: *Medieval Cities, Their Origins and the Revival of Trade*, chap. 1. (Trans. by F. D. Halsey) Princeton University Press: Princeton, 1925.

[90] Lot, F.: *The End of the Ancient World and the Beginnings of the Middle Ages*, 248. (Trans. by P. Leon and M. Leon) Kegan Paul, Trench, Trübner & Co., Ltd.: London, 1931.

[91] Thompson, J. W.: *The Literacy of the Laity in the Middle Ages*, 11 *ff.* University of California Press: Berkeley, 1939; Specht, F. A.: *Geschichte des Unterrichtswesens in Deutschland von den ältesten Zeiten bis zur Mitte des dreizehnten Jahrhunderts*, 2. J. G. Cotta: Stuttgart, 1885.

[92] *The Letters of Sidonius*, Introduction, liv-lix. (Trans. by O. M. Dalton) 2 vols. Clarendon Press: Oxford, 1915.

of the Empire."[93] Frankish royalty and the lesser aristocracy
were often well educated, and merchants and public func-
tionaries were probably possessed of letters sufficient to their
domain.[94]

Learning was declining, however. Decline was a slow, cu-
mulative process, as were growth and flowering. Already in
the time of Diocletian, says Tenney Frank,[95] books were rot-
ting in the libraries. Near the end of the fourth century
Marcellinus sadly noted[96] the libraries, "shut up forever like
tombs." Sidonius[97] saw this progressive decline, as did Gregory of Tours. The second half of the seventh century appears
to have seen the disappearance of those "pale" shadows of
the once-vigorous Roman schools in Gaul. Formal schooling
in some degree, however, was to be carried on in monastic
isolation from the worldly scene. There, too, the world of
learning was not unacquainted with the heavy hand of violence
and ignorance. Danish raids in England and on the mainland
from the late eighth to the mid-ninth century are credited with
general destruction of monastic life.[98] Numerous monastic
institutions suffered from Norman sallies into the river valleys
of France in the ninth century; and, in south Germany and
Italy, at the hands of Magyars in the early tenth.[99]

Into the broad seedbed of Latinity which had been pre-

---

[93] "De l'État de l'Instruction des Laïques à l'Époque Mérovingienne." *Revue
Bénédictine* (1934) XLVI, 172 *f.*

[94] Thompson: *op. cit.,* 4-9.

[95] *Rome and Italy of the Empire. An Economic Survey of Ancient Rome,* V,
303. Johns Hopkins Press: Baltimore, 1940.

[96] *Ammianus Marcellinus,* XIV, 6, 18. (Trans. by J. C. Rolfe) 3 vols. Harvard
University Press: Cambridge, 1935-39.

[97] *Letters,* II, 10; IV, 17.

[98] Thorndike: *op. cit.,* 220.

[99] Waddell: *op. cit.,* 62 *f.;* Sellery, G. C., and Krey, A. C.: *Medieval Foundations of Western Civilization,* 79 *f.* Harper & Brothers: New York, 1929; Thompson, J. W.: *The Medieval Library,* 222, 650 *f.,* 657. University of Chicago Press:
Chicago, 1939.

pared, a new seed was cast—the bookishness of Christianity. Founded on a Book, the new faith was logically committed to the fostering of some knowledge of letters. Christian extremists, notwithstanding their attacks on worldliness, the evils of secular literature and public schools, were insistent on knowledge of their own *Word*. Zeal for this spiritual message infused new content and fervor into Latin letters in Western Europe, in sharp contrast to the emptiness which marked the works of late pagan authors.

Christian concern for learning to read was consistent, but its defense often resembled walking a tight rope. Tertullian, whose bitter invective against pagan poets and philosophers knew no bounds, sought to resolve the Christian's dilemma respecting a foundation in letters. His critique "On Idolatry"[100] concluded that literary learning is partly unavoidable, for it is necessary to the pursuit of divine studies. Hence, Christians may study letters, but they should not teach them. Augustine, too, saw that Christians must borrow letters from the heathens, though poor is all the useful knowledge to be gathered from their books, compared with knowledge of the Holy Scriptures.[101] Jerome wrote to Eustochium, "Read often, learn all that you can";[102] and little Pacatula, he advised, must "learn the alphabet, spelling, grammar, and syntax."[103] Paula, strictly guarded from the world, was to be schooled in Greek and Latin; but the Psalter, Proverbs of Solomon, Gospels, Acts, and Epistles of the Apostles, the Heptateuch, Kings, Chronicles, Ezra, Esther, the Song of Songs, Cyprian, Athanasius, and Hilary were to make up her curriculum.[104]

100 Chap. 10. *Ante-Nicene Fathers*, III, 66 *f*.

101 *Christian Doctrine*, IV, chaps. 2-6. *Nicene and Post-Nicene Fathers*, ser. 1, II, 575 *ff*.

102 *Letters*, XXII, 17. *Nicene and Post-Nicene Fathers*, ser. 2, VI, 28.

103 *Ibid.*, CXXVIII, 1. *Loc. cit.*, ser. 2, VI, 258.

104 *Ibid.*, CVII. *Loc. cit.*, ser. 2, VI, 189-95.

Despite pitfalls in the path of letters, the Christian clerk who
would "gladly lerne, and gladly teche" was to become a feature of the Age of Faith and Eternity.

A deep devotion to secular authors, an inner bondage to
their human subject matter, which was felt by numerous ad-
herents of the new faith, despite professed disapproval of
such transient values, contributed measurably to the preservation of the old pattern of studies. Throughout the Age of
Faith runs a thread of individual confessions, revealing the
cleavage of loyalty. Jerome, in fear of the Judgment, promised
never again to read Gentile authors; Augustine, near death,
retracted his earlier emphasis on liberal arts. Alcuin, in old
age, regretted his one-time love of Virgil, and advised pupils
that "sacred poets" were sufficient. Hroswitha, fearing the
dangerous thralldom of Terence, wrote comedies to take his
place.[105] Chaucer asked forgiveness for his "translations and
editings of worldly vanities."[106] Deathbed repentance, however effective otherwise, could not undo the influence of years
devoted to letters. The very anathemas of the most literarily
inclined Christian Fathers were so laden with references to
pagan writers as to constitute a means of their survival. A
monastery, formed as a refuge from the world, was destined
to help preserve that world, when some who sought its shelter
brought with them profane authors—the most indestructible
tie with the world just fled. And though a monk must scratch
his ear like a dog, if he would read a book of pagan unbe-
lievers, he did scratch!

Continuity of culture is a remarkable phenomenon in
human history. Men find it difficult, indeed impossible, to
live without the past. Its transmission, its continuing contem-

105 Waddell: *op. cit.*, 76.
106 Coulton: *Chaucer and His England*, 72.

poraneity, though it may be consciously promoted, is often accomplished through unforeseen and unpredictable ways. A transmission belt carried the pattern of liberal education from antiquity to modern times—incidentally, rather than by design. The faith of an obscure Jew, crystallized and metamorphosed into the Roman Church and its peripheral adjuncts, became a part of that mechanism of transmission, although that faith knew nothing of the arts, and leading churchmen, knowing or unknowing, feared and scoffed at them. Donatus, Priscian, Capella, Boethius, Cassiodorus, Isidore, the Rule of Cassian and that of Benedict, and the institutions under their sway, were all—men and institutions—servants of their own day, some pagan, others Christian. Capella was pagan; Boethius, a professed Christian, but pagan in devotion to scholarship. Cassiodorus, Cassian, Benedict and Isidore were, above all, devoted to the immediate, utilitarian labor of salvation. Yet, through the concatenation of events, pagan and Christian constituted, with their hosts of imitators and commentators, the main channel of transmission of the arts for a thousand years.

Incomprehensible as it may seem to us, Capella's arid allegory, *The Marriage of Mercury and Philology*, a verse and prose product of the first third of the fifth century, became the most popular textbook of the seven arts in the Age of Faith. Drawing his materials largely from Varro's *disciplinae*, and in lesser degree from Romanus, Solinus, Cicero, Pliny, and Aristides Quintilianus, Capella devoted seven books to grammar, rhetoric, logic, arithmetic, geometry, music, and astronomy. Architecture and medicine, which Varro had included, found no place in this highly fanciful, mythological treatment, which was to leave its stamp on later encyclopedic formulations of the realm of learning. Though the terms

trivium, for the first three arts, and *quadrivium*, for the other
four, were apparently first so employed in the seventh century,
or even the eighth, the authority of Capella's seven arts left
its impress on the work of Cassiodorus and Seville, and on
later lesser lights. Though the "canonical seven" were to be
regarded as the foundation of all medieval learning, attention was not evenly distributed. The *trivium*, regarded as
elementary and general, was more widely studied than the
quadrivium; and of the *trivium*, grammar, *i.e.*, language and
literature, was the only art that could command universal
application.[107]

Donatus, fourth-century grammarian and teacher of
Jerome, became to the learned world a synonym for grammar, or even any elementary text. Priscian's more advanced
Institutiones Grammaticae, copied by Theodorus about 526,
bore in its well-packed pages fragments of ancient poets
otherwise forgot, as well as more copious borrowings from
the greatest names in Latin literature. Known to Aldhelm,
Bede, Alcuin, Maurus, and other luminaries of the eighth
and ninth centuries, Priscian is still extant in about a thousand manuscripts.

If Donatus, Priscian, and Capella provided foundation and
framework for the medieval temple of learning, Boethius
built out and ornamented the superstructure. To change the
figure, they gave a skeleton; he, with skillful soul surgery,
endowed it with a critical mind—a pagan mind, essentially
Aristotelian and Platonic—and feeling. As Terence and
Cicero had thought it not beneath them to translate, paraphrase and interpret the literature and philosophy of Greece

---

[107] Sandys, J. E.: *A History of Classical Scholarship*, I, 228, *pass.* 3 vols.
University Press: Cambridge, 1903-08; Laistner, M. L. W.: *Thought and Letters
in Western Europe*, 22 *f.*, 169 *f.*, *pass.* Dial Press: New York, 1931; Taylor,
H. O.: *The Mediaeval Mind*, I, 71 *f.* 2 vols. Macmillan & Co., Ltd.: London, 1938.

to Romans of their day, Boethius held it his proper care, in his own, to instruct "the manners of our State with the arts of Greek wisdom" by translating and interpreting all the works of Aristotle and Plato's dialogues, whose essential unity on important matters he sought to show.[108]

This grandiose undertaking, left incomplete, due to Boethius' imprisonment and execution, had far-reaching consequences, for his translations and commentaries on Aristotle— Porphory's *Introduction* to the *Categories,* the *Categories* themselves, and *De interpretatione*—were the basic treatises on logic in Western schools until the mid-twelfth century. The most imposing display of intellectual fireworks of the Age of Faith, the conflict of Realists and Nominalists, which illuminated the five centuries from Eriugena to Occam, was set off by a Boethian spark—his translation and commentary on a passage of Porphory's *Introduction* relating to the mooted matter of universals. As Howard R. Patch remarks,[109] it was Boethius, rather than the Arabs, who introduced Aristotle to the Western world.

Besides his labor of love for logic, Boethius' *De arithmetica, De musica,* and *De geometrica* were favorites of succeeding centuries. Beyond all these *De consolatione philosophiae,* composed in prison, was admired, loved, paraphrased, interpreted, and translated, and is so even today. It is not remarkable, therefore, that indebtedness to Boethius has been ranked high. Gibbon called the *Consolatione* a "golden" book, worthy of a Plato or a Cicero. Charles E. Mallet[110] thought Boethius "the greatest name among the teachers of the Middle Ages";

108 Taylor: *op. cit.,* I, 91 *f.*
109 *The Tradition of Boethius,* 31. Oxford University Press: New York, 1935.
110 *A History of the University of Oxford,* I, 7. 3 vols. Methuen & Co., Ltd.: London, 1924-27.

and Taylor considered him the chief "purveyor" of early medieval "intellectual grist."[111]

On the institutional side, Cassian, Benedict, and Cassiodorus made important decisions that affected learning throughout the Age of Faith. Cassian, disciplined in the ascetic life of the East for ten years, returned to Marseilles, where he established Saint Victor and compiled his *Institutes* and *Conferences* (*c.* 419-28), which gave guidance to monastic foundations that had been developing since St. Martin's mid-fourth century innovation.[112] Far from encouraging broad study, however, Cassian's advice was to read the Fathers as zealously as one once read pagan authors, in order to stifle all memory of the latter.[113] It has been suggested, and with some reason, that the *Institutes* "seconded the destroying arm of the Frank."[114] The low level of education in monasteries, which Charlemagne later sought to remedy, may well be credited in part to the limited scope of learning encouraged by the *Rule*.

Benedict of Nursia, leaving the world and its studies to lead a life of retirement at Subiaco and at Monte Cassino, promulgated his *Rule* about 526, which, whether designed, as recent scholars say, not for Italy alone but for the monasteries of Western Christendom, became "all but universal in the West by the Carolingian age."[115] He, though imperfectly educated, was acquainted with the Scriptures, the monastic

---

[111] *Op. cit.,* I, 102.

[112] *Ibid.,* I, 351; Coulton, G. G.: *Five Centuries of Religion,* I, 19. 4 vols. University Press: Cambridge, 1927-50; Sandys: *op. cit.,* I, 207.

[113] *Cassian's Conferences,* XIV, 12-13. *Nicene and Post-Nicene Fathers,* ser. 2, XI, 441 *f.*

[114] Mullinger, J. B.: *The Schools of Charles the Great and the Restoration of Education in the Ninth Century,* 31. G. E. Stechert & Co.: New York, 1911.

[115] Laistner: *op. cit.,* 67 *f.*

rules of Cassian and Basil, and the Western Fathers, Augustine and Jerome. Though the *Rule* gave no detailed direction as to studies, the assignment of part of the day to sacred reading, and provision for reading aloud at meals, and a book at Lent, gave a definite, albeit limited function to letters in institutions whose primary purpose had been to offer a refuge from the world.[116]

Cassiodorus (*c.* 490-585), who devoted his early life to political affairs and his later years to religious labors, embodied in himself the transition of learning from the world to the cloister. At Squillace, where he returned when past middle life, he founded Vivarium. There, more than any predecessor, he established a pattern of scholastic labors—gathering an excellent library, compiling, editing, copying manuscripts—whose influence was profound. His own literary output was bulky, consisting in part of *Epistulae*, a *Chronicon*, a *History of the Goths*, *De anima*, a *Commentary on the Psalms*, and the *Historia tripartita*—a compilation of Socrates, Sozomen, and Theodoret.

Of major importance for education was Cassiodorus' chief work, the *Institutiones divinarum et saecularium literarum*, produced about the middle of the sixth century. Therein he laid down a pattern of study for the brethren at Vivarium, showing the grammar, spelling, history and the Scriptures most worthy of their time. The great end of learning was to speed the work of salvation. To copy a word of the Lord was to strike a blow at Satan. But to that end, education was necessary, even knowledge of classical authors; and Cassiodorus gave careful attention to spelling, binding, as also to devices to facilitate the copyist's labor. A treatise, *De orthographia*, derived from Priscian, was prepared for his monks

---

[116] *Rule*, 38, 42, 48. Henderson: *op. cit.*, 291 *f.*, 294, 297 *f.*

before he died. In the second part of the *Institutiones*, Cassiodorus surveyed the seven liberal arts, giving half the space
to logic. His treatise, Sandys says, "by emphasizing the sanctity of the number 'seven,' by giving a new meaning to the
saying that 'Wisdom hath builded her house, she hath hewn
out her seven pillars,' and by connecting the seven arts with
the education of his monks," probably helped to popularize
the pagan treatise of Capella.[117]

In Isidore of Seville, paraphrase, selection, and compilation, which had been going on for centuries, reached its
zenith. Though widely famed for many works, a Gothic History, a Chronicle, *De viris illustribus*, *De natura rerum*, *Syn-
onyma*—a devotional book—and others, it was Isidore's
Etymologiae which became a standard reference in every
institution of learning of any importance in Western Europe.
This famed summation of all that should be known, as its
author characterized it, brought together "all such dead remnants of secular learning as had not been absolutely rejected
by the superstition of his own and earlier ages" and furnishes
us with "a cross-section of the debris of scientific thought at
the point where it is most artificial and unreal."[118] Being an
epitome of knowledge, secular and divine, the *Etymologiae*
is an invaluable, yet depressing, witness to the low estate to
which man's knowledge of his universe had fallen in the
seventh century. Apart from religious and pseudo-scientific
content, Isidore resummarized the seven liberal arts, following
the tradition of Capella and Cassiodorus, and included also
law and medicine. Notwithstanding modern judgments, the
very aridity of this compilation, itself based largely on previous ones, made it palatable to medieval minds. As Sandys[119]

---

[117] Sandys: *op. cit.*, I, 253; Taylor: *op. cit.*, I, 95 *f.*; Laistner: *op. cit.*, 68 *ff.*
[118] Brehaut: *op. cit.*, 16.
[119] *Op. cit.*, I, 443.

observed, its authority "as an encyclopaedia of classical learning" was so great that it "superseded the study of the classical authors themselves." A factor in this unhappy preference of an "authority" for the originals, however, lay in Isidore's own prescription that his monks limit themselves to the reading of grammarians.

It has been observed that men and peoples draw to themselves the kind of learning they desire. Therein is much truth; yet the whole social economy of the day into which men are born predetermines in broad lines some of the things they will most desire. In short, the character of intellectual effort and accomplishment is a resultant of interacting *desire* and *compulsion*. Under propitious circumstances, men relish and make good use of freedom, hazardous adventure, gay, courageous traffic of the mind; under less favorable conditions of a troubled, uncertain, decaying order, they crave security, fair certainty, and submit more willingly to authority. Thus, millions of men and women fled an unstable, declining world and accepted cloistral security and authority until the outer world, having put itself in better order, again beguiled them to essay a life more venturesome and independent.

Such a bright morn was long in dawning. Yet, centuries before the pulsing New Life was sensed and expressed by Dante, centers of secular power emerged in Frankland and in England which drew to themselves the best scholarship that could be found, and fearlessly and generously encouraged it. From then on, educational life quickened in two diverse channels: in schools—monastic, cathedral, and ultimately those of university grade; and in the gay, worldly society of the feudal order. The present purpose requires neither the story of formal, educational institutional expansion nor that of the social set. It will suffice to call attention to the influence of secular power and society in promoting broader, more meticulous devotion to certain long-neglected intellectual arts; and in rehabilitating the cult of physical excellence which had once been part of a liberal education.

Two centuries had elapsed since Gregory of Tours lamented the decay of letters in Gaul, when Charlemagne, enjoying a degree of order and relative leisure, derived from his own efforts and that of his predecessors, surveyed education and found it bad. Recognizing the goodness of God, the importance of religion, and the need of sound, liberal learning for a true understanding thereof, Charlemagne lent the full weight of his prestige and authority to the task of improving them. To that end, a capitulary, commonly assigned to 782, ran: ". . . we impose upon ourselves the task of reviving, with the utmost zeal, the study of letters, well-nigh extinguished through the neglect of our ancestors. We charge all our subjects, as far as they may be able, to cultivate the liberal arts, and we set them the example."[120]

It had been centuries since any potentate had spoken as forcefully on behalf of liberal learning. Moreover, suiting action to word, Charlemagne brought Alcuin from York, where broader learning was still flourishing, to the Palace School. There he redeemed his promise by setting an example of devotion to learning, not only for his court but for the realm as well.

To the heads of monasteries and bishoprics, entrusted to his care, Charlemagne addressed a directive, pointing out the dependence of true knowledge of religion upon mastery of letters. Many communications from monasteries had been received, he said, filled with due sentiments of piety and devotion, but expressed in uncouth language, for "what pious de-

120 Mullinger: *op. cit.*, 101.

votion dictated faithfully to the mind, the tongue uneducated on account of the neglect of study, was not able to express ... without error." Whence, he had begun to fear that, "as the skill in writing was less, so also the wisdom for understanding the Holy Scriptures might be much less than it rightly ought to be." Yet, if error in speech be dangerous, error in understanding is more so. Therefore, the monarch exhorts them "not to neglect the study of letters," and to study zealously in order more correctly to interpret the mysteries of Sacred Writ. For the Scriptures are full of tropes and similar figures, which can only be understood properly by one "fully instructed in the mastery of letters." To promote this end, therefore, those men are to be chosen who "have both the will and the ability to learn and a desire to instruct others."[121] And, the monarch adds, in the performance of this let your zeal equal ours in recommending it. Two years later (789) a capitulary advised every monastery and abbey to have schools, "where boys may be taught the Psalms, the system of musical notation, singing, arithmetic, and grammar; and let the books which are given them be free from faults. . . ."[122]

A century after Charlemagne's effort, Alfred judged the decay of learning in England so great that "very few on this side of the Humber," and not many beyond it, could understand rituals in English, or translate letters from Latin into English. He therefore besought Waerferth's aid in advancing learning, proposing the translation of books into English, that freeborn youths, "rich enough to be able to devote themselves to it," should learn English, and that those destined for

---

[121] Munro, D. C.: *Laws of Charles the Great*, 13. *Translations and Reprints from the Original Sources of European History*, VI, no. 5. Department of History of the University of Pennsylvania: Philadelphia, 1900.
[122] Mullinger: *op. cit.*, 102.

higher rank should continue with Latin.[123] From Gaul, on in-
vitation, came Grimbald and John to assist in this design.
Alfred's youngest son, Ethelwerd, was directed to such learning along with others.[124]

The significance of Alfred's and Charlemagne's reforms
lay in their positive, favorable attitude toward learning, the
encouragement of personal example, the influence of their
high station. Studies, their content relatively elementary, followed the traditional pattern. Alcuin viewed the liberal arts
as the seven pillars of the house of wisdom, the seven steps
leading to theology. But Charlemagne's directives raised
learning from a casual occupation to a basic responsibility
of religious institutions, and brought a somewhat reluctant
scholarship from the cloister into the service of society.

The promise of the awakening seems greater than its immediate performance. If Alcuin's interpretation of grammar
was limited, and his love of pagan poets turned to condemnation in his later years, that of Rabanus Maurus, his pupil at
Tours, was more expansive, and included the interpretation
of poets and historians. Most heavily fraught with significance
for future centuries was the encouragement of dialectic. What
Tertullian and many another Father had condemned as hurt-
ful to the Faith, Charlemagne found fascinating and encouraged, as did Charles the Bald. Alcuin's dialectic truly had no
edge. Rabanus, however, elevated the art of knowing how to
know, the discipline of disciplines, and urged the clergy to
master it in order to rout heretics.[125]

---

[123] *King Alfred's West-Saxon Version of Gregory's Pastoral Care*, 3 *ff*. (Ed.
by H. Sweet) Early English Text Society: London, 1871.

[124] Asser: "Annals of the Reign of Alfred the Great," in *Six Old English
Chronicles*, 68, 70. (Ed. by J. A. Giles) George Bell and Sons: London, 1896.

[125] Mullinger: *op. cit.*, 144; Taylor: *op. cit.*, I, 222.

Whether by reason of remoteness from invasions, never being part of the Roman Empire, isolation from the centers of authority, tough resistance of the Irish, or from some combination of these and other factors, Irish monks, as Adamson put it, "avoided the stupid pedantry" of the continentals and still cherished Greek letters at a time when even Latin learning was at low ebb in Gaul and elsewhere.[126] Indeed, the discrepancy between Ireland and the continent, in respect to Greek learning, reputedly gave rise to a common assumption that if one knew Greek he came from Erin. From such a background, though his precise birthplace is unknown, came John Scotus Eriugena, who served at the Palace School under Charles the Bald (c. 845). This renowned scholar, well versed in Plato's *Timaeus* and acquainted with the *Celestial Hierarchy* of Pseudo-Dionysius, the latter of which he was commissioned to translate into Latin, vastly enlarged the scope of dialectic in Christian controversy. Independent in mind, familiar with Greek philosophers and early Greek Fathers, whom he supported in maintaining the identity of true religion and philosophy, Eriugena unequivocally espoused reason against mere authority, and thus gave impetus to a scholarship long unfamiliar in Western Christendom. "Authority," he maintained, "sometimes proceeds from reason; but reason never from authority."[127] Two centuries later the intellectual harvest ripened in the conflict of Realism and Nominalism, the upshot of which was to clothe religious dogmas in the logic of that pagan philosopher whom the Western Fathers had once most roundly condemned.

[126] J. W. Adamson, "Education," in F. J. C. Hearnshaw (Ed.), *Mediaeval Contributions to Modern Civilisation*, 198. Henry Holt and Company: New York, 1922; Sandys: *op. cit.*, I, 438 *f.*

[127] Taylor: *op. cit.*, I, 231; Fitzpatrick, B.: *Ireland and the Foundations of Europe*, 178, 208. Funk & Wagnalls Company: New York, 1927.

Physical aspects of education survived the Age of Faith, but not without strenuous opposition. The ancient Greeks sought a harmony of mental and physical culture in their conception of a liberally educated citizen.[128] In practice, however, physical culture degenerated into professionalism before the Christian era—a degeneracy which invited criticism. Against indulgence in games, competitive athletics and other pleasures of the gymnasium, baths, and stadium, Christian ascetics loosed a vigorous attack. In the place of physical sports, Christians exalted the virtues of hard physical labor—long forgot by leisure-class Greeks and Romans—which they justified partly as an economic necessity to sustain life, in part as a moral discipline.

Clement of Alexandria probably came nearer than any other churchman to accepting the old Greek ideal of proportion, admitting, as he did, the propriety of certain physical sports for men.[129] His statement, however, was carefully guarded. Manual labor—drawing water, cutting wood, and hoeing—he thought respectable and approved. Even Pittacus turned a mill; and Biblical characters hallowed toil. Women, too, require physical exercise; and they are to get it, Clement says, as if he had an eye on Xenophon, not in running and wrestling, but by spinning, weaving, cooking, making beds, running errands, and at the mill.[130]

Clement's leniency toward sports had little effect upon the Fathers; more and more the emphasis on labor grew. Jerome urges spinning in the training of Paula and Pacatula.[131] A young monk is advised to have always some work, "that the

---

128 *Supra*, 21 *ff.*, 42 *f.*, 51 *ff.*
129 *Supra*, 94.
130 *Instructor*, III, 10. *Ante-Nicene Fathers*, II, 283.
131 *Letters*, CVII, 10; CXXVIII, 1. *Nicene and Post-Nicene Fathers*, ser. 2, VI, 193, 258.

devil may find you busy." Make creels and baskets, hoe, plant, water, tend fruit trees, care for bees, twist fish lines, copy books, that "your hand may earn your food and your mind may be satisfied with reading."[132]

Monastic life, in some ways a back-to-nature, back-to-the-soil movement, returned men and women to a primitive democracy of labor. The "athletes of Christ" learned to labor rather than to play. Biblical justification was not wanting, in the words of the Apostle and the Psalmist: "If any will not work, neither let him eat"; and "Thou shalt eat the labor of thine hands." When certain hearers of Holy Writ found justification for eating the bread of idleness, in the "lilies" that "labor not, neither spin," and the birds that "sow not, nor reap," Augustine gave his pen to judgment in *De opere monachorum*.[133]

On rich and poor, noble and plebeian, Columbanus imposed agricultural labor. Even the sick threshed wheat. An abbot, like the rest, might labor in the field, as did Equitius.[134] Basil's *Rule* emphasized labor. Fasting, though useful, must not stand in the way of labor; if it does interfere, "it is better to eat like the workmen of Christ that you are."[135] Cassian's *Institutes* stressed dual utility, the economic and moral value of labor: one must work or not eat; "a monk who works is attacked by but one devil; but an idler is tormented by countless spirits."[136] Benedict echoed the same principle, but with more moderation in application: "Idleness is the enemy of the soul. And therefore, at fixed times, the brothers ought to be occupied in manual labour . . . for . . . they are truly monks

---

132 *Ibid.*, CXXV, 11. *Loc. cit.*, ser. 2, VI, 248.
133 Sec. 2. *Nicene and Post-Nicene Fathers*, ser. 1, III, 504.
134 Montalembert: *op. cit.*, I, 354, 553; II, 502.
135 *Ibid.*, I, 204.
136 Bk. X, 12, 14, 23. *Nicene and Post-Nicene Fathers*, ser. 2, XI, 271, 274.

if they live by the labours of their hands; as did also our fathers and the apostles."[137] Cassiodorus, true to his broad literary bent, which meant much for the future, gave scholastic labor first place, urging even the classics, that one might better understand Scripture, and providing that those monks who had no inclination for such intellectual endeavor should devote themselves to gardening and agriculture, but accompany that labor with reading of Martialis, Columella, and Macer.[138]

While "Christian Athletes" applied themselves to labor in the cloister, the outer world, wearing the Cross lightly, pursued its joyful, often somewhat hilarious, way. Commoners ran races, fought with fists and staves, wrestled, leaped, played ball, danced, shot, threw the stone, engaged in cock-fighting, bull- and bear-baiting, jousted in boats, went sliding and sledding on the ice, fished, and hunted—though this lordly sport was often denied them, even when animals from the lord's preserves destroyed their crops.[139] In some localities, burghers engaged in armed contests, in imitation of the tournaments of their betters, as in the *toupineures* in France.[140] Hunting, hawking, horse-racing, tennis, and tournaments embodying the activities of warfare in feudal times were the chief physical recreations of nobility, some of them enjoyed by women as well as men.

Thus sporting life went on, despite the fact that tournaments were condemned by church anathemas, and sometimes forbidden by secular law.[141] Moralists condemned dancing, but

---

137 *Rule,* 48. Henderson: *op. cit.,* 297.

138 Sandys: *op. cit.,* I, 251.

139 Stephen, W. F.: "A Description of London," trans. by H. E. Butler with F. M. Stenton, *Norman London,* 28 *ff.* Historical Association Leaflets, nos. 93, 94. London, 1934; Coulton, G. G.: *The Medieval Village,* 115 *ff.* University Press: Cambridge, 1925.

140 Meller, W. C.: *A Knight's Life in the Days of Chivalry,* 149 *f.* T. Werner Laurie: London, 1924.

141 Coulton: *Social Life in Britain,* 400 *f.*

people danced and sang outside the cathedral door, and sometimes within. As Havelock Ellis remarked, "In English cathedrals dancing went on until the fourteenth century."[142] One
wonders whether there was not many a parish clerk who, like
Chaucer's, could "in twenty manere" "trippe and daunce . . .
and with his legges casten to and fro."[143]

In optimum cases, physical sports and training mingled
with intellectual culture. Charlemagne and Alfred combined
both. Charles' sons and others at court joined learning, manly
sports, and the arts of war. Ethelwerd, son of Alfred the Great,
learned with others of the nobility, to read and write Saxon
and Latin, becoming thus schooled in the liberal arts "before
they were of an age to practice manly arts, namely, hunting
and such pursuits as befit noblemen."[144] Of others in high
position it might have been said, as it was of Charles the Bald,
that he gave himself to scholarly as well as to martial exercises.[145] As Thompson's survey, *The Literacy of the Laity in
the Middle Ages*, shows, though their learning varied vastly
in respect to place and period, the worldly nobility of Europe
were by no means as illiterate as the tradition of learned
churchmen and illiterate laity once encouraged us to believe.
Chaucer's portrait of the Squire—

> Wel coude he sitte on hors, and faire ryde.
> He coude songes make and wel endyte,
> Iuste and eek daunce, and wel purtreye and wryte.[146]

was more than a poet's fancy. The day was not far off when
liberal learning, after centuries of celestial service pointing to
the stars, would be reunited to the secular realm of practical

[142] *The Dance of Life*, 44. Houghton Mifflin Company: Boston, 1923.
[143] "The Miller's Tale," *The Canterbury Tales*.
[144] Asser: *op. cit.*, 68.
[145] Mullinger: *op. cit.*, 173.
[146] "The Prologue," *The Canterbury Tales*.

reason, in Aristotle's sense—a reunion epitomized in the phrase, "a gentleman and a scholar." The worldly nobility and the burghers of the free cities that rose to power in the eleventh and twelfth centuries were to constitute the social milieu in which liberal learning was to be fully restored to its original rôle befitting free men and fitting them for freedom.

CHAPTER SIX

NEW LIFE AND EDUCATION

1. *The New Life*

INCIPIT VITA NOVA—the New Life begins. Thus Dante captioned the autobiographical poetry of his youth, portraying the new sense of life welling within him. Apart from its revelation of personal experience, *La Vita Nuova* breathes the spirit of a new epoch to which the poet was keenly sensitive,[1] an age in which medieval culture reached its maturity and gave way to that of modern times. Dante felt the pulse of change already in process, and to it gave added impetus.

In this metamorphosis there was no swift maturing of the new culture, no sudden collapse of the old. The new epoch came slowly, like a rosy-fingered dawn. Far from being a cataclysmic phenomenon of the fourteenth and fifteenth centuries, or even of the thirteenth, foreshadowings of the new era are discernible in the time of Charlemagne, of Alfred, of Otto, and in the eleventh and twelfth centuries. Moreover, far from being limited to, or originating in, a mere revival of classical letters, the new era, many-sided as life itself, grew out of the life of peoples, and manifested itself in subjective

---

[1] Vossler, K.: *Die göttliche Komödie*, I, 513 *ff*. 2 vols. Carl Winter's Universitätsbuchhandlung: Heidelberg, 1907-08; *The New Life of Dante Alighieri*, 96. (Trans. by C. E. Norton) Houghton Mifflin Company: Boston, 1909.

and objective, economic, political, philosophical, religious, aesthetic, literary (vernacular as well as classical), and scientific tendencies. Nevertheless, being centrally concerned with man and his earthly *Tun und Streben,* in contrast with the otherworldliness of medieval Christianity, it is not surprising that the new life discovered a kinship with pagan antiquity; and that it found its most perfect educational ideal and stimulus in a rehabilitation of the ancient mode of liberal education, more or less modified from time to time to suit different nations and the ever-changing conditions of the modern world.

Viewing the New Life thus broadly, rationalism in religion, the vernacular movement, the classical revival, the development of modern science and a naturalistic philosophy of life all appear as successive phases of the evolution of man's struggle for freedom through mastery of himself and his universe. Each age, rebelling momentarily against its predecessor, as though sufficient to itself, betimes sees fit to incorporate something once denied. The most scientifically disposed of modern nations embodies more concern for man than did the thirteenth or the fifteenth century, provides him learning in his mother tongue, as Dante anticipated, and with its science reads the classics. Properly considered, in its full meaning, *La Vita Nuova* is still an unfinished book.

What, fundamentally, was this new life emerging in Western Europe? At heart, it was a subjective change, a shift of mental view—conditioned by external factors. Man rediscovered himself and reasserted his right to think for himself, in face of the claims of fixed patterns of authority which had for centuries ruled him. John Scotus Eriugena, Roscellinus, and Abelard, asserting the prior claims of reason over dogma, enhanced the dignity of man as an individual. Such arrogance was scarcely to be tolerated. John's forthright championship of reason made him a heretic.[2] Centuries of rationalism would at length make heresy a commonplace of the New Life; would, despite even the repressive measures of the Inquisition and death by burning, disrupt the Church and end in the fragmentation of Christendom, leaving the individual absolutely free in the sphere of religion to choose for himself.

From the small circle of medieval intelligentsia, the quest for freedom broadened. Ultimately it flowed through many channels. By the thirteenth century, man's sense of self-esteem was all but ready to eclipse his once proclaimed self-abnegation. Far from fearing to be himself, man comes to flaunt his self-assertion. Desire for fame takes hold of him; he yields to it, though not without conflict. He wants to be first; he wishes to excel. *L'uomo universale,* all-sided, universal man, becomes the grand ideal. Priority in dealing with the science of the vernacular appeals to Dante.[3] He would do something not done before. Aristotle has been explained. Why expound Euclid again? After Cicero, a work *On Old Age* would be superfluous. He turns to *De Monarchia,* that he may not be guilty of burying his talent. It will be of value to the world; besides, he hopes to win for his "glory the palm of so great a prize."[4] To be sure, Dante knows the world's renown is like a breath of wind that comes and goes; and that *lo gran desio dell' eccellenza* pays its tax in purgatory.[5] Nevertheless, he longs and labors for the poet's crown.[6] Petrarch, like Dante,

[2] *Cf.* Vossler: *op. cit.,* I, 152.

[3] *The De Vulgari Eloquentia,* I, 1. (Trans. by A. G. F. Howell) *A Translation of the Latin Works of Dante Alighieri.* J. M. Dent and Co.: London, 1904.

[4] *The De Monarchia,* I, 1. (Trans. by P. H. Wicksteed) *A Translation of the Latin Works of Dante Alighieri.* J. M. Dent and Co.: London, 1904.

[5] *Purgatory,* 11. *The Divine Comedy of Dante Alighieri.* (Trans. by C. E. Norton) 3 vols. Houghton Mifflin Company: Boston, 1892.

[6] *Paradise,* 25.

reveals the conflict between desire for fame in human accomplishment and the conception of ascetic renunciation. "What," he asks Augustine, would you rob me "of my most splendid preoccupations," condemn to darkness the brightest portion of my soul?[7] True to the spirit of the new age, he refuses even the counsel of Augustine to forget his *Africa* and fix his mind on death.

Perhaps in no area was subjective change more striking than in man's view of woman and human love. What early Christian ascetics had held vile, a snare of Satan, "the chief impediment to holiness,"[8] to be avoided at any cost, emerged now in full splendor and respectability. Instead of leading to perdition, woman becomes an inspiration to excellence, an angel-guide to paradise. Far from hiding romantic love, the greatest and the least figures of the New Life revel in its revelation before all the world. Love poetry flourished in the worldly court of advancing chivalry and became the favorite "form of distraction."[9] The religious hymned the Blessed Virgin. In scholastic circles one heard the wandering student singing,

> Love flies all the world around. . . .

Dante was not unacquainted with these foreshadowings of a new age. Guinicelli, he called his teacher in songs of love. Inspired by Beatrice, Dante surpassed his predecessors, and immortalized the story of his love in *La Vita Nuova*. At her death, he mourned: "How doth the city sit solitary that was full of people!"[10] Thereafter, obedient to a vision, he formed

[7] Robinson, J. H. (with H. W. Rolfe): *Petrarch*, 404 *f*. G. P. Putnam's Sons: New York, 1899.

[8] Symonds, J. A.: *Wine, Women and Song*, 3. Chatto & Windus: London, 1925.

[9] Grandgent, C. H.: *Dante*, 93. Duffield & Company: New York, 1916.

[10] Gardner, E. G.: *Dante*, 43, 50. J. M. Dent and Co.: London, 1900.

a resolution that, "if it shall please Him through whom all
things live, that my life be prolonged for some years, I hope
to say of her what was never said of any woman."[11] Beatrice,
transfigured, was the inspiration of the *Commedia*, Dante's
guide to Paradise; what he said of her was at once "the Auto-
biography of a soul,"[12] and a gifted, imaginative revelation
of the medieval mind.

Love, inspired by women, real or imagined, became the
theme of a poetry of unprecedented proportions. Petrarch
immortalized the charms of Laura and thereby left a name in
creative literature, as more than four hundred editions testify.
In later years, devoted to scholarship and Latin poetry of an
epic strain, he deprecated these early "trivial verses, filled
with the false and offensive praise of women." He tells his
brother he has learned to fear "association with women,"
once desired, "more than death."[13] But it was vain to regret;
he could not recall his sonnets; he had set the whole world
singing. The learned and unlearned alike, Petrarch ruefully
remarks, are versifying. Even his farm hand dreams on Mount
Parnassus. The kine, he fears, will soon be lowing numbers
and ruminating sonnets!

Subjective change manifested itself in historiography as
well as in poetry. Lives of saints, and occasionally secular
figures of eminent status, had been the favorite themes of
Christian chroniclers. Chiefly they were more noteworthy for
alleged revelations of God's Providence than for delineation
of individual portraits. Now, however, in keeping with a
growing sense of human worth, a fresh tendency appeared—
secular, individualistic, inclined more and more to natural

11 Norton: *The New Life*, 89 *f*.
12 Grandgent, C. H.: *Dante Alighieri: La Divina Commedia*, I, xxvi. 3 vols.
D. C. Heath and Company: Boston, 1909-13.
13 Robinson: *op. cit.*, 23, 403.

and material in place of miraculous and supernatural causation, which was seen increasingly as empty, unprovable allegation. "An acute analysis of individual characters and interests," Benedetto Croce observes,[14] took the place of divine intervention and papal action. Even religious wars were to be seen in a political, utilitarian light. Biography emerged as an eminently proper form of history, justified, as Jacob Burckhardt said,[15] simply "if and because" a man was in himself "remarkable." Joinville, sometimes called Saint Louis' Boswell, is remembered primarily for his *Histoire,* distinguished for its emphasis on character portrayal. Boccaccio, full of enthusiasm for the great Florentine poet, set his hand to a life of Dante. Not only recent men found interpreters. Cities, formerly concerned chiefly with their saints, recalled the ancient pagans who had made them famous. In keeping with the age, a city itself becomes worthy of attention, as Bruni's *History of Florence* shows.

Aesthetically, the subjective metamorphosis is reflected in graphic arts, as well as literature. As Christian asceticism had persuaded man to see evil lurking behind the mask of natural beauty, early Christian art shunned realistic imitation of nature, in which Greek art had found its ideal, and exalted the abstract and universal. "Through love of universality," says Venturi, "the individual became indifferent, and was reduced to an anonymous instrument of religious exaltation."[16] Art was absorbed in God. Now, keenly sensitive to human exaltation and the excellence of nature, painters and sculptors began a return to realistic, natural, humanistic ex-

[14] *History, Its Theory and Practice,* 224. (Trans. by D. Ainslie) Harcourt, Brace and Company: New York, 1921.

[15] *The Civilisation of the Renaissance in Italy,* 329. (Trans. by S. G. C. Middlemore) George Allen & Unwin Ltd.: London, 1921.

[16] Venturi, L.: *History of Art Criticism,* 64. (Trans. by C. Marriott) E. P. Dutton & Company: New York, 1936.

pression, and freed art from excessive devotion to the abstract. The art of both ages may be religious, but the difference "between the religiosity of the Middle Ages and that of the Renaissance" is that one denied and the other affirmed humanity. Giotto emancipated and humanized painting. Niccola Pisano gave new vitality to sculpture. Ghiberti said of Giotto that he united "natural art and gentleness" without going to extremes, discovered "what had been buried" for almost six centuries, and "led art to the greatest perfection."[17] Devotion to nature grew and inspired the greatest artists of the age. Leonardo maintained that "it is always best to have recourse to Nature."[18] A painter who imitates another is the grandchild, not the child, of Nature.

Natural grace of form and a keen sense of individuality and movement supplanted the stiffness of medieval art. The difference between medieval and Renaissance conceptions is well exemplified in portrait statues and equestrian monuments. Medieval horsemen, W. R. Valentiner says,[19] are "obviously not portraits" but symbolic figures. The equestrian statues of Verrocchio (Colleoni) and Donatello (Gattamelata), on the contrary, are realistic and natural. Portrait statues reflect the individualism of the new age. Donatello's "David" is the first nude statue of the Renaissance, executed realistically in the round, independent of architectural setting. As secular tendencies advanced, portrait monuments, "unknown to the Middle Ages," became highly popular, being generally designed to perpetuate the memory of "temporal heroes."[20]

Man's aesthetic quest led ultimately to theoretical, schol-

17 *Ibid.*, 84 *f.*, 87.

18 Da Vinci, L.: *A Treatise on Painting*, CCCLIV. (Trans. by J. F. Rigaud) J. Taylor: London, 1802.

19 *Origins of Modern Sculpture*, 109 *ff*. Wittenborn and Company: New York, 1946.

20 *Ibid.*, 165.

arly study. In this, as in so many other phases of its development, the new age sought and found inspiration and guidance
in classical antiquity. Alberti, as gifted in music, poetry, and
philosophy as in painting, and famed as restorer of the
ancient architectural style, wrote two treatises, *De Pictura*
and *Della Statua,* besides his most important *De Re Aedifi-
catoria.* Ghiberti's *Commentari* reflects experience, careful
study of antiquity, and a readiness to glean truth from pagan
as well as Christian sources. He drew from Vitruvius and
others to formulate a philosophy of painting and sculpture,
being convinced that without rational theory there can be no
sound art. Leonardo da Vinci's *Trattato della pittura*[21] emphasized the indispensable rôle of theory: "Practice must
always be founded on good theory," for those without it are
like mariners without rudder or compass.

A significant alteration of attitude toward the world of
things marked the New Life. Though, at the outset, the new
realism was unable to match the growth of speculative reason
in scholastic circles, it paralleled and ultimately transcended
it in its transforming effect on the modern world. The shift
was essentially one of outlook and of method. Early medieval
folk did not lack an explanation of the natural world. Their
"knowledge," however, was bookish, derived from previous
"authorities," garnered in neat compends such as those of
Capella, Cassiodorus, Isidore, and their imitators. "Science"
served theology. The world of the theologian was a fixed universe. The early encyclopedists selected and arranged the
world of things in harmony with religious scruple, or theological concepts, and told what was known, or should be
known.[22] They did not look for new discoveries.

21 *Op. cit.,* CXII.
22 Taylor, H. O.: *The Mediaeval Mind,* I, 103 *ff.* 2 vols. Macmillan & Co., Ltd.:
London, 1938; Brehaut, E.: *An Encyclopedist of the Dark Ages, Isidore of
Seville,* 16. Columbia University: New York, 1912.

To a great degree the clerical-minded encyclopedists of the twelfth and thirteenth centuries continued the old tradition, following authorities and serving religion. Neckam's *De naturis rerum* was "a vehicle for moral instruction."[23] Thomas of Cantimpré offered in *De natura rerum* a highly uncritical collection from "diverse writings."[24] Bartholomew Anglicus' *On the Properties of Things*, though marked by fresh, original observation in some areas, was largely a compilation from saints and philosophers, designed to explain the mysteries of Holy Writ. Though widely popular for three centuries, it represented "on the whole" a state of knowledge "already superseded" when written.[25] In Vincent of Beauvais' *Speculum majus*, the *Speculum naturale*, though superior to other compilations in its coverage and novel in plan, still served the cause of religion and theology, and made no original contribution to science.

Stimulated by many forces—the growth of commerce, intercourse with distant parts, new knowledge of Aristotle, and increasing contact with Moslem scholarship which had far outdistanced Christendom—a new science grew with, and served, a new world that was gradually emerging—a world of dynamic movement, engaged in practical concerns, desirous of wealth and power. In essence, the new science involved new sources and new methods, substituted the Book of Nature for the Word, and elevated reason, observation, experience, and experiment above authority. But the deviation from the

23 Thorndike, L.: *A History of Magic and Experimental Science During the First Thirteen Centuries of Our Era*, II, 192. 2 vols. Macmillan Company: New York, 1923.
24 *Ibid.*, II, 375, 380; Sarton, G.: *Introduction to the History of Science*, II, 593. 2 vols. Williams & Wilkins: Baltimore, 1927.
25 Sarton: *op. cit.*, II, 586; Steele, R. (Ed.) : *Medieval Lore: An Epitome . . . of Bartholomew Anglicus on the Properties of Things.* Elliot Stock: London, 1893; Thorndike: *op. cit.*, II, 401 *ff.*

old tradition was gradual and piecemeal: new methods mingled with the old; accurate observation rubbed elbows with wild credulity and superstition. For many, the new science was still the servant of theology. Even in the nineteenth century, some considered various sciences valuable only as a proof of Holy Writ.[26]

Science was about to forsake the cloister. Its full emancipation would wait upon its going. Meantime, however, progress was made amongst clericals, despite obscurantism and repressive measures, by a few who looked with unaccustomed interest and freshness of vision on the world of things. A new geography appeared; mathematics, physics, astronomy, biological and medical science began to move forward. Adam of Bremen, "first German geographer," gave in his *History of Hamburg Diocese* (*c.* 1075) a valuable, direct account of north European trade, based largely "on oral information," yet for certain areas he relied on fabulous lore.[27] Adelard of Bath, rebelling against the wordy sophisms and verbosity of the schools of Gaul, broadened his learning by travel to Salerno, Graecia Maior and the Mohammedan world, and enlarged the West's learning with a treatise on the astrolabe, another on the abacus, an astrological work, and, most important, a treatise on *Natural Questions,* wherein he defended human science and put reason above authority. William of Conches, contemporary of Adelard, similarly defended human reason against authority in his *Dragmaticon,* holding that "a reason should be sought in every case, if one can be found." Though compelled to recant

[26] Bolzau, E. L.: *Almira Hart Lincoln Phelps, Her Life and Work,* 248 *ff.* Science Press Printing Co.: Lancaster, 1936; Le Duc, T.: *Piety and Intellect at Amherst College,* 78 *ff.* Columbia University Press: New York, 1946.

[27] Sarton: *op. cit.,* I, 767; Haskins, C. H.: *The Renaissance of the Twelfth Century,* 336. Harvard University Press: Cambridge, 1927.

his theological heresies, he stood his ground in defense of natural science.[28] Peter of Spain, author of many medieval treatises and commentaries, set forth a defense of experimental method in his *Commentary on Isaac*. Albertus Magnus deviated in his scientific works from the ruling position regarding "universals," saying that one must know each thing's "peculiar characteristics for this is the best and perfect kind of science." Natural science depends on "investigation of causes."[29] In a limited degree, Albertus employed experiment in the study of animals, and often, though by no means always, exhibited a critical attitude toward authorities. Grosseteste, at Oxford, appealed to reason, experience, and experiment in his mathematical, physical, and astrological work. His pupil, Roger Bacon, recognized subservience to faulty, unworthy authority, custom, prejudice, and concealment of ignorance under ostentatious display of knowledge, as the chief sources of error,[30] and sought especially to advance experimental science. Though he himself made "few if any experiments, and no invention,"[31] he had some vision of mechanical improvements that might come, if science were applied to practical problems. Thorndike, certainly not uncritical of Bacon's claims to distinction, nevertheless calls his *Opus maius* "one of the most remarkable books of the remarkable thirteenth century."[32]

Fluctuation in individual mental states may be conditioned by internal factors, as well as by external forces. When alteration in outlook characterizes whole populations, or classes,

---

28 Thorndike: *op. cit.*, II, 53, 59 *ff.*; Taylor: *op. cit.*, II, 402 *f.*
29 Thorndike: *op. cit.*, II, 535, 541 *ff.*; Taylor: *op. cit.*, II, 452 *ff.*; Haskins: *op. cit.*, 310.
30 *The Opus Majus of Roger Bacon*, I, 4 *ff.* (Trans. by R. B. Burke) 2 vols. University of Pennsylvania Press: Philadelphia, 1928.
31 Sarton: *op. cit.*, II, 953; Thorndike: *op. cit.*, II, 654 *ff.*
32 Thorndike: *op. cit.*, II, 678,

and assumes such proportions that it becomes a movement, one looks for external causes, which, because they are external and general, may readily affect the many. What lay back of the subjective change, that rising tide of intellectual and aesthetic revolt, the increased sense of freedom, which became so conspicuous a phenomenon of European life from the twelfth century onward, and ultimately transformed social, political, religious, and educational conceptions and institutions? Many forces contributed to the change. Most fundamental in its effect upon all others, however, was the alteration of economic life and its related politico-social patterns; for intellectual life, in anything more than a minimal degree, depends in the aggregate for its nurture and expansion on surplus wealth and a certain stability for its acquisition and preservation.

Decline of learning in Western Europe had paralleled the disintegration of the old Roman order. It ebbed lowest where the surplus, created and maintained in that economy, was exhausted; when security and stability, which made commerce possible, reached the vanishing point. Cities were not all suddenly destroyed by barbarians. Rather, they shrank with a progressive anemia as their life-blood—trade—diminished and was finally reduced to merely local exchange of goods. This vital flow persisted longer than was once believed. Foreign commerce through Mediterranean ports, especially Marseilles, though declining in the seventh century, was still active in the early eighth. Shortly after the mid-eighth century, when advance of the Moslems into Spain and France closed the Mediterranean, Marseilles became an empty port; and Provence, once the richest, became the poorest of Gallic provinces.[33]

[33] Pirenne, H.: *Medieval Cities, Their Origins and the Revival of Trade*, 29. (Trans. by F. D. Halsey) Princeton University Press: Princeton, 1925.

Commerce in Charlemagne's empire was almost wholly local, serving the town, the monastery, and the court with local products. The Roman gold *solidus* gave way to the silver *deniers*. The concentration of power effected by Charlemagne, though remarkable, was sharply limited in time and territory. What Saracens had done to Mediterranean ports, the Norse invasions inflicted sporadically upon western and northern coasts from the ninth to the eleventh century. Cut off from commerce with the outside world, the Carolingian empire became almost wholly an agricultural economy, wherein money was of little value, and production was chiefly for use rather than sale.[34] In this feudal, agricultural society, immobility of population was a conspicuous trait. Learning had slight meaning for such an economy, and enjoyed only a slim, precarious existence in monasteries and cathedrals. Charlemagne did much to stimulate intellectual effort in these circles. Feudal and clerical dominion went hand in hand. The purpose, character, and extent of education continued relatively fixed until a ground-swell of external forces—expansion of production, increased commerce, growth of cities, and contact with the outer world—ultimately undermined the feudal order of northern Europe, and gave increasing numbers of people a new freedom. The "New Life" was preeminently a phenomenon of the city.

Rehabilitation of trade and cities was first marked in Italy, where life, after Imperial collapse, was subject to factors from which northern Europe was long cut off. Strengthened by contact with eastern commerce via the Mediterranean, certain old Italian cities were sustained, and new centers of commerce developed. While Sicily fell to the Moslems,

---

[34] Knight, M. M., *et al.*: *Economic History of Europe*, 87. Houghton Mifflin Company: Boston, 1928.

southern Italy successfully staved off conquest. In Amalfi, East and West continued to meet. Venice, sprung from native peoples who sought refuge amid the islands and lagoons at the head of the Adriatic, when forced back by encroaching barbarians in the fifth century, was favored throughout the Middle Ages by her situation in the orbit of Constantinople. Nourished by continuing commerce, cities not only survived but became, despite sharp struggles against popes and emperors, the dominant power in Italy. A commercial aristocracy came to be as conspicuous a feature of Italian life—even nobles participated in commercial affairs—as was the feudal landed aristocracy in northern Europe. The Crusades, launched for a variety of other reasons at the end of the eleventh century and continuing sporadically for two hundred years, provided new stimulus to Italian ports—Genoa, Pisa, and most of all, Venice, which reaped the chief harvest when Constantinople was captured in 1204.[35] Not only was foreign shipping increased; new industries—silk, glass, dyes, sugar, flax, and hemp—were brought to Italy. Commerce fostered industry; and industrial growth stimulated further expansion, southward from Lombardy into Tuscany, and northward through Alpine passes to France and Germany. Italian traders were in Paris as early as 1074; in the early twelfth century they were participating in Flanders fairs. Venice had a "brisk commerce" in England by the thirteenth century.[36]

Commercial activity in the northern Lowlands began to develop in the early tenth century when the Norse turned to peaceful pursuits. Bruges became the center of a great commercial and industrial area. Flanders' coins of the tenth and

---

[35] Day, C.: *A History of Commerce*, 90 *ff*. Longmans, Green and Co.: New York, 1924.
[36] *Ibid*., 96 *f*.

eleventh centuries, found in Denmark, Prussia, Russia, and in London toll records, show the channels through which the trade of Flanders passed. By contact with Russia, Byzantine trade, expanding through Kiev and Novgorod, was tapped to enrich the cities of the north. The basic Lowlands product which fed this trade was wool. Participating in this commercial expansion of the tenth and eleventh centuries were Ghent, Ypres, Lille, Arras, Tournai, Cambrai, Valenciennes, Liège, Huy, Dinant, Mainz, and Cologne. By the twelfth century commerce and industry were profoundly altering the life of Western Europe; and mobility became as prominent a feature as immobility had been in the centuries past.[37]

Formed under the impetus of economic interests, commercial and industrial cities had far-reaching, sociopolitical consequences. They were at once the creation and the home of a new social class, a bourgeois order. Merchants were of necessity a mobile element; their life made them, in fact, free men. As their depots prospered, they exerted a power of attraction on surrounding rural areas; quite unintentionally, they undermined feudalism and freed men from the soil. Before the eleventh century north European artisans were serfs, serving secular or ecclesiastical lords. But serfs who fled the country, and managed to dwell in town for a year and a day, came to be free men. Germans began to say, *"Die Stadtluft macht frei"*—city air makes free![38] Living within these burgs, people became known as burghers. Increasing wealth of the burghers was an attractive prize for highwaymen. To protect themselves, in an age when strong national governments did not as yet exist, townsmen armed themselves,

[37] Pirenne: *op. cit.*, 97 *ff.*, 103 *f.*; Baynes, N. H., and Moss, H. St. L. B.: *Byzantium: An Introduction to East Roman Civilization*, 63 *ff.* Clarendon Press: Oxford, 1948.
[38] Pirenne: *op. cit.*, 201.

built palisades and, ultimately, firm-walled fortresses that could withstand even robber-kings. The Hansa League maintained armed forces numbering many thousands. Danzig, according to Aeneas Sylvius, could put fifty thousand men under arms.[39]

Attached to the agricultural village economy of feudalism, craftsmen labored alone or in small numbers, owing allegiance to their masters. In the emergent cities, the central feature of the economy was the increase of artisans in each craft, greater specialization, and the formation of guilds, or corporations, whose rôle was at once economic, educational, social, legal, and religious. Life under these altered conditions was itself a new education, transforming men's minds and enhancing self-appreciation. Organized, the artisans— men and women[40]—ceased to be nonentities; indeed, in many cities, they became for a time the government itself. Paris had six great guilds. Florence, a city of ten thousand in 1200, and embracing some ninety thousand by 1329, saw the rise of seven leading guilds and fourteen smaller ones. By 1293, Florentine guilds had become practically synonymous with city government, nominating its officials. Without this triumph of citizens, Vossler[41] thinks, the whole Italian Renaissance would be inconceivable. Florence, Burckhardt declared, was the cradle of the Renaissance, "the first modern State."

The influence of guilds varied vastly one from another, in different cities, and from time to time in the same city. In general, the *Universitas Mercatorum*—of which the Floren-

39 Zimmern, H.: *The Hansa Towns*, 87. G. P. Putnam's Sons: New York, 1903; Knight: *op. cit.*, 212.
40 Renard, G.: *Guilds in the Middle Ages*, 20. (Trans. by D. Terry; ed. by G. D. H. Cole) George Bell and Sons: London, 1919.
41 *Op. cit.*, I, 530.

tine Calimala, Flemish and German Hanse, Paris merchants, and English merchant guilds[42] were the earliest and most powerful—the very nature of whose enterprise established connection between producing craftsmen and distant markets, rose to supremacy in the expanding world of commerce and industry, and ultimately destroyed the democracy that once existed. As Renard says, "capital" came to rule "labour without tact or consideration." The later "liberal movement against the guilds emanated from the merchant aristocracy," and its exponent, Gournay, was "director of commerce."[43]

Interests of the burgher class conflicted with those of the two older orders, clerical and feudal. Commerce required a ready, standard medium of exchange, promoted banking and lending money. Florence first minted florins in 1252; Venice coined ducats; in the North, gulden became standard exchange. Capitalist houses—Ricciardi, Bardi, Perruzi, Scali, and the Fuggers—ruled the world of trade, and could, in necessity, ease financial woes of popes and kings. Cupidity and great risks made interest high, sometimes as much as 100 per cent. Feudal lords had little use for money in their small domains. The Church opposed usury. Actually, Templars, Benedictines, and Franciscans engaged in loaning money. Ultimately, the Church compromised and approved interest covering industrial and commercial risks, and helped the bankers collect.[44] As for the feudal lords, municipal growth undermined their agricultural economy and favored the rise of sovereign powers, whose interests, too, like those of merchants, were best served by standard coinage. Saint

[42] Ashley, W. J.: *An Introduction to English Economic History and Theory*, I, 68 *ff*. 2 vols. G. P. Putnam's Sons: New York, 1892-93.
[43] Renard: *op. cit.*, 23, 118.
[44] O'Brien, G.: *An Essay on Mediaeval Economic Teaching*, 166-212. Longmans, Green and Co.: London, 1920.

Louis prohibited use of all save royal coin in his domain, as English kings had done earlier. Thus, in the triangular struggle, commercial interests triumphed over clerical and feudal orders.

In its political aspects, the New Life exhibited two major trends—both fed by increasing commerce and industry—the development of free cities, and the emergence of the national state. In Italy, where free cities struggled against papal dominion and northern imperialists, the Lombard League won independence from Barbarossa at the Peace of Constance in 1183, and Tuscan cities achieved a similar autonomy despite papal and imperial pretensions. When doctors disagree the patient goes free! Italian cities were free; but Italy achieved no national unity. Animosities of Guelph and Ghibelline, partisans of the Church and Empire, respectively, became submerged in internal struggles of cities and provinces of Italy. Shortly, in many cases, the "freedom" of cities became nominal rather than real. Thus, Florentine government became a family possession, a political instrument of the Medici whose banking houses could make and unmake governments. Similarly, at Mantua the house of Gonzaga, at Verona the della Scala, at Milan the Visconti, and at Padua the Carrara, held government in their hands. Among these tyrants and city bosses, crime and "culture," good and evil, often went hand in hand. The new humanism found in them its leading patrons; and a great humanist, Petrarch, offered ideological support to their paternalistic tyranny, set forth the pattern of their totalitarian powers, and urged "stern justice" against those citizens who might seek a change.[45] But voices of protest were not lacking. Against such arbitrary, unrestricted power some saw only

45 Burckhardt: *op. cit.*, 9.

one logical remedy: tyrannicide. Now Thomas Aquinas, the most respected scholastic authority, had agreed that the people must bear even tyranny "for conscience sake," and must trust "some higher authority," whence comes all government, to rid them of bad rulers.[46] In flat contradiction of such submission, Boccaccio declared that arms, conspiracy, spies, fraud, and ambush are "sacred and necessary" means. "There is no more acceptable sacrifice than the blood of a tyrant."[47]

In the North, in contrast with Italy, national sovereignty grew consistently in England, consolidating control over towns and feudal lords. In France, progress was more fitful, sovereigns playing clerical, feudal, and town authorities against each other, as circumstances dictated. Finally, summoning burgesses to the first Estates General in 1302, Philip at one stroke weakened town autonomy and strengthened himself in the struggle against papal power. In both England and France, the contest between papacy and national sovereigns centered in the investiture conflict—a struggle for pelf, power, prestige—just as in Germany, where the war for supremacy (1059-1122) was even more violent.

Theoretical formulations reflected the struggle taking place, the decline of papal authority, the rise of national sovereignty. Between the political thought of John of Salisbury and that of Machiavelli is the difference between the Middle Ages and modern times. Salisbury's *Policraticus* (1155-59) opposed sharply all encroachments of temporal on clerical authority, and maintained the supremacy of spiritual over temporal power. The two swords belong to the Church; the prince receives the material sword from the Church.[48] In the day of

---

[46] Phelan, G. B.: *Saint Thomas Aquinas On the Governance of Rulers*, I, 6. Sheed & Ward: London, 1938.

[47] Burckhardt: *op. cit.*, 56.

[48] Carlyle, R. W., and Carlyle, A. J.: *A History of Mediaeval Political Theory in the West*, IV, 330 *ff.* 6 vols. William Blackwood & Sons: Edinburgh, 1903-36.

Aquinas the struggle had become more acute. He argued the question nicely, but his doctrine seems to have varied from time to time. Despite different interpretations, his assignment of supreme authority to the Pope is perfectly clear, though, in regard to the *bonum civile*, the spiritual must obey the secular power. The end of society is to "live virtuously," and ultimately to attain God. To promote these ends, secular and spiritual authorities coöperate; but "those to whom pertains the care of intermediate ends" (secular rulers) "should be subject to him [spiritual authority] to whom pertains the care of the ultimate end, and be directed by his rule." "Consequently in the law of Christ, kings must be subject to priests."[49] Elsewhere, he says, the Pope may depose apostate kings, intervene in "temporal matters in which the secular power is subject to it," and when "the secular is combined with the spiritual authority, as in the case of the Pope, who holds the highest place in both powers," the latter is supreme.[50] Clearly the whip hand is papal.

Dante, in whom the flame of patriotism and love of Florence burned as brightly as his love of Beatrice, fought for his city at Campaldino (1289), participated in her civic life, bore his banishment with stoical fortitude, and then, when practical political activity was closed to him, gave in the *De Monarchia* a clear-cut answer to the greatest political question of his day. The Bull *Unam Sanctam* (1302) had pushed the claim of papal power to the utmost. Dante was profoundly sensible of his duty to the public weal.[51] Of problems that matter, he held, that of "temporal monarchy is most important and least explored"; yet, being no source of gain, no one attempts it. He will explore its depths. He finds gov-

---

[49] Phelan: *op. cit.*, I, 14.
[50] Carlyle: *op. cit.*, V, 349 *ff.*
[51] *De Monarchia*, I, 1.

ernment must be judged by its relation to the end of civiliza-tion—the full realization of human potentialities. The claim of clerical supremacy in temporal, as well as spiritual, affairs and the consequent strife of parties frustrate the fulfillment of that end. He concludes that clerical claims to universal supremacy (spiritual and temporal) are unfounded; that secular power comes to emperors direct from God; that no emperor has the right to alienate that power; that the Church has no right to receive it; therefore, it cannot dispose of that over which it has no jurisdiction.[52]

The abstractions of the clerical scholar and the imperial vision of the patriot-poet fall short of the revolutionary thinking of Marsiglio of Padua's *Defensor Pacis* (1324) and the ruthless realism of Machiavelli's *Prince*. Marsiglio defends imperial supremacy, and exposes the vanity of papal usurpations. In Machiavelli's eyes the Empire is obsolete: clerical tyranny vies with secular. Patriotic and anticlerical, he calls for a strong man, able to conquer all rivals and weld national unity.[53] The *Discourses on Livy*, *The Prince*, and the *Art of War* reveal a man schooled by experience of politics and inspired by ancient history. Machiavelli's political philosophy is a precursor of the *Real-Politik* of modern, national sovereign states. Cesare Borgia is idealized. The Prince must be able to act like a beast, or like a man, whichever serves his ends. Machiavelli's appeal is to realism, not idealism; politics is not a matter of ethics. One must reckon with man as he is. Men are evil; no one does good but by compulsion. It is better to be feared than loved. Desires are unlimited; power to satisfy them, limited. War is indispensable to the

---

[52] *Ibid.*, III; Carlyle: *op. cit.*, VI, 111-23.
[53] *The Prince*, 26. *Machiavelli: The Prince and Other Works*. (Trans. by A. H. Gilbert) Packard and Company: Chicago, 1941.

Prince; it is his first and only specialty. By war one wins position; by the same, maintains it. "Nothing is so weak and unstable as a reputation for power not based on force."[54] Religion is useful to unite a people. It is an aid to military strength. The Prince should encourage religion, to make his sway easier. He need not ask that the faith be true; he may protect a false one, and use it for the state's preservation. Unfortunately, those nearest the Roman Church "have least religion," their example robs all of piety, divides the country and "keeps it so."[55]

In its linguistic and literary aspects, the New Life was two-fold—vernacular and classical. Throughout medieval times Western Europe exhibited two distinct levels of culture, a lower and a higher. One was local, indigenous, natural, close to the life and experience of native populations; the other, foreign, universal, artificial, superimposed by the sway of Imperial Rome and her clerical successor, and little comprehended by the people, save as a few were elevated in the social scale, and came to use Latin more or less readily as a medium of intellectual exchange. At the close of the Middle Ages, after centuries of inconspicuous growth, the indigenous cultures exhibited a fuller vigor and disrupted the alien growth. Now, more articulate, they began to lay claim to the allegiance of men's minds. As an expression of the maturing soul of nations, the vernacular movement was democratic in character and ultimate consequence. As educational instruments, the mother tongues and literatures at first appeared only as elementary studies. Gradually, however, rising in estimation, they elbowed Greek and Latin classics from

[54] *Ibid.*, 13, 14, 17, 18, 23.
[55] Machiavelli: *Discourses on Livy*, I, 12.

the halls of higher learning. Centuries were required for this development. The end is not yet.

Literature is the soul of a people. "Poets," it has been said, "are the unacknowledged legislators of the world." By such a measure, Dante, above all others, laid the foundations of modern Italy, fashioned the soul of her people. His work had predecessors, indeed: Italian authors of Provençal poetry, similar to that of France; and the Italian poetry of Guinicelli and Cavalcanti. But Dante's *Commedia* gave the Tuscan tongue preëminence in the formation of modern Italian. In *De Vulgari Eloquentia* Dante turned to a study of "the science of the vernacular," heretofore neglected, despite its great importance, being used by all—men, women, and children. The primary, the mother tongue, which one learns to speak naturally, he held, is nobler than the secondary, artificial, grammatical language, acquired by virtue of much study. But there are many mother tongues. Which is the true one? It is that language which illustrious poets have employed, and is known to all Italy. This true Italian vernacular would be fit to use at court, "if we Italians had a court."[56] In the *Convivio*, a popularization of philosophy, Dante again offered a hearty defense of the vernacular, because of his love of it, its nearness to him, its beauty, excellence, and utility. All men desire knowledge; yet, partly owing to their own shortcomings, in part due to family and public cares which leave no leisure for learning, and because of isolation from centers of study, well-nigh countless are they who are famished for this food. Dante is impelled to teach the many. To this end, only the mother tongue is suitable; written in Latin, his commentaries would serve only a few.[57]

56 *De Vulgari Eloquentia*, I, 1, 18, 19.
57 *The Convivio*, I, 1, 5, 9-13. (Trans. by P. H. Wicksteed) J. M. Dent and Co.: London, 1903.

Elsewhere, indigenous cultures grew and found expression in vernacular literatures. The primitive Germans had songs in praise of gods and heroes, as Tacitus noted.[58] Ulfilas translated Holy Writ into his folk tongue, in the fourth century. The *Hildebrandslied* of the eighth century, and many works, chiefly on Christian themes, in the Carolingian Age, further enriched German literature. Stimulated by the Crusades, flowering of chivalry, the splendor of the imperial court, and the example of French poetry, a new literary life burgeoned in the twelfth and thirteenth centuries. Its greatest monuments were the national epic, *Nibelungenlied;* courtly epics, fashioned by Heinrich von Veldeke (Aeneid), Hartmann von Aue (Erek and Enite), Wolfram von Eschenbach (Parzival), and Gottfried von Strassburg (Tristan and Isolde) from foreign themes—Arthurian, Spanish Grail, Trojan, and Carolingian; and the ballads of the *Minnesänger*. In Walther von der Vogelweide, most significant of the *Minnesänger*, is heard a serious, vigorous German voice, a champion of Frederick, and counselor of all, great and small, as to their duty. Bitter critic of papal vice and misrule, his queries and judgments anticipate the coming storm:

> Why are the chastisements of Heaven delayed?
> How long wilt thou in slumber lie, O Lord?
> Thy work is hindered and thy word gainsaid,
> Thy treasurer steals the wealth that thou hast stored.[59]

Three centuries later, religion found in Luther a reformer, German nationalism an advocate, the German tongue a skillful, effective artist, and universal vernacular education its foremost spokesman. For the translation of the Bible (1521-

---

[58] *Germania*, 2, 3. *Agricola and Germania.* (Trans. by M. Hutton, with the *Dialogus*, by W. Peterson) William Heinemann: London, 1925.
[59] Lea, H. C.: *A History of the Inquisition of the Middle Ages*, I, 54. 3 vols. Harper & Brothers: New York, 1888; Taylor: *op. cit.*, II, 62 *f.*

32), as in his church hymns, Catechism, letters to mayors and aldermen, and other writings, Luther employed the "common tongue," which both the Uplands and the Lowlands could understand.[60] Under the impetus of religious fervor and national self-interest, and aided by the new-found art of printing, universal vernacular education—a portentous phase of the New Life, much neglected in Europe since the bright vision of Dante—was to be realized in Germany long before the patriot-poet's dream could come true in Italy.

Beyond the Channel, indigenous culture early found voice in Widsith or "The Wide-Wanderer," Deor's Lament, and the heroic adventures of Beowulf. Caedmon, first Christian gleeman; Cynewulf; Alfred's translation of Boethius' *Consolations of Philosophy* and Gregory's *Pastoral Care;* Bede's *Ecclesiastical History* and *The Anglo-Saxon Chronicle*—all enriched the vernacular treasure chest, mingling therein pagan and Christian elements. These early linguistic and literary elements fused with French and courtly letters to form the flexible instrument with which Chaucer wrought. His England, like Dante's Italy, pulsed with vigorous life. A large part of it he spread with brilliant color and fidelity upon a broad canvas. What he touched slightly, or not at all—the suffering, poverty, peasant turmoil, and earnest religious striving of the fourteenth century—Wyclif and Langland sensed and voiced in rumbling tones. Piers the Plowman's vision of toilers and wasters, Wyclif's English Bible, and the wandering Lollards prepared the mind of Englishmen for changes long before their masters were ready for them.

Secular and religious events of the sixteenth century raised English national consciousness to heights previously un-

[60] Kluge, H.: *Geschichte der deutschen National-Literatur*, 81. Oskar Bonde: Altenburg, 1911.

known. Therewith came a remarkable creative activity in vernacular literature and an increased loyalty to the mother tongue itself. Universal culture was giving way to particularism. A sense of national superiority and national destiny showed itself. Despite their classical training, their indubitable debt and devotion to the learning of antiquity, the authors of *The Scholemaster, Toxophilus, The Boke Named the Gouernour,* the *Elementarie,* and the *Positions* wrote in English for Englishmen. Roger Ascham speaks proudly in the *Toxophilus* of an English matter, archery, in English, because it is pleasant, and profitable both to personal well-being and to the nation in time of war.[61] The "Italianated Englishman" is beginning to be suspect. Ascham does not advise going to Italy for education, for *"Italy* now, is not that *Italy,* that it was wont to be," and "not so fit a place, as some do count it. . . ."[62] Richard Mulcaster urges vernacular schooling and defends employment of the native tongue in his treatises. "I do write," he says, "in my natural English tongue, because though I make the learned my judges, which understand Latin, yet I mean good to the unlearned, which understand but English." "My meaning is principally to help mine own country, whose language will help me, to be understood of them, whom I would persuade. . . ."[63] Elsewhere, he asks, "is it not in deed a marvelous bondage, to become servants to one tongue for learning sake . . . ?" English is "the joyful title of our liberty and freedom"; Latin, a reminder of "thralldom & bondage." "I love *Rome,* but

[61] *Toxophilus,* 2, 4 f. *The Whole Works of Roger Ascham.* (Ed. by J. A. Giles) 3 vols. John Russell Smith: London, 1864-65.

[62] *Roger Ascham: The Scholemaster,* 148 f. (Ed. by E. Arber) D. C. Heath and Company: Boston, 1910. (Spelling modernized.)

[63] *Positions,* 2 f. (Ed. by R. H. Quick) Longmans, Green and Co.: London, 1888. (Spelling modernized.)

London better, I favor *Italy*, but England more, I honor the Latin, but I worship the *English.*"[64]

Among many other things, the New Life gave a sharp impetus to a recovery of cultural materials of classical antiquity and a new appreciation of the spirit of Greek and Latin authors. So stimulating was the quest, so great the reward, so profound the influence of this return to ancient sources, many came to identify the New Life almost wholly with the classical revival, and thought of it as a fourteenth-sixteenth-century phenomenon. From a distance one sees the mountain tops first. A closer view reveals the low approaches through the foothills; and sometimes, too, a heretofore mist-hidden peak. Viewed as an increasing identification of West European minds with ancient ideals and authors, and a gradual loosening of the hold of patristic literature and otherworldliness of medievalism, the New Life was stirring before Dante and Petrarch. Moreover, considered solely as an enthusiastic search, recovery and dissemination of classical letters, the New Life still goes on. If Poggio Bracciolini and Leonardo Bruni rejoiced to find a dusty, filthy, neglected copy of Quintilian at St. Gall, in 1416, kindred minds felt rapture when a manuscript of Bacchylides of Ceos and Aristotle's Constitution of Athens were brought to light in Egypt in the last decade of the nineteenth century. If translation of Greek and Latin authors made them known to some, yet unacquainted with the original—as Leo Pilatus made Homer speak to Petrarch in Latin[65]—translation today opens the same authors, and a host besides, to a mass audience, all but universal.

Poggio's enthusiasm at finding Quintilian highlights an

---

[64] *Mulcaster's Elementarie*, 269. (Ed. by E. T. Campagnac) Quoted by permission. Clarendon Press: Oxford, 1925. (Spelling modernized.)
[65] Petrarch: "To Homer," Robinson, *op. cit.*, 253.

essential matter: The New Life is within us. Quintilian had long lain neglected at St. Gall. The interest of a new era made him and other great authors of antiquity seem worthy of utmost respect and laborious study. Men of the new era had slight sympathy with the attitude of their forbears. Petrarch condemned their neglect: "Each famous author of antiquity whom I recall, places a new offence and another cause of dishonour to the charge of later generations, who, not satisfied with their own disgraceful barrenness, permitted the fruit of other minds and the writings that their ancestors had produced by toil and application, to perish through insufferable neglect. Although they had nothing of their own to hand down to those who were to come after, they robbed posterity of its ancestral heritage."[66]

Petrarch's ire was not without justification. Yet medieval neglect of antiquity had never been so complete as his condemnation suggests. A fitful, furtive interest in certain pagan classics had survived. Virgil was ever popular, though, as Comparetti demonstrated, he was to the Middle Ages a prophet of Christianity, a magician—anything Christian minds could fancy.[67] Dante, himself a great creative artist and keenly sensitive to national revival, elevated the appreciation of Virgil immensely, yet his Virgil is still medieval, not the true poet of the Augustan Age. Men in time to come, oblivious to medieval moralizing, would see Virgil and his contemporaries in a clearer light.

A century and more before Dante, interest in classical study had risen to notable proportions—particularly at Orleans and Chartres—though it was never quite freed from

[66] Robinson: *op. cit.*, 25 *f.*

[67] Comparetti, D.: *Vergil in the Middle Ages,* 101 *f.*, 168, 195 *ff.*, *pass.* (Trans. by E. F. M. Benecke) Swan Sonnenschein & Co.: London, 1895.

the influence of clerical associations.[68] The classical revival of the eleventh century, which had forerunners in that of Charlemagne and in the labors of Gerbert, reached its height in the twelfth century. Gerbert outdistanced all others of his day in devotion to studies of a broad, generous nature. Like Cicero, he would join the good and the useful. There is nothing nobler, he held, than a knowledge of those who have been most distinguished. According to one of his students, Gerbert explained Virgil, Statius, Terence, Horace, Juvenal, Persius, and Lucan in his teaching at Rheims, and also drew from Cicero, Caesar, Sallust, and Suetonius.[69] Chartres felt his influence through Fulbert. There, Thierry composed his *Eptateuchon*, a treatise on the seven arts, and used parts of Cicero's works—*De inventione rhetorica, Ad Herennium, De partitione oratoria dialogus*—to supplement Donatus and Priscian. Bernard of Chartres, brother and predecessor of Thierry, gave instruction in grammar and rhetoric, with careful attention to diction, choice of figures, memorizing select passages, and the daily writing of verse and prose. As to books, only those of "distinguished authors" were to be read. John of Salisbury, to whom we owe a description of Bernard's teaching, was himself a genuine humanist, possessed of much knowledge of classical authors, and full of contempt for the Cornificians of the day who, scorning classical letters, would limit Latin study to what was useful. The benefits of letters, John held, are all-embracing: they banish tedium, solace grief, refresh the weary, cheer in poverty, encourage modesty amid wealth and pleasure, redeem the soul from vice, bring friends together. Above all, they preserve for posterity

---

[68] Poole, R. L.: *Illustrations of the History of Medieval Thought,* 113 *ff.* Williams and Norgate: London, 1884.

[69] Sandys, J. E.: *A History of Classical Scholarship,* I, 489 *f.,* 645 *ff.* 3 vols. University Press: Cambridge, 1903-08; Taylor: *op. cit.,* II, 143.

that which is worthy of remembrance and would otherwise certainly perish.[70]

Clouds soon obscured the bright dawn of humanism. Gerbert had been damned as anti-Christ and deposed for his traffic with poets and philosophers. Theological interests, aided by the advent of the *New Logic* and the triumph of Aristotle at Paris by 1254, eclipsed the humanities.[71] Henri d'Andeli's "Battle of the Seven Arts," written in the second quarter of the thirteenth century, reveals the conflict between the new dialectic and the authors of *belles lettres*. "Paris and Orleans are at odds," he tells us. "Logic, . . . always wrangling, calls the authors authorlings and the students of Orleans mere grammar-boys." "They," in turn, "call Dialectic . . . a cock-a-doodle-doo," and consider Paris clerks not "worth a button." Too bad they can't agree! Only the surgeons profit from the strife! Meanwhile,

> However, Logic has the students,
> Whereas Grammar is reduced in numbers.

The evil trend will last,

> Until a new generation will arise,
> Who will go back to Grammar,

>   *   *   *

> For in every science that master is an apprentice
> Who has not mastered his parts of speech.[72]

The "new generation" interested in grammar arose in the

[70] Norton, A. O.: *Readings in the History of Education: Mediaeval Universities*, 26 f. Harvard University Press: Cambridge, 1909; Taylor: *op. cit.*, II, 140 f., 158, 403 *ff.*; Sandys: *op. cit.*, I, 517 *ff.*

[71] Rashdall, H.: *The Universities of Europe in the Middle Ages*, I, 71 *ff.* (Ed. by F. M. Powicke and A. B. Emden) 3 vols. Clarendon Press: Oxford, 1936; Norton, A. O.: *op. cit.*, 45 f.

[72] Paetow, L. J. (Ed. and trans.): *La Bataille des VII Ars of Henri D'Andeli and the Morale Scolarium of John of Garland*, 34, 37 *ff.*, 60. University of California Press: Berkeley, 1927.

next century, but in Italy rather than in France. The humanities, languishing in cathedral schools and universities, under
the pressure of dialectic, theology, and other professional
interests, were to find generous encouragement in secular
circles in Italian cities. Vergerius, Guarino, and Vittorino
were spiritual kin of Gerbert, Little John, and Bernard. But
the later humanists were part of a more general movement.
Boundless effort and vast resources of Niccoló de Niccoli, the
Medici, and others were spent to collect and copy manuscripts. Fragmentary texts were perfected; others, unknown
or nearly so, were again put into circulation. Even stones
speak to those who have ears to hear. The ruins of Rome, as
Dante knew,[73] could speak to men who were sympathetic to
the spirit of her ancient builders.

2. *In Quest of a Liberal Education*

In the matrix of these forces was generated a quest for a
liberal education. New, in its contrast with ascetic and theological patterns of the preceding epoch, and in that it was
a progressive adjustment to a new world in process of becoming, it was, in principle, as old as Graeco-Roman antiquity. As the forces which called the new ideal forth were
various, in a degree conflicting and constantly changing, the
new education, though pursuing a central tendency, was variously conceived, depending on individual bias, locality, the
lapse of time and the changes wrought. One may readily
descry the universal man, the scholar, the gentleman-scholar,
the scientist, the citizen, as the several ideal products sought
by the new education in its mutations since the thirteenth
century. The types are not exclusive; they tell of shifting
emphasis, broadening interpretation and application. The

[73] *Convivio*, IV, 5,

scholar's gown harbored a citizen of some sort—at best, a citizen of the world; at worst, the servant of a tyrant. The free citizen of today is heir to all of them, has something of them in himself, and seeks *en masse*, though often with dubious title, the scholar's gown.

The central tendency of the new education centers on man and his social sphere. Swiftly grew the conviction, echoed by Pope, that "The proper study of mankind is man." Whether the ideal be formulated as *l'uomo universale*, prince, courtier, governor, complete gentleman, Christian scholar, or citizen, the heart of the matter is the same. True, the ideal all-round man, by whatever name, was scarcely consummated. Castiglione portrayed a courtier such as never was, perhaps never could be. Milton knew his scheme was "not a bow for every man to shoot." Even the theorists leaned, one to a scholarly, another to a social, and still others to a religious emphasis.

Yet man and social *utilitas* hold the center of the stage. At Florence, says William H. Woodward,[74] action and precept decreed "well-being of the community" as the goal of humanistic studies. To humanists, language and literature were not ends in themselves. One who has nothing but language, says Thomas Elyot, is no more to be praised than a popinjay.[75] Educated after his pattern, men would be noble counselors in the commonweal. "Language is but the Instrument" to convey useful knowledge, says Milton.[76] Montaigne is pleased to quote Seneca: "We learn not for life, but for the school."[77]

[74] *Studies in Education During the Age of the Renaissance, 1400-1600*, 30. University Press: Cambridge, 1906.
[75] *The Boke Named the Gouernour*, I, 13. (Ed. by H. H. S. Croft) 2 vols. Kegan Paul, Trench & Co.: London, 1883.
[76] *Milton's Tractate on Education*, 4. (Ed. by O. Browning) University Press: Cambridge, 1905.
[77] "Of Pedantry," in *Montaigne: The Education of Children*, 101. (Trans. by L. E. Rector) D. Appleton and Company: New York, 1899.

The idea of a citizen, a term retired from service in medieval, otherworldly education, returns to active duty. It is all-embracing: man is to be educated as a personality, to serve his community and God. The ideal man is a synthesis of pagan, Christian, and medieval warrior. One hears anew of a liberal education, fit for free men, competent to fit men for freedom. "We call those studies *liberal* which are worthy of a free man . . ." says Vergerius.[78] Guarino's *studia humanitatis* embraced "learning and training in virtue," the activities and pursuits that are proper to man.[79] Palmieri's *ottimo cittadino* is the *Orator* of Quintilian's day, the best citizen. Da Feltre declares that "all of us are created for the life of social duty."[80] His school stressed the citizen rather than the scholar. Vives condemns "empty dilettantism"; all branches of learning should be applied "to the practice of life" and for the common good.[81] Melanchthon saw "private virtue" and "public weal" as the end which "liberal disciplines" were to serve. Saxon *Fürstenschulen* (1543) were organized so that learned men might be prepared to perform the duties of church and state.[82] Milton's complete and generous education is "that which fits a man to perform justly, skilfully and magnanimously all the offices both private and publick of Peace and War."[83]

Humanist educators praised man—man writ large. Mirandola's *Oratio de hominis dignatate* proclaimed the universal in man, and that he might develop according to his free will.

---

[78] Woodward, W. H.: *Vittorino da Feltre and Other Humanist Educators*, 102. University Press: Cambridge, 1921.

[79] *Ibid.*, 177.

[80] Woodward: *Education During the Renaissance*, 13.

[81] *Vives: On Education: A Translation of the De Tradendis Disciplinis of Juan Luis Vives*, I, 6; II, 2. (Trans. by F. Watson) University Press: Cambridge, 1913.

[82] Woody, T.: *Fürstenschulen in Germany after the Reformation*, 14 f. George Banta Publishing Co.: Menasha, 1920.

[83] *Tractate*, 8.

It has been said that "differences of birth" lost their significance in Italy.[84] In this there is much exaggeration. In general, letters and social station found an affinity. According to J. A. Symonds,[85] "an almost complete separation between the cultivated classes and the people" existed in the fifteenth century. Schools at courts faithfully reflected the stratification of society and the prevailing preference for princely rule. The class character of humanistic education is stamped in the title of many of the most important treatises and pervades their pages. Theorists and teachers, generally, wrought for an aristocracy of birth and of wealth—those who were free, and were possessed of the means to support themselves in leisure. In Franklin's satire on Harvard College, "two sturdy porters named Riches and Poverty" guard the gate.[86] Birth and wealth alone, however, would not suffice, though the presumption was in their favor. The title conferred by birth must be confirmed and guaranteed by intellectual accomplishment. Leisure should be adorned by letters.

Without leisure, one could not master ancient authors. Advocates of the new education frequently reveal contempt for commoners, or ignore their education. Milton's studies are for "our noble and our gentle youth."[87] Montaigne frowns on education in the hands of base persons: learning and philosophy are for princes and noblemen; gentlemen will learn more in a year than base fellows in seven.[88] Elyot prefers, as there is one God in heaven, "the best and most sure governance" of one king or prince, rather than "a monster with

[84] Burckhardt: *op. cit.*, 354.
[85] *Renaissance in Italy*, IV, 234. 5 vols. Smith, Elder, & Co.: London, 1875-81.
[86] Woody, T. (Ed.) : *Educational Views of Benjamin Franklin*, 105. McGraw-Hill Book Company: New York, 1931.
[87] *Tractate*, 17.
[88] *Education of Children*, 26.

many heads." He would provide an education fit to form the "gentle wits of noblemen's children" that they may be serviceable thereto.[89]

Some there were, indeed, who sought to promote liberal learning among those designed for lesser station. Vittorino, himself the son of a noble family which had suffered reverses, provided, at Padua, Venice, and Mantua, for the children of poor parents, and put them on a basis of equality with those of aristocratic birth. Guarino was the son of a metal worker. Saxon *Fürstenschulen* provided for the education of children of poor people, as well as those of nobility.[90] But these were the exceptions, not the rule. Even when accessible, classical studies were of dubious value to men of practical affairs. So Melanchthon learned at the *Oberschule* of Nuremberg. Men of wealth, whose sons were destined for business, were ill content with ten years' liberal education in letters, if at the end of it, they were not fitted for the world of commerce.[91] Dissatisfied, they sent their sons elsewhere, to learn the languages of the commercial world. Academies in England, and in American colonies, and *Realschulen* in Germany arose to satisfy that need. The study of Latin and Greek letters, encouraged by the classical humanists, Renard concluded, established "a clear line of demarcation between the children thus brought up, who were destined to hold the highest social positions, and the others doomed to inferior tasks and studies. . . . It swelled the tide which was carrying society towards class division. . . ."[92]

Liberal education, as conceived by early humanists, was committed to certain central principles, which have been current in

[89] *Gouernour*, I, 2, 4.
[90] Woody: *Fürstenschulen*, 8, 13.
[91] Woodward: *Education During the Renaissance*, 226.
[92] Renard: *op. cit.*, 91.

the literature of educational reform to the present, despite changing patterns of curriculum. Foremost in importance was their recognition of individual nature, variability of capacities and interests, and the necessity of adjusting education to them. Vittorino da Feltre knew that taste and capacity differed in each person. Whatever the teacher might desire, he must "follow Nature's lead." No one is apt for all sorts of studies; few have even three or four talents, yet each has a "gift." To discover and develop it is the teacher's purpose. Vittorino is said to have devoted endless pains trying to satisfy the need of even the least capable student.[93] Vergerius, likewise keenly observant of individual traits, considered alertness, industriousness, eagerness for study, thoroughness, obedience, love of praise, emulation, sensitiveness under punishment and disgrace, and sociability, as indices of great promise in a student. Native capacity is the teacher's guide; a youth of limited talent should devote himself to the subject in which he can progress.[94] Alberti would give to every naturally promising mind its best opportunity for development. One may recognize it in speech, gesture, glance, dislike of inactivity, zeal in accomplishment of work begun, frankness, flexibility, and willingness to forgive.

Erasmus recognized reason as common to the nature of man. Individuals, however, are more or less strongly disposed to different studies. One has a bent to mathematics, another is inclined to divinity, poetry, rhetoric, or war, and is reluctant, even hostile, to other pursuits. The wise teacher will give heed to such a natural disposition, which, Erasmus thinks, may even be read in the face and bearing of youths. Where minds have a strong determination, one should not

93 Woodward: *Vittorino*, 62, 203.
94 *Ibid.*, 109.

run counter to "their instinct." A cow cannot learn boxing; donkeys will never play the fiddle. Nevertheless, Erasmus is of the opinion that the mind is so adaptable that it may master any subject, if the method be sound and if teaching be joined with practice.[95] Ascham is fully aware of the difference between "quick and hard wits," and their potentialities for life and learning. Good memory, love of learning, "lust to labor," willingness to learn from others, boldness in questioning, and love of praise are among the natural gifts that give educational promise.[96]

Mulcaster would always follow nature's lead, "For as she is unfriendly, wheresoever she is forced, so is she the best guide, that any man can follow, wheresoever she favoreth." If those fitted by nature to excel fail of advancement, is not education to blame? And for those to whom nature has given little, the best training is that which is obedient to her design. "If nature in some children be not so pregnant, as they may take the full benefit of this whole train, yet by applying it wisely, there may be some good done, even in the heaviest wits, & most unapt bodies, though nothing so much as in the very quickest."[97] The time to begin education differs with individuals, according to physical strength and the "quickness of their wits." It is not a matter of years: "Some be hastings and will on, some be hardings, and draw back."[98] As not all corn ripens at the same time, neither do children's capacities.

Comenius and Pestalozzi were scarcely more concerned with adapting education to the nature of the learner than

[95] Woodward, W. H.: *Desiderius Erasmus Concerning the Aim and Method of Education*, 195 *f.* University Press: Cambridge, 1904.

[96]*Scholemaster*, 72 *ff.*, 87 *ff.*

[97] *Elementarie*, 30, 41. Quoted from *Mulcaster's Elementarie*, edited by E. T. Campagnac, by permission of The Clarendon Press, Oxford.

[98] *Positions*, 18 *f.*

were leading humanists. Vives' preoccupation with the study of human capacity led to results of far-reaching consequence. His *De Anima et Vita* (1538), whose psychological principles were appealed to as basic laws in the *De Tradendis Disciplinis*, charted a new course. Vives has been called the "father of modern psychology."[99] Influenced by Aristotle, he nevertheless relied on observation and experience to discover new knowledge of the mind. Observation of nature "is at once school and schoolmaster." "The senses open up the way to all knowledge."[100] His psychology is empirical. One must know what the soul does. Quick comprehension, fidelity in memory, and abilities revealed at play are useful indices of educational promise. Masters should assemble every two or three months to pool their judgments of their pupils' minds and send each one to that for which he shows himself best fitted. Thus will "incredible advantage" accrue to the human race. "Nothing would then be done badly and perversely by those who now do it under compulsion and against their desires. . . . When unwilling minds are driven to uncongenial work, we see that almost all things turn out wrong and distorted."[101]

Vives' *De Anima* may have given impetus to Juan Huarte's *Examen de Ingenios,* wherein he argued:

. [Examination of children by expert] *Triers* appointed by the State, Men of approved Sagacity and Knowledge, to search and sound the Abilities of Youth, and after due Search, to oblige them to the Study of that Science their Heads leaned most to, instead of abandoning them to their own Choice. Whence would proceed in Your Majesty's

---

[99] *Vives: Tratado del Alma,* XIII. (Trans. by J. Ontañón; introduction by F. Watson) Clasicos Castellanos: Madrid, 1923; *cf.* W. A. Daly: *The Educational Psychology of Juan Luis Vives.* Catholic University of America: Washington, 1924.
[100] Vives: *De Tradendis Disciplinis,* IV, 1.
[101] *Ibid.,* II, 4.

Kingdoms and Dominions, the most inimitable Artists in the World, as well as the most Accomplish'd Works, by this way of suiting Art and Nature. I would have the same thing Practised in all the Universities in Your Kingdoms, seeing they allow not the Student to proceed to another Faculty till he be first well entred in the Latin Tongue; for even there should also be *Triers*, to discover if he that designed to Study Logic, Philosophy, Physic, Theology, or the Law, had a *Genius* adapted to each of those Sciences; if not (besides the detriment accruing from such a one to the State, exercising a Profession he is incapable of) 'twould be a shame to see a Man slave and beat his Brains for a thing impossible ever to be extracted thence.[102]

The new humanist appeal to natural capacity as a guide in education should logically have effected a revolution in girls' education. Application of that principle four hundred years later did do so. Humanism of the fourteenth and fifteenth centuries actually accomplished much less, being limited by its class relationship, entrenched religious doctrines, patriarchalism, and a sociopolitical economy which assigned no significant public function to women. The new education, at its best, was to prepare the free person for a life of freedom. It could scarcely hope for, and humanist educators did not advocate, the emancipation of women from patriarchal and other forms of subjection. Burckhardt's phrase, "women stood on a footing of perfect equality with men"[103] at that time, is apt to be somewhat misleading. Alberti's patriarchal doctrine, expressed in *Della Cura della Famiglia*—"Never would I allow my wife to regard me as other than the master"[104]—doubtless struck a responsive chord in a vast majority of families, as did Cato's view of the place of women in

---

[102] *Examen de Ingenios: or, the Tryal of Wits*, a3. (Trans. by E. Bellamy) Sare: London, 1698.
[103] *Op. cit.*, 395.
[104] Woodward: *Education During the Renaissance*, 58.

ancient Rome. A few women of highest station, a few not so high, were educated after the new fashion in Italy, and a lesser proportion elsewhere. Vittorino, Guarino, and Ascham taught women of social standing. In certain instances, women taught in Italian and Spanish universities.[105] But, generally lacking the larger sphere of men, women's learning could scarcely escape dilletantism. Middle-class families were not yet able to afford the luxury.

Theory ran, naturally, far ahead of practice. When other advocates of the cause were lacking, humanists—Bruni, Barbaro, Erasmus, Vives, More, Ascham, and Agrippa—were like voices in the wilderness. Bruni's thought, expressed early in the fifteenth century, when, as he says, learning in women was unknown, is indicative of the trend of early humanism, which espoused a view that has echoed through succeeding centuries: "what men can know, the same can women also." Bruni placed religion and morals first in educating a "Christian lady." Grammar (Servius, Donatus, and Priscian), thoroughly mastered, will open the way to the best authors— poets, historians, and orators—from whom facts and principles may be learned, and an excellent style formed. Among the Fathers, Lactantius, Jerome, Augustine, Ambrose, and Cyprian are recommended; Gregory Nazianzen, Chrysostom, and Basil may be read, in good translations, if desired. All that antiquity has said of the virtues—continence, temperance, modesty, justice, courage, and greatness of soul—deserves attention. History, because it enables us to understand our development, is first among the studies necessary for genuine culture. Livy, Sallust, Curtius, and Caesar are in-

[105] Dennistoun, J.: *Memoirs of the Dukes of Urbino*, II, 123. 3 vols. Longman, Brown, Green, and Longmans: London, 1851; Woody, T.: *A History of Women's Education in the United States*, I, 24 f. 2 vols. Science Press: New York, 1929.

dorsed as being "within the comprehension of a studious lady." Cicero, always a pleasure, richest in ideas, and best in style, has everything an author can give. Poetry is an indispensable element in a true education. Did not Aristotle and Cicero show how highly they regarded poets? Virgil, Homer, Hesiod, Pindar, Euripides, Ennius, Accius, Statius, and Seneca are acclaimed. As for restrictions, Bruni thinks some discrimination in subjects is necessary: subtleties of arithmetic, geometry, astrology, and even rhetoric are unworthy of a "cultivated mind."[106] Rhetoric has no practical use, is even unbecoming to women, whose sphere never includes public discussions and all the arts that pertain to them.

Fidelity to human nature would logically require recognition of physical culture as a phase of liberal education. Obviously, man is neither all mind, nor all body. Greeks had recognized their mutual interdependence; Christians had denied it. The rise of physical culture to favor was not, however, a mere matter of logic. Negatively, it was a reaction against the warfare of mind and body, an erroneous dogma which Christian asceticism had espoused for a thousand years. Positively, the concern for sports, gymnastics, and military training depended on increasing understanding of the rôle assigned to them in ancient philosophy and practice, and from the identification of liberal education with the life of courtier or citizen, on whom might fall the duty of military service.

In harmony with the many-sidedness and individualism of the New Life, several aspects of physical culture received varying stress by different authors, and in different localities. Of first importance, a matter on which there was general agreement, was the relation of physical culture to the educa-

---

[106] Woodward: *Vittorino*, 126 *ff.*, 132.

tion of the whole man, as a means of balance, as fashioner
and preserver of health, and as a source of personal pleasure.
Vittorino appears to have been equally concerned with physical and mental culture. In respect to physical well-being, he
laid a sharp stress on suitable diet, exercise, and the avoidance of artificial comforts and refinements. He himself was
at home on the playground as in the classroom, and refused
to permit pupils in health to abstain from games.[107]

Aeneas Sylvius would educate mind and body side by side.
Physical training must aim, above all things, at "a certain
hardness," avoiding all excesses and luxuries. Games and
exercises must be employed which will develop muscles, cultivate graceful carriage, and promote healthy organic functioning.[108] Alberti would have intellectual exercise alternate
with physical activities, especially those that demand dexterity, strength, and endurance. Nothing ranks higher than
health, for moral, mental, and social usefulness depends
upon it. Since exercises are means to ends, rather than ends
in themselves, excessive emphasis on physical attainment,
even in approved sports, would be unworthy, for it would
defeat the purpose of right education.[109] Erasmus is concerned that there be health and a good constitution. Health
must be secured and safeguarded in childhood especially,
but the common fear that early study injures health, he thinks,
is groundless. He is not stirred by the Greek ideal of physical
perfection. He neither wishes to develop athletes, nor to form
"the physique of a Milo."[110]

Elyot, in agreement with Italian humanists, and following
ancient authors, particularly Galen, turns from his "com-

107 *Ibid.*, 35 *f.*; *Education During the Renaissance*, 22 *f.*
108 Woodward: *Vittorino*, 136 *ff.*
109 Woodward: *Education During the Renaissance*, 60.
110 Woodward: *Erasmus*, 202.

mendation of learning" to "some manner of exercise," without which the "spirits vital" are shortly exhausted, digestion hindered, the body sickened, and life shortened. Exercise preserves health, increases strength, exalts the spirits, whets the appetite, and facilitates physical processes. This part of "physic" is, therefore, not to be "neglected in the education of children," particularly after thirteen.[111] Ascham will not have "young Gentlemen" always poring over books, and missing pleasures and pastimes. He is neither Stoic nor Anabaptist. His own inclination and habit have been to play. Athenian practice set an excellent example. He would, therefore, have a suitable time set and observed constantly for "Courtly exercises, and Gentlemanlike pastimes," even as for intellectual pursuits.[112] In the *Toxophilus*, he declares that "to omit study some time of the day, and some time of the year" makes "as much for the increase of learning as to let the land lie some time fallow, maketh for the better increase of corn."[113]

Mulcaster considers the soul and body "copartners in good and ill." How can they, or should they, be separated in education, the one made strong, the other left weak and a prey to infirmity? Since both are good, he cannot neglect the body which is "so near, and so necessary a neighbor unto the soul." His whole labor, therefore, is designed to discover what is necessary for the "training and exercising of the body, that it may prove healthy, and live long: and be ready to assist, all the actions of the mind." The same masters should train the body and frame the mind.[114] Montaigne expresses a monistic view of education, oft repeated in present philosophy: "It

111 *Gouernour*, I, 16.
112 *Scholemaster*, 132 *f*.
113 *Toxophilus*, 14.
114 *Positions*, 40 *ff*., 124.

is not the mind, it is not the body we are training: it is the man, and we must not divide him into two parts." His exercise and recreation "will be a part of his study."[115]

Physical culture as training for war, with special emphasis on peculiarly valuable military sports, held a prominent place in humanists' views of education. Particularly stressed in schemes of courtly education, such as Castiglione's *Courtier* and Elyot's *Gouernour* (which portray chivalric training plus the newly discovered letters of antiquity), the military end is recognized as valid in Milton's *Tractate*,[116] Ascham's *Scholemaster*[117] and *Toxophilus*,[118] and a host of treatises on the ideal liberal education. Vittorino, Guarino, Palmieri, Vergerius, and Aeneas Sylvius, to name no more, defend it in writing, or practice military arts in their schools. Sylvius links military training with one's duty to defend Christendom against Turks.[119] Schools conducted at courts and supported by tyrants were naturally disposed to honor the supreme art of their patrons. Defense of prince and of country and the notable examples of antiquity are appealed to for justification and guidance. In general, the more ardently patriotic and nationalistic the writer, the more the stress on the virtues of military training.

The chief and true profession of a courtier, says Castiglione, "ought to be in feats of arms." He should practice them "lively," and be known for his "hardiness." The more excellent he be in this art, the more is he worthy of praise. He must handle all sorts of weapons, on foot and on horse. Fencing, wrestling, management of rough horses, tilting,

---

[115] *Education of Children*, 61.
[116] *Op. cit.*, 8.
[117] *Op. cit.*, 134.
[118] *Op. cit.*, 51 *ff*.
[119] Woodward: *Vittorino*, 138.

hunting (for its likeness to war), swimming, leaping, running, and throwing the stone are specially recommended. Tennis and vaulting are also approved. Tumbling and rope climbing are unworthy of a courtier.[120]

Elyot describes at length those exercises, fit for a gentleman, which may be his safeguard "in war or other necessity."[121] Wrestling, running, swimming, use of sword and battle-ax, riding great horses, hunting, and shooting the long bow are of great value. The last is especially praised, for it is "most excellent artillery for wars," and by it the English have struck dread into enemies and gained admiration from their allies. Tennis is excellent for young men. Hawking is approved of, for it is "delectable," gives appetite for supper, and keeps a man from worse sports, though it is not of as much use for war as is hunting. Dancing is justified, despite divines and other learned folk who judge it "repugnant unto virtue." Pins, coits, and football are unfit for gentlemen.[122]

Erasmus and Vives, whose social philosophy was universal and international rather than ardently patriotic or nationalistic, were opposed to war and its training. Pacifism has been called "one of the most valuable" features of Erasmus' thought.[123] A good prince should never engage in war, unless he has tried everything else. If he were of this mind, "there would hardly be a war."[124] Parents are condemned for training "their sons to a love of war."[125] In *The Education of a Christian Prince,* as in many other works, Erasmus argues

[120] *The Book of the Courtier . . . of Count Baldassare Castiglione,* 48, 53 ff. (Trans. by T. Hoby) David Nutt: London, 1900.

[121] *Gouernour,* I, 16.

[122] *Ibid.,* I, 18, 19, 27.

[123] Smith, P.: *Erasmus,* 198. Harper & Brothers: New York, 1923.

[124] Erasmus, D.: *The Education of a Christian Prince,* 249. (Trans. by L. K. Born) Columbia University Press: New York, 1936.

[125] Woodward: *Erasmus,* 189.

the folly of war, stresses the rational aspects of education for the conduct of state affairs, and neglects military sports and exercises which bulk so heavily in most portrayals of princely education. All forms of idleness in the state must be reduced to the minimum. "In the military service there is a busy sort of time wasting, and it is by far the most destructive, for from it result the complete cessation of everything worth while and the source of all things evil."[126] Vives favors games whose aim is pleasure and recreation and which do not "make boys wild and ferocious." All that promotes the *mens sana in corpore sano* is to be judged worthy. Arts, such as "the military art which belongs to the attacking and slaughtering of men," are wrong. Physical education should avoid them.[127]

Humanists found sound pedagogy in the play tendency. The utility of games, as a concession to physical nature, whereby youths might be refreshed and brought back to their studies with renewed zeal and effectiveness, was commonly recognized. Lessons were regularly interrupted by periods for play at Vittorino's school at Mantua. Erasmus represented the idea in the colloquy of Nicholas, Jerome, and master Cocles, wherein the boys, quoting to him the little Quintilian they remember, "moderate play quickens the wit," beg for a playday. Chagrined, that they recall so well what suits their purpose, Cocles gives in; but he expresses doubt that they will, on their return, really make up for past delinquencies in study.[128] Vives, too, sees play as a necessary pedagogical device. For the powers of mind and body, weak and limited, must be nourished in order that further work

---

126 Erasmus: *op. cit.*, 226.
127 Vives: *De Tradendis Disciplinis*, I, 4; III, 4.
128 *The Colloquies of Desiderius Erasmus*, I, 80 *f.* (Trans. by N. Bailey) 3 vols. Gibbings & Co.: London, 1900.

may be accomplished; otherwise they are exhausted and "become good for nothing." Recreation is a form of food for the
body. Boys need recreation frequently, since the age is one
of growth and development. The mind is naturally inclined
to freedom. It can be put to work, but it cannot be compelled.
If driven constantly to study, without rest from attention, boys
may "begin to hate work before they begin to love it."[129]
Mulcaster's doctrine is the same: "stillness more than ordinary," which is required in school for the sake of study, must
be offset by "stirring more than ordinary" through properly
directed exercise.[130]

Following Quintilian, their mentor, play was seen by
many humanists as an index of educability, a means of its
discovery. Vives would have children exercise at play, especially with those of their own age and likeness, in order that
everything may be natural and unfeigned, for thereby "their
sharpness and their characters" are revealed.[131]

Early humanists reintroduced pleasure as a principle of
education. The school itself should be a pleasant place. Vittorino named his institution at Mantua "La Casa Giocosa,"
The Pleasant House. Mulcaster wanted as large a room as
possible for the elementary school; the grammar school
should be in the outskirts of town, near to the fields, in order
to have sufficient range for playing. Milton's academy needs
a spacious house and grounds. Montaigne would strew classrooms with green boughs and flowers, and "paint the school
with pictures of joy and gladness."[132] Vives chooses a country
site for his academy, removed from noisy clamor, with good
air, and free of all pestilence, for good health is indispensable

---

[129] Vives: *De Tradendis Disciplinis*, III, 4.
[130] *Positions*, 23.
[131] Vives: *De Tradendis Disciplinis*, II, 4.
[132] *Education of Children*, 62 f.

for good work. Still inclined somewhat toward an ascetic view of sensuous pleasures, however, and keenly aware that beauteous nature may easily distract from studies, he would "not choose a verdant or pleasant place" which might tempt scholars to wander.[133]

Recognizing the tendency of human nature and the natural difficulties involved in school learning, humanists often readily accepted it as a sound principle of teaching that interest and pleasure should be associated with learning, wherever possible. Erasmus is keenly sensitive to the rôle of interest. Nature points the path by which "the toil of learning is reduced." It should be followed, not ignored or contraried. A pleasant story from Aesop is recommended. Circe, Ulysses, and the swine will catch a boy's attention. Names of natural objects should be learned in Latin. Pictures of strange animals may be used effectively. It is desirable always "to discuss what is naturally attractive to the youthful mind." "Brightness" and "attractiveness" make the only appeal to boys in learning. Nothing in all this hinders "utility" from going "hand in hand with delight." Erasmus knows that some will say: "*I* had to learn Latin in this [hard] manner when I was a boy; what was good enough for me must do for him." But he thinks the ancients were wiser: their doctrine was that "excellence in true learning" is only "attained by those who find pleasure in its pursuit; and for this cause the liberal arts were by them called 'Humanitas.' "[134]

Vives employed Latin dialogues, dealing with many facets of home, school life, and children's games, so as to insure the interest of pupils.[135] Games and the practice of Latin

---

133 Vives: *De Tradendis Disciplinis*, II, 1.
134 Woodward: *Erasmus*, 212 *ff.*, 217.
135 *Tudor School-Boy Life: The Dialogues of Juan Luis Vives*. (Trans. by F. Watson) J. M. Dent and Co.: London, 1908,

may well be joined on the playground.[136] Elyot,[137] citing Quintilian, advises luring pupils by praise and with gifts they like, the use of painted letters, and learning the Latin names of all things seen, for there should be no violence or forcing of children in learning. Mulcaster wishes "to lighten the course of study by making of it plain."[138] Montaigne is convinced that teachers must study the strength and pace of pupils, else everything will be spoiled. Sophists, "by making the study difficult," have made philosophy a thing of reproach, even among those of understanding. Profit and pleasure should go together; whatever is useful and proper for children to know ought to be "seasoned with sugar," the opposite "with gall."[139]

In harmony with their advocacy of appeal to interest and the use of play for the encouragement of study, the foremost humanists uniformly condemned harsh disciplinary methods, particularly corporal punishment. General practice doubtless ran counter to enlightened theory. Erasmus tells of a Churchman who selected his teachers from "the more accomplished wielders of the birch." Beating, in his philosophy, was the first means to the purification of nature.[140] Ascham refers to the common use of beating in the schools of England. Against this, Vittorino's practice was seldom to employ physical punishment, preferring expulsion instead. German *Fürstenschulen* regulations permitted use of the rod only as a last resort.[141] Guarino condemns corporal punishment roundly. It is an indignity to "free-born youth," turns them against learning, encourages evasions. The result is injury, moral and intellectual. It should be used only as a last resort.

[136] Vives: *De Tradendis Disciplinis*, III, 4.
[137] *Gouernour*, I, 5.
[138] *Elementarie*, 42.
[139] *Education of Children*, 28 f., 51, 63.
[140] Woodward: *Erasmus*, 206.
[141] Woody: *Fürstenschulen*, 25.

According to Aeneas Sylvius, teaching should not require the rod.[142] Ascham is convinced that "your great beaters, do as oft punish nature, as they do correct faults." Faults must be corrected; but masters mar rather than mend pupils by beating.[143] Vives is less outspoken; he thinks some boys may have to be brought to "duty by blows," like slaves; yet masters should reserve corporal punishment for "rare occasions," and never do anything to cause "permanent injury."[144] Erasmus, greatest humanist of all, wishes masters to resort seldom even to the harsh language of blame. As for beating? "Teaching by beating . . . is not a liberal education."[145]

Large-scale defection in the ranks of educators from an established pattern of education betrays the decay of the old social order and the emergence of its successor. The new order calls for a new education, and it is in turn fashioned in part by it. The humanistic pattern of liberal studies constituted a revolt against the spirit, curriculum, and institutions of medieval education. Otherworldly, ascetic self-renunciation was supplanted by joy in life, self-appreciation, and devotion to mundane affairs. Italy's court schools, Germany's *Fürstenschulen* and *Gymnasien,* England's Great Public Schools, and other institutions took the place of once dominant monastic and cathedral institutions. Old medieval universities were long hostile to the new age and the new learning; Petrarch ridiculed them as "nests of gloomy ignorance" where illiterates won doctors' degrees.[146] Erasmus heaped scorn upon monasteries and colleges as seats of idleness and vain pretensions to learning. Their number ought to be re-

---

[142] Woodward: *Vittorino,* 34, 137, 163.

[143] *Scholemaster,* 70 *ff.*

[144] *De Tradendis Disciplinis,* III, 4.

[145] Woodward: *Erasmus,* 208.

[146] Mullinger, J. B.: *The University of Cambridge,* I, 382. 2 vols. University Press: Cambridge, 1873-84.

stricted by the state. Divines play the fool in their schools, as if the heavens would fall but for their "Syllogistical Buttresses."[147] Ramus, more "extreme in his opposition to medieval and scholastic thought" than any of the humanists, devoted his life to a radical reform of college and university teaching, and died at the hands of assassins as a result of the hostility his reforms had stirred.[148] Only in new university foundations—Ferrara, created in the spirit of the New Life (1442), and Wittenberg (1502), for example—were poetry and eloquence at home.

In respect to curriculum, the humanists struck at theology and dialectic, particularly the cult of Aristotelianism, regnant in universities since the dawn of the thirteenth century. Petrarch saw Aristotle as a truly great philosopher, but thought him in error all his life, not only in small matters but in many of greatest importance. The poet's chief complaint, however, is against the slavishness of Aristotelians, which disgraces their master. Ramus, with humanistic zeal, carried the attack on Aristotle to absurdity, defending the thesis that "All that Aristotle has said is false."[149]

In the thirteenth century Henri d'Andeli had sighed for a "new generation" that would "go back to Grammar." The fourteenth century saw the beginning of grammar's restoration as chief of the seven arts. As Augustine, when Rome crumbled, had turned his eyes to the City of God, humanists turned now from the temple of learning, which medieval scholastics had erected in defense of faith, and looked back to the Rome of Augustus—a Golden Age, they thought, which

---

[147] Erasmus: *Education of a Christian Prince*, 226; *The Praise of Folly*, 114-38. (Trans. by J. Wilson; ed. by P. S. Allen) Clarendon Press: Oxford, 1925.
[148] Graves, F. P.: *Peter Ramus and the Educational Reformation of the Sixteenth Century*, 105 f., 205. Macmillan Company: New York, 1912.
[149] *Ibid.*, 26.

a barbarian world, in its quest for true culture, must rehabili-
tate. Said Agricola: "Regard as suspect all that you have
been taught hitherto; ban and cast away as an imposture anything and everything that professes to be knowledge, unless
its title can be vouched for by the evidence of the great writers
of old."[150] In the literatures of Greece and Rome, Erasmus
held, is "all the knowledge that we recognise as vital to mankind." Melanchthon observed solemnly, a "world in which
the monuments of Greek learning are unknown is a world
where men are always children."[151] Vives, admonishing youth
to learn Latin, called it "the treasure-house of all erudition,
since men of great and outstanding minds have written on
every branch of knowledge in the Latin speech. Nor can any
one attain to the knowledge of these subjects except by first
learning Latin."[152]

The break, naturally, was not absolute. Beccadelli, Vallo,
and Lorenzo, who scandalized the church and established
customs, represent an extreme feature of the new day. Humanists, generally, did not discard Christian faith but humanized it. Classical authors did not entirely rout the Fathers.
Rather, the *summae* and ponderous theological commentaries
lost vogue. Subtleties of Realist and Nominalist found fewer
disciples. Return to antiquity meant appeal to original
sources, in some degree a fresh interest in early patristic
authors. Some of them—Lactantius, Augustine, Jerome,
Chrysostom, Gregory of Nazianzus, and a few others—because of their learning and eloquence, found a place in instruction. Parts of the Bible were used for reading and
memorization. As for the compact compends of the seven

---

150 Woodward: *Education During the Renaissance*, 101.
151 *Ibid.*, 114.
152 Vives: *Tudor School-Boy Life*, xxi.

arts, pleasing to medieval palates, they seemed lifeless and tasteless when full texts of ancient authors were at hand. After the rediscovery of Plutarch's *Education of Boys,* Quintilian's *Institutes,* and Cicero's *On Oratory,* in the early fifteenth century, educators found deviation from their *dicta* difficult. Appeal to their authority became universal. Quintilian, practical schoolmaster that he was, became especially the schoolmaster's guide. Some, indeed, urged critical use of authorities. As Mulcaster observed, because Plato, Aristotle, Quintilian, or Cicero favored something or other is no proof that "it is for us to use."[153]

Progress in recovery of the classics was initially slow. Rising to the sources, always difficult enough, required unusually arduous effort of early humanists. Greek, despite its prior importance as the source of Roman letters, lagged long behind Latin in the process of rehabilitation—for obvious reasons. Medievalism corrupted and obscured the classical tongue, but did not obliterate its memory. Roman life and letters remained nearer, not only to Italian but also to other Western humanists. Nevertheless, prodigious application was necessary even for such men of genius as Petrarch, Boccaccio, and their successors to regain the classical tongue of their forbears. Despite the effort, Symonds calls Petrarch's Latin verse "lifeless" and his prose "far from pure."[154] Greek, unlike Latin, was all but unknown in Western Europe, save to a few, from the sixth century to its localized revival in the twelfth. The phrase, "It's Greek to me," was familiar to medieval copyists, who by-passed Greek passages, noting simply *Graeca sunt, non legenda.* In southern Italy and Sicily, however, a Greek element in the population and Byzantine

---

153 *Positions,* 11.
154 *Renaissance in Italy,* II, 86.

influence preserved the spoken tongue. There it was that Plato's *Meno* and *Phaedo* were first translated in the mid-twelfth century.[155]

Yet knowledge of Greek did not then spread. Petrarch mourned his lack of it, save for a smattering gained from Barlaam. Boccaccio, on Petrarch's urging, learned Greek badly under Leo Pilatus, from whose dictated Homer he turned out a much-prized, though poor, Latin version. Not till learned Manuel Chrysoloras came to teach Greek at Florence (1396), then in Milan, Rome, Venice and elsewhere, were many of great talent—Strozzi, Bracciolini, Guarino, Bruni, Rossi, Barbaro, Marsuppini, Manetti, and others— able to drink from a pure Hellenic spring. Then, for the first time in seven hundred years, said Bruni, was there in Italy a real "master of Greek letters."[156] Shortly thereafter Aurispa, Filelfo, and Guarino sought a knowledge of Greek directly in Constantinople. Through Vergerius, who studied under Chrysoloras, Vittorino da Feltre, a student of Guarino, and a number of others, the pathway to Hellenic culture was thus broadened for a host of successors, in Italy and beyond the Alps.

Agricola, having imbibed learning for almost a decade in Italy, spread the Hellenic fire among the Germans. Hegius, inspired by him, gave Erasmus a beginning in Greek at Deventer. In England, though knowledge of Italian humanism had been gained earlier through the beneficence of Duke Humphrey of Gloucester, and the journeys of Free, Grey, Gunthorpe, Flemming, Tiptoft, Hadley and Selling, it was with Linacre, Grocyn, and Latimer, who returned from Italy

---

[155] Haskins: *op. cit.,* 292.
[156] Symonds: *Renaissance in Italy,* II, 90 *ff.,* 109 *ff.*; Mullinger: *op. cit.,* I, 393.

to teach at Oxford, that an impetus theretofore unknown was given to classical study in England.[157]

Thus the first pattern of a liberal education got under way, founded largely, if not wholly, on translation and study of two foreign languages. Theorists and particular schools varied the pattern, but the heart of it was the same. Curiously enough, though Greek was the major source and inspiration both for Roman and modern humanists, it might parallel, but never exceeded and seldom equalled, Latin in respect to time and attention devoted to it.

The pattern of a truly liberal education, as set down by Vergerius (*c.* 1404) in *De Ingenuis Moribus,* a most influential document, widely read for a hundred and fifty years, emphasized religious and moral training in childhood. As for the large areas of study, first place is given to history, for its utility and interest to men of affairs; the second, to moral philosophy which reveals the meaning of true freedom; the third, to eloquence. Then follows a defense of letters (grammar and literature), logic, rhetoric, poetry, music, arithmetic, geometry, astronomy, and nature study—very pleasing to youth. Medicine, theology and law are professional studies. Law may be a liberal study, though a "mere trade" when practiced. A liberal education, Vergerius thought, did not require all of these, for mastery of one would require a lifetime. One, of course, cannot be fully understood, save in relation to the rest; but most of us have limited capacities. It is best, therefore, to be guided by intelligence and taste. In study, one should use only authors of first rank. Military affairs, especially for a prince, will include strategy, discipline, supplies, camp arrangement, engines of war, reading

---

[157] Einstein L.: *The Italian Renaissance in England,* 17 *ff.,* 29 *ff.* Columbia University Press: New York, 1935.

of books on war, as well as physical training for courage and endurance, practicing swordsmanship, spear, club, swimming, running, jumping, wrestling, boxing, javelin-throwing, archery, and horsemanship. As recreations for the scholar, ball-play, hunting, hawking, fishing, easy riding, walks, music, and tabulae are approved, while dancing and dice are condemned.[158]

From Battista Guarino's *De Ordine Docendi et Studendi* (*c.* 1459), which professes to summarize the practice of several teachers, especially that of his father, may be learned the authors and some of the texts considered most necessary for a liberal education at a time when Greek had become well established in the curriculum, and was, in the author's opinion, "of at least equal importance" with Latin—though some, still ignorant of Greek, do not consider it necessary. The course outlined, he says, will prepare one to do his own reading and also qualify him as an efficient teacher. Battista divides his curriculum into two parts: elementary and advanced. Grammar is the foundation of all education. Elementary training *(methodice)* is concerned with the mastery of parts of speech, accidence, syntax, and prosody. In Latin grammar, the *Regulae Guarini,* a compend prepared by his father, is to be learned thoroughly, supplemented by Alexander de Villa Dei's long-popular *Doctrinale,* and for further study, Priscian. Virgil is to be learned by heart. Writing Latin verse, an essential for an educated man, is to be practiced. Some of Cicero's letters may be memorized to develop style and purity of expression. Greek, without which Latin scholarship is impossible, will rest on Chrysoloras' *Erotemata.* Despite Quintilian's advice, it is impossible now to study Greek before Latin. The *Iliad* and *Odyssey* are followed by

158 Woodward: *Vittorino,* 94, 99 *ff.*, 108 *ff.*, 114 *ff.*

"Heroic poets" and "Dramatists." Elementary composition should be stressed from the beginning, and students should soon begin translation of Latin authors into Greek, for the "faithful translator" will not ignore delicate nuances of thought.[159]

Advanced studies *(historice)* begin with the historians (Justin and Valerius Maximus are named, to be followed presumably by Livy and Plutarch), to familiarize one with customs, laws, and institutions. Parallel with this there is to be further study of Virgil, now supplemented by Statius *(Thebais),* Ovid *(Metamorphoses, Fasti),* Seneca (Tragedies), Terence, Juvenal, Plautus, Horace (Art of Poetry, Satires). Persius is mentioned, but he is "less clear." Lucan may be postponed. With the poets it is necessary to study also Pomponius Mela, Solinus, and Strabo. After this solid foundation, rhetoric will be studied in Cicero *(Rhetorica ad Herennium,* credited to Cicero in the Middle Ages, and other works), without neglecting Quintilian. Logic, the *Ethics* of Aristotle, and Plato's *Dialogues* are required, apparently because they are necessary for comprehension of Cicero, rather than for their inherent value. The *De Officiis* and *Tusculans* are preferred to anything Plato wrote. Roman law is suggested as an aid in reading Latin authors. In discussing methods useful to the self-taught, Battista mentions Aulus Gellius, Macrobius, Pliny's *Natural History,* and Augustine's *De Civitate Dei.*[160]

Beyond the Alps, Sturm's Strassburg *Gymnasium* (1538), offering a ten-year course almost wholly of classical letters, gave only a beginning of mathematical studies in the last two years. Latin was begun in the first year; Greek, begun in the

---

[159] *Ibid.,* 164 *ff.*
[160] *Ibid.,* 169 *ff.*

fifth, was studied for six years. Balance of mind and body, emphasized by Italian humanists, seems to have been forgotten. Melanchthon's "Visitation" likewise ignored it.[161] *Fürstenschulen* offered a similar course of Latin and Greek authors.[162] The ten-year course at the Collège de Guyenne, Bordeaux, in the time of Vinet (1556-70), began Latin in the first year, and Greek in the seventh, to which was added two years in the Faculty of Arts. Curricula at Strassburg and Bordeaux omitted some authors and added a few not mentioned by Guarino. Strassburg gave a place to elementary mathematics in the ninth year, and continued with the first book of Euclid and elementary astronomy in the tenth. Guyenne, similarly, began arithmetic in the ninth year, and gave attention to simple proportion, squares and cubes in the tenth. Here, too, the claims of health and physical education seem to have been neglected, save as boys may have played between school hours.

Eton, in 1560, had seven forms. The following texts were used: 1) Cato's *Disticha de Moribus;* Vives' *Exercitatio Linguae Latinae;* 2) Terence; Lucian's *Dialogues,* in Latin; Aesop's *Fables* (Latin); 3) Terence; Aesop's *Fables* (Latin); Sturm's *Epistles* of Cicero; 4) Terence; Ovid's *Tristia; Epigrams* of Martial; Catullus, and Thomas More; 5) Ovid's *Metamorphoses;* Horace; Cicero's *Epistles;* Valerius Maximus; Florus; Justin; Susenbrotus' *Epitome Troporum;* 6 and 7) Caesar's *Commentaries;* Cicero's *De Officiis* and *De Amicitia;* Virgil; Lucan; *Greek Grammar.*[163] Though some scope was allowed for games, a historian of Eton says there were no provisions made in statutes of the early public

---

[161] *Barnard's American Journal of Education,* IV, 749 *ff.*

[162] Woody: *Fürstenschulen,* 29 *f.*

[163] Lyte, H. C. M.: *A History of Eton College,* 145. Macmillan & Co., Ltd.: London, 1911.

schools for time to be set aside for play. Intervals not filled with studies and meals were free for games, but they were not numerous. At the mid-sixteenth century, an hour (4-5) for play was allowed in winter, and an extra hour in summer.[164]

As a phase of the New Life, classical humanism made a profoundly important, lasting contribution to Western culture, both as liberal education and as scholarship. Many who do not recognize their indebtedness are nevertheless indebted. Singularly, both the "progressives" of later centuries and the teaching classicists, warring against each other, seem wholly oblivious of the fact that many basic principles of humanist education are the same that "progressives" espoused. In respect to principles, the humanist conception of liberal education still lives, obscured under other subject matter, and now applied, or seeking application, in a broad social scene which the wildest dreams of early humanists could not anticipate. Recognition of this significant truth would serve a useful end.

In every human movement there are elements of decay. The grounds of ultimate failure of the classical humanist pattern of education lay partly within itself, partly in external factors. As for the latter, as it served best a small, select class, its destinies were somewhat limited by the fortunes of that class and its spokesmen. The petty bourgeoisie and commoners generally, finding it of slight attraction, save as a luxury, an adornment, which most felt they could ill afford, turned to vernacular languages and literatures, and to the sciences as these were developed. Against a living, dynamic culture it was impossible to oppose, save for the brief historic

[164] Cust, L.: *A History of Eton College*, 233, 236. Duckworth & Co.: London, 1899; *cf.* Lyte: *op. cit.*, 139, 142.

moment, another which, no matter how excellent, had ceased to grow. It is significant that in his vernacular poetry Petrarch lives, whereas he is entombed in those laborious Latin works on which he hung hope of immortality. Greek and Latin letters, like rain on thirsty soil, watered indigenous shoots, but could not take their place. As for the science of antiquity it might profitably displace medieval lore, but must itself sink in the swirling wake of modern science.

Internally, classical studies suffered from a tendency, common to other systems: Means became ends. It is a fresh instance of an old truth: "The letter killeth, the spirit maketh alive." Originally designed to effect the all-sided development of *l'uomo universale,* a wide range of authors was read and interpreted in the quest for ideas and enlightenment. "Let education be for the quickening of independent thought" —Wimpfeling's expression—was in full accord with the high ideal of humanism. Great authors, properly studied, serve well that end. But, having found the "best" authors, schools transmuted them into ends. Style is by no means unimportant. But slavish devotion to imitation of the style of others jeopardized the higher end of human enlightenment. When Italian humanists "had finally learned how to polish prose," as Symonds says,[165] the interests of liberal learning were already endangered. If style becomes the end, the best stylists should certainly be followed. Cicero seemed by all odds the best model. Schools and masters found fidelity to Tully the mark of excellence. "Where the child does well, either in choosing, or true placing of *Tully's* words," Ascham admonishes, "let the master praise him, and say here you do well."[166] Erasmus did not tilt at windmills when he flayed the

165 *Renaissance in Italy,* II, 108.
166 *Scholemaster,* 62.

Ciceronians. Nosoponus, he tells us, is suffering from a dread disease, worse than jaundice or any fever, having spent a decade learning every word and phrase of Cicero, that he may be able to write and speak like the master. Yet, if one consider the matter, it is obvious that "one cannot walk well, who always puts his foot in the tracks of another," nor swim if one always clings to the cork. The Erasmian prescription is age-old. When the disease attacks, only one cure is sure: "Reason."[167] Notwithstanding his admonition, Ciceronianism throve and still drew fire in the nineteenth century. "It is not good," the foe declared, "to imitate the copiousness and sub-articulation of Cicero's periods, because they never have been imitated successfully even by the best scholars, and because the habit of writing that kind of Latin is likely to hinder the formation of a direct, lucid, and solidly impressive . . . [style]." The effort has even less reward than writing Latin verse. "Few things can be more difficult than to get a boy to appreciate the best Ciceronian prose; and as it is after all one of the curiosities of literature it seems strange that it should be so very highly valued at Oxford."[168]

[167] Erasmus, D.: *Ciceronianus, or a Dialogue on the Best Style of Speaking*, 130. (Trans. by I. Scott) Teachers College, Columbia University: New York, 1908.

[168] Farrar, F. W. (Ed.): *Essays on a Liberal Education*, 330 *f*. Macmillan & Co.: London, 1868.

CHAPTER SEVEN

DISCIPLINARY
INTERLUDE

WHAT shall we teach? What is a liberal education? There is "disagreement about the subjects," as Aristotle said.[1] These perennial pedagogical questions have been answered variously in millenniums past by appeal to two main principles of selection: *utility* and *discipline*. *Decoration*, recognized by some as an independent principle, may be viewed as a sort of utility. Prior in point of time, *utility* has been a constant determiner of the content of education, in respect to skills of body, letters, and science. *Discipline*, a later discovery of philosophers in quest of universal improvement of mind, has had unsteady employment, at times none at all. Now it is well to understand that each of these principles is utilitarian: one, immediate and concrete; the other, abstract and remote. There is no question of useful versus useless education. Plato's philosopher will serve the state. Seneca's philosophy is a stairway to the stars. A ladder is really useful if it reaches!

Of *utility*, immediate and practical, there has been no uncertainty as to its meaning. The proof of the pudding is in the eating; peasant, artisan, man of affairs, and philosopher

---

[1] *Politica*, VIII, 2. *The Works of Aristotle.* (Trans. under the editorship of J. A. Smith and W. D. Ross) 11 vols. Clarendon Press: Oxford, 1908-31.

too, could test it as they would. The principle of general discipline, so far accessible to but a few for testing, has been variously interpreted, and has occasioned much doubt. Widely divergent studies have claimed approval in its name. Plato sought mental discipline in music, arithmetic, geometry, astronomy, dialectic. Modern theorists championed Latin, Greek, algebra,[2] and other subjects as mental whetstones. That Greek should be taught for formal disciplinary value seems never to have occurred to Plato. Utility alone sufficed to give Greek grammar and literature their place in Hellenic education. It was on the same principle, not for formal mental discipline, that Romans learned Greek letters. Later, when the Greek cycle of studies was emphasized, the philosopher's doctrine of formal discipline was restated.[3] Similarly, humanists of the fourteenth century steeped themselves in the literatures of Greece and Rome for the sake of illuminating content—ideas, meanings, and vital interpretations of human life.

Such fluctuations in values assigned to certain studies suggest an important inference: skills which are imperatively required by immediate circumstances of life are taught without appeal to general disciplinary grounds. Erase the immediate practical considerations which call for a skill, and its cultivation must find support in some formal, general value;

---

[2] See Robert Recorde, *The Whetstone of Witte*, 1557. The disciplinary virtues of the "Whetstone" are suggested by the author's dedication, quoted in part:

> The grounde of artes did brede this stone:
> His use is greate, and moare then one.
> Here if you list your wittes to whette,
> Moche sharpenesse therby shall you gette.
> Dulle wittes hereby do greately mende,
> Sharpe wittes are fined to their fulle ende.
> Now prove, and praise, as you doe finde,
> And to your self be not unkinde.

[3] *The Institutio Oratoria of Quintilian*, I, 10. (Trans. by H. E. Butler) 4 vols. Harvard University Press: Cambridge, 1921-36.

or, perhaps, as a pleasant employment of leisure time. Latin was a practical necessity in the Middle Ages. The classical humanistic phase of the New Life in Western Europe invested the Roman tongue with even greater utility, and discovered that Greek as well was indispensable to everyone who would know the life of antiquity. The practical value of Latin and Greek to the world of scholarship continues today. Latin was long a necessity in church, in state, and in business. When these broad areas of indisputable utility shrank, and some of them vanished entirely, formal disciplinary values were increasingly emphasized in justification of Latin study.[4]

The modern dogmas of formal discipline, though often applied to quite different studies, found their original sources in Plato's theory of the value of certain subjects,[5] and Aristotle's doctrine of faculties of the rational soul—reason, memory, *et al.*, whose activity is the highest good.[6] Plato's choice of disciplinary studies harmonized with his doctrine of a world of perfect truth, or reality—absolute ideas, universals, eternal patterns—transcending the material world, without beginning and without end. Aristotle rejected this doctrine of ideas,[7] though he agreed with Plato in dividing the soul into rational and irrational parts.[8]

Difficult of access, Plato's world of true being could be apprehended only by gifted minds, properly schooled to deal with pure abstraction. The best disciplines are arithmetic, geometry, music, astronomy, and dialectic. Arithmetic and other members of the quadrivium may serve immediately

---

[4] Von Raumer, K.: *Geschichte der Pädagogik*, Pt. III, *Erste Abt.*, 55. 2 vols. Verlag von S. G. Liesching: Stuttgart, 1843-47.

[5] *Republic*, VII, 515, 525; *Laws*, V, 747. *The Dialogues of Plato*. (Trans. by B. Jowett) 5 vols. Oxford University Press: New York, 1892.

[6] *Magna Moralia*, I, 1-5.

[7] *Ethica Nicomachea*, I, 6.

[8] *Magna Moralia*, I, 1.

useful ends, of course. But arithmetic is not to make a shop-keeper; nor is geometry to measure a field. Education, as Aristotle also taught,[9] must not be concerned with preparation to make money. But direct military utility ranks higher, and is approved. Plato's view of studies centers in their philosophical aspects, through which the soul will be most readily brought to know true being. Arithmetic elevates the soul, compels it to reason with abstract number, and to rebel against the intrusion of tangible and visible objects. Through it pure intelligence advances in the attainment of absolute truth. Arithmetic is a difficult study; few can be found to match it. Moreover, it is a ready *index* of native capacity. The naturally quick are adept at calculation. Arithmetic is a *stimulant:* the study of number arouses the mind. It improves mental capacities: even dim wits, having had the discipline of arithmetic, are quicker in learning and more retentive than they would be without it, though they may gain nothing else. Obviously, then, those who are naturally most able ought to have the benefit of such training. Similarly, geometry quickens apprehension and leads to a knowledge of the eternal. Astronomy and music are conducive to the same end. In the last analysis, however, these four correlated studies are only a preparation for a higher discipline, dialectic, which is the sole science that deals directly with first principles. Without dialectic even mathematicians are seldom "capable of reasoning."[10]

Surveying the modern groves of *Academe*, one finds no such economy of disciplines as in Plato, but rather a host of them, old and new: arithmetic, geometry, algebra, Latin, Greek, astronomy, chemistry, botany, geology and, ultimately,

[9] *Politica*, VIII, 2.
[10] *Republic*, VII, 531.

even manual training and domestic science. Both ancient and recent whetstones of mind found more or less distinguished counselors to argue the legitimacy of their claims. Nevertheless, it was first and foremost the classical languages and mathematics in whose behalf disciplinary arguments were advanced. Later arrivals, the new sciences and modern languages, could scarcely do better than claim for themselves certain formal values, over and above their obvious, direct utility. Thus, W. Johnson, in his paper "On the Education of the Reasoning Faculties," concluded that "the Latin language must be a hindrance to the full culture of the reason," but he professed to find "enough grammar in French for coercive discipline and for the shampooing of a dull mind."[11]

Transition from the cultivation of *l'uomo universale*, the ideal of classical humanism at its best, to formal discipline of mind was not difficult. One means to perfection gave way to others which, if their claims were sound, would provide better, readier, more economical modes of education. The rich array of authors, the varied content of their thought and information, first degenerated into imitation of the best models of poetry and prose; this, in turn, when writing as Cicero or Virgil wrote fell under suspicion of barrenness, met increasing competition from the spread of faculty psychology and belief in the general discipline of faculties. In an age when once-accepted authority had crumbled, man sought a universal guide in reason, his highest faculty. What could more profitably engage one's time than a process which professed to perfect reason itself? The permanent improvement of other, less regal faculties would be desirable in proportion to their relative importance.

[11] Farrar, F. W. (Ed.) : *Essays on a Liberal Education*, 332, 362. Macmillan & Co.: London, 1868.

In Germany, the disciplinary theory gained impetus from the rationalism of Christian Wolff[12] and the philological movement. Locke's praise of mathematics for training the reason evoked Wolff's special comment and approval.[13] Gedike, following Wolff's psychology, was a firm advocate of formal discipline of the faculties. As rector of a prominent Berlin school, he did much to popularize a pattern of thinking which long held sway in German higher education. The content of studies, he recognized, is of moment, but it is commonly forgotten, even by those who are most successful in their chosen spheres of life. The time and effort spent, however, are never wasted. Even though Greek and Latin be forgotten, "you still have the advantage of having given your mind a training and discipline that will go with you into your future occupation."[14]

This doctrine of a permanent value, derived from the gymnastic of the mental faculties, came to dominate German *Gymnasien*. Paulsen wrote of them, that their purpose "is the development of all the faculties in every possible direction. To this end, a study of the ancient languages is regarded as of the utmost importance; for, by cultivating the Greek and Roman languages and literatures, we acquire skill in all mental operations. . . . The study of mathematics ranks next in importance, and also furnishes an excellent training to the faculties. The new era despises the utilitarian and encyclopedic attainments so highly valued by the preceding epoch.

---

[12] His *Vernünfftige Gedancken von den Kräfften des Menschlichen Verstandes* (1712), which set forth the value of mathematics and logic, reached the fifth edition in 1727; the *Philosophia Rationalis sive Logica* appeared a year later. Ueberweg, F.: *History of Philosophy*, II, 93, 116. (Trans. by G. S. Morris) 2 vols. Charles Scribner's Sons: New York, 1893.

[13] *Vernünfftige Gedancken, Vorrede*, a4. Magdeburg, 1727.

[14] Russell, J. E.: *German Higher Schools*, 74. Longmans, Green and Co.: New York, 1907.

True human culture, and not utility, is its aim."[15] Paulsen continues with another thought from antiquity, namely, that ignoble minds look only to the utilitarian end, oblivious to the value of perfect inner culture. It was this preoccupation with mental gymnastics that Emperor William opposed at the end of the nineteenth century:

> If any body enters into a discussion with these gentlemen [teachers of the *Gymnasien*] on this point [whether their teaching fits for life's activities] and attempts to show them that a young man ought to be prepared, to some extent at least, for life and its manifold problems, they will tell him that such is not the function of the school, its principal aim being the discipline or gymnastic of the mind, and that if this gymnastic were properly conducted, the young man would be capable of doing all that is necessary in life. I am of the opinion that we can no longer be guided by this doctrine.[16]

Locke, widely read, if not always thoroughly and rightly, provided schoolmasters with persuasive passages, frequently drawn upon to explain the general discipline of reason, and to justify physical hardening and moral training as well. Divergent or conflicting ideas were apt to be conveniently neglected by those who were intent on a universal substitute for authority. Right or wrong, they found in Locke a good stock of phrases that were useful ammunition in the war of *content* versus *discipline*. The body needs hardening, and "use alone hardens it."[17] Morally, children require "restraint and discipline." Self-denial must be "wrought into the mind." As virtue consists in power to deny desires, when not authorized by reason, Locke advised that, first of all, children

15 "The Evolution of the Educational Ideal.—I." *Forum* (July, 1897) XXIII, 606 f.

16 From the Emperor's Address to the Commission on School Reform, in the *Reichs-anzeiger*. *Educ. Rev.* (Feb., 1891) I, 202 f.

17 Locke, J.: *Some Thoughts Concerning Education*, 2 et seqq. University Press: Cambridge, 1913.

should learn to "submit their desires, and go without their longings," getting nothing because it pleases them, but only that which their elders judge fit.[18]

As for intellectual discipline, "We are born with faculties and powers capable almost of any thing. . . ."[19] Exercise of them alone leads to perfection. Locke speaks approvingly of a "universal taste of all the sciences," which is to guard against that narrowness which is found in those who are "seasoned only by one part of knowledge."[20] This and other passages suggest the desirability of breadth and variety of subject matter. Yet Locke makes it clear that it is not content, or range of information that he desires, but a schooling in thinking that "gives the mind a freedom" and exercises "the understanding in the several ways of inquiry and reasoning," teaching "sagacity and wariness," and imparting a "suppleness" in application.

Clearly, it is schooling in the processes of reasoning that is so important. "The faculty of reasoning seldom or never deceives those who trust to it. . . ."[21] Above all agencies for perfecting the reason, Locke prized mathematics, in which he included algebra, for it "gives new helps and views to the understanding."[22] Mathematics, he thinks, will prove useful, even to grown men, by showing them what is necessary "to make any one reason well."[23] To make men professional mathematicians or algebraists is not his aim; instead, he wants a training in reasoning—"to settle in the mind a habit of reasoning closely and in train"—that they, "having got

[18] *Ibid.*, 38, 40, 45.
[19] *Locke's Conduct of the Understanding*, IV. (Ed. by T. Fowler) Clarendon Press: Oxford, 1901.
[20] *Ibid.*, XIX.
[21] *Ibid.*, III, 3.
[22] *Ibid.*, VII.
[23] *Ibid.*

the way of reasoning, which that study necessarily brings the mind to," may "transfer it to other parts of knowledge as they shall have occasion."[24] All who have time and opportunity should study mathematics "to make them reasonable creatures," for though "we are born to it if we please," it is only by "use and exercise" that we become "rational creatures."[25]

One anticipates, and finds, praise of utility of certain mathematical studies in Franklin. Though he failed arithmetic under Brownell, he went through Cocker's *Arithmetic* independently, studied geometry, and read on navigation. His "English School" included arithmetic and accounts, along with geography, globes, drawing, and mechanics. Such vocationalism would not have pleased Plato, or have satisfied Locke. But Franklin, too, looked beyond immediate use. His Academy, a more ambitious project, would teach "the several branches of the mathematics," including "some of the first principles of geometry and astronomy." In its defense he followed Plato's lead, though he thought him "unreasonable and unjust" in condemning as irrational anyone who failed to comprehend Euclid XIII, 17. The general disciplinary value of mathematics he summed up with his usual clarity in a single sentence: "Mathematical demonstrations are a logic of as much or more use, than that commonly learned at schools, serving to a just formation of the mind, enlarging its capacity, and strengthening it so as to render the same capable of exact reasoning, and discerning truth from falsehood in all occurrences, even subjects not mathematical."[26]

[24] *Ibid.*
[25] *Ibid.*, VI.
[26] Woody, T. (Ed.) : *Educational Views of Benjamin Franklin*, 129, 159, 183, 232. McGraw-Hill Book Company: New York, 1931. In his article, "Of the Usefulness of the Mathematicks," *Pa. Gaz.*, Oct. 30, 1735, Franklin presumably

The disciplinary view of linguistic and mathematical studies, generally held by colleges in the nineteenth century, was precisely put by the University of Pennsylvania (1824): "Liberal education must rest for its basis on an accurate and extensive knowledge of the learned Languages, when the acquisition of them has cultivated the taste, strengthened the memory and stored the mind with terms and the capacity to analyze them. Adapted to every branch of knowledge an introduction of the *precise sciences,* of mathematics and the art of reasoning is peculiarly seasonable." Again, five years later, the University amplified its doctrine negatively, as it concerned preparation for professions: "It [a liberal education] is not designed . . . to qualify the student in a special manner for any particular profession or pursuit . . . but to aid in the development of all his faculties in their just proportions; and by discipline and instruction, to furnish him with those general qualifications, which are useful and ornamental in every profession. . . ."[27] Yale's formulation (1827) was in the same vein: "The two great points to be gained in intellectual culture are the *discipline* and the *furniture* of the mind; expanding its powers, and storing it with knowledge. The former of these is, perhaps, the more important of the two." The object of a collegiate course should therefore "be . . . [the] daily and vigorous exercise" of "the faculties of the student."[28]

---

meant the 17th Proposition (not 117th): "To construct a dodecahedron and comprehend it in a sphere, like the aforesaid figures, and to prove that the side of the dodecahedron is the irrational straight line called apotome."—T. L. Heath, *The Thirteen Books of Euclid's Elements,* III, 493. 3 vols. University Press: Cambridge, 1926. Franklin's ascription of this particular view to Plato is seemingly an error. Euclid's *Elements* had not yet appeared. Plato himself spoke disparagingly of the status of solid geometry in his day, and wanted the state to foster its study.—*Republic,* VII, 528.

[27] Mulhern, J.: *A History of Secondary Education in Pennsylvania,* 321. Science Press Printing Co.: Lancaster, 1933.

[28] *Am. Jour. Sc. and Arts* (Jan., 1829) XV, 297, 300.

Women's colleges echoed men's, professing faith in general, and opposing special, training. The teacher, as Graves of Mary Sharp College stated, "marshals these powers [of the mind], not for a single field but for life's campaign."[29] Said Lida R. McCabe (1893): "We do not aim to train a woman for a sphere, profession or calling. . . ." "When men complete the college curriculum they rarely have definite ideas of what course they will pursue. Why should women be expected to have definite plans? All must await developments, and whatever . . . [they] may be the college-bred woman is better equipped to meet them."[30]

Emma Willard, Almira Hart Phelps, John Todd and a host of others laid great stress on disciplinary values in the education of girls. The discipline of mathematics, Willard held, had been the chief cause "of that stronger intellectual power by which the American women have now shown themselves capable of teaching, not only high subjects in the schools, but of investigating new ones, and of managing high schools as well as those for children."[31] While Mrs. Phelps would have blushed if her pupils failed to show a profit from arithmetic in practical affairs, she recognized a higher general value in mathematics, and its transference to other sciences:

The study of mathematics has, by philosophers, been considered the most direct way of controlling the imagination, perfecting reason and judgment, and inducing a habit of method and love of order. . . . Mathematics is peculiarly a science of comparisons; these comparisons are always exact and may be made manifest to the senses. . . . Suppose of two young persons of equal talents, and who have devoted equal time to study, the one is a geometrician, and the other

---

[29] Woody, T.: *A History of Women's Education in the United States*, II, 194. 2 vols. Science Press: New York, 1929.

[30] McCabe, L. R.: *The American Girl at College*, 4 f., 14. Dodd, Mead & Company: New York, 1893.

[31] Woody: *History of Women's Education*, I, 405 f.

has given her time more to other branches of knowledge—suppose these two commencing together some new science, botany, chemistry, or mental philosophy, we shall soon perceive the great advantage which the knowledge and practice of mathematical reasoning gives the one, over the other, in the mode of arranging facts, of developing truth, and performing such mental analyses as are necessary to disentangle, and bring to light the most complicated subjects.[32]

Todd's general defense of disciplinary education included training in power of commanding *attention,* continual application of mind "as long as is necessary," strengthening the memory, developing "balanced judgment," cultivating "the taste," storing the mind with knowledge, and cultivating endurance of "what we naturally dislike."[33] No less inclusive was Phelps' theory of mental discipline:

We may now consider the human mind as a garden laid out before us: he who created this garden, planted in it the seeds of various faculties; these do indeed spring up of themselves, but without education, they will be stinted in their growth, choked with weeds, and never attain that strength and elevation of which they are susceptible. In one part of our garden the germ of reason is seen to unfold itself, in another appears that of memory, in another that of judgment, until all the faculties of the intellect are in their full progress of development. The emotions and passions are mingled with powers of slower growth: while the intellectual gardener cultivates the latter with assiduous care, he knows that the passions need his most vigilant attention; that if they grow rank and unpruned, like the fatal Bohan Upas, they will poison and destroy the vital principle of virtue, and root out the moral harmony on which the beauty of the whole depends. Leaving the passions and emotions to be hereafter considered, our concern now is with those mental germs which belong to the intellectual department. The skilful gardener knows that his roses require one mode of culture, his tulips another, and his geraniums

32 Bolzau, E. L.: *Almira Hart Lincoln Phelps: Her Life and Work,* 279. Science Press Printing Co.: Lancaster, 1936.
33 Woody: *History of Women's Education,* I, 407 ff.

another; and that attention to one of these, will not bring forward the other. So ought the mental cultivator to understand that the germs of the various faculties should be simultaneously brought forward. This truth seems not to have been understood by those, who, bending all their efforts towards the cultivation of the memory, neglected the other powers of the mind.[34]

Tarver, an English master who saw nowhere the "smallest trace of enthusiasm for sound intellectual training," went to some length to explain that learning Latin or Greek was not an end but a means: "what is important is the process of acquiring it." If the "mere acquisition" of a language were an "end in itself," the position of Latin and Greek could not be defended; but "we learn Greek or Latin, so that we may be prepared to learn something else." "My claim for Latin, from the point of view of an Englishman and a foster parent, is simply that it would be impossible to devise for English boys a better teaching instrument. There may be as good, but I have not yet come across better. Misused it unquestionably has been, and will continue to be so, and in such a case its failure is more obvious than the failure of a less complicated piece of machinery; but it must be judged by what it is capable of doing at its best, not by the achievements of the bungler."[35]

Bennett and Bristol accepted "training in English" as the "most important reason for studying Latin," but they recognized other "excellent reasons" of a general disciplinary nature. "Latin trains the observing faculty"; it involves a constant observation and mental recording; it is as "severe an exercise of the reasoning powers as anything" known;

[34] Phelps, A. H. L.: *Lectures to Young Ladies*, 69 *f*. Carter, Hendee & Co.: Boston, 1833.

[35] Tarver, J. C.: *Some Observations of a Foster Parent*, xii, 75 *ff*. Archibald Constable & Co.: Westminster, 1897.

finally, translation necessitates continuous "practice in expressing the results of one's observing, recording, and reasoning," the excellence of the process being determined by the teacher.[36]

A central thesis of the general disciplinary school of thought emphasized the importance of difficulty. Locke said that strength of body, and of the mind, too, lay "in being able to endure hardships."[37] It became a commonplace, as the disciplinary defense of ancient language developed, to stress the hardness of its mastery. Madame d'Epinay's correspondent, Abbé Galiani, wrote (1770):

> Education is the same thing for man and for beast. It can be reduced to two principles, to learn to put up with injustice, to learn to endure *ennui*. What does one do when one breaks in a horse? Left to himself, the horse ambles, trots, gallops, walks, but does it when he wishes, as he pleases. We teach him to move thus or thus, contrary to his own desire, against his own instinct—there is the injustice: we make him keep on at it for a couple of hours—there is the *ennui*. It is just the same thing when we make a child learn Latin or Greek or French. The intrinsic utility of it is not the main point. The aim is that he should habituate himself to obey another person's will. . . . All pleasant methods of teaching children necessary knowledge are false and ridiculous. It is not a question of learning geography or geometry: it is a question of learning to work, of learning the weariness of concentrating one's attention on the matter in hand. . . .[38]

Mr. Dooley seems to have had this aspect of the disciplinary theory in mind when he said, "It makes no difference what you teach a boy so long as he don't like it."

When girls' education began to claim serious attention, it

---

[36] Bennett, C. E., and Bristol, G. P.: *The Teaching of Latin and Greek in the Secondary School*, 11, 12, 23, 24, 26. Longmans, Green and Co.: New York, 1906.

[37] *Thoughts*, 33.

[38] Boyd, W.: *The Educational Theory of Jean Jacques Rousseau*, 306 f. Longmans, Green and Co.: London, 1911. (Courtesy of the author.)

donned the same cloak which prevailing fashion had decreed for the mental discipline of boys. Todd's *Daughter at School* (1854) stressed "habits of patient toil."

> How much patience is needed to get one lesson in Latin, or to make a single good recitation in algebra! Now you must multiply this toil as many times over as you have lessons. In the course of a week, and a year, how much is the patience exercised! And this toil, this perseverance, this endurance of what is hard and what we naturally dislike, is the very discipline which we must meet all the way through life. Toil, patient toil, is our lot, and there is no place where the young can learn it so well as at school. . . .[39]

A century and more after Galiani, Tarver declared: "The one great merit of Latin as a teaching instrument is its stupendous difficulty."[40] Bennett and Bristol stressed the indubitable fact that, *"Translation is a severe exercise."*[41] These are but a few of a multitude of variations on Newman's theme: "Consider, for instance, what a discipline in accuracy of thought it is to have to construe a foreign language into your own; and what a still severer and more improving exercise it is to translate from your own into a foreign language." Cardinal Newman broadened the field, however, to speak of the discipline of "memory and discrimination" in "getting up" a "chapter of history," the value of mastering "definitions," the value of "exercise in logical precision" in Euclid and mastering "the great arguments for Christianity" so as to stand an examination, and "so of any other science," whether chemistry, anatomy, natural history —"it does not matter what it is, if it be really studied and

---

[39] Todd, J.: *The Daughter at School*, 49 f. Hopkins, Bridgman, and Company: Northampton, 1854.
[40] *Op. cit.,* 79.
[41] *Op. cit.,* 12. Italics mine.

mastered, as far as it is taken up."[42] In short, any subject could be made a good discipline.

Huxley facetiously pushed the argument of discipline to a logical conclusion in his comparison of paleontology and linguistic sciences:

> It is wonderful how close a parallel to classical training could be made out of that paleontology to which I refer. In the first place I could get up an osteological primer so arid, so pedantic in its terminology, so altogther distasteful to the youthful mind, as to beat the recent famous production of the head-masters out of the field in all these excellences. Next, I could exercise my boys upon easy fossils, and bring out all their powers of memory and all their ingenuity in the application of my osteogrammatical rules to the interpretation, or construing, of those fragments. To those who had reached the higher classes, I might supply odd bones to be built up into animals, giving great honor and reward to him who succeeded in fabricating monsters most entirely in accordance with the rules. That would answer to verse-making and essay-writing in the dead languages.
>
> To be sure, if a great comparative anatomist were to look at these fabrications he might shake his head, or laugh. But what then? Would such a catastrophe destroy the parallel? What, think you, would Cicero, or Horace, say to the production of the best sixth form going? And would not Terence stop his ears and run out if he could be present at an English performance of his own plays?[43]

The Report of the Committee of Ten on Secondary School Studies (1893) recognized certain practical claims which a changing society made upon educational institutions, but bowed most deferentially to the long-accepted doctrine of mental discipline. Indeed, the Committee stamped with approval the extension of discipline's domain. Advocates of certain newer branches of study, as yet "imperfectly dealt

---

[42] *The Idea of a University*, 501 *f*. Longmans, Green and Co.: New York, 1910.
[43] Huxley, T. H.: *Science and Education*, 90 *f*. American Home Library Company: New York, 1902.

with," made "the longest and most elaborate reports, ardently" desiring "their respective subjects" to be made "equal to Latin, Greek, and mathematics," yet, at the same time, knowing that "many teachers and directors of education felt no confidence in these [newer] subjects as disciplinary material."[44]

In respect to Latin, the Report noted, it had "been more successfully employed" in England, Germany, and France, "than with us 'as an instrument for training the mind to habits of intellectual conscientiousness, patience, discrimination, accuracy, and thoroughness,—in a word, to habits of clear and sound thinking,' " due to more time being given to it. "Latin is a difficult language," and only long study will "yield its best fruits." It should begin not later than fourteen, and continue for not less than four years, five forty-five-minute periods a week.[45] The conference on mathematics saw the chief claim for geometry in its "discipline in complete, exact, and logical statement."[46] In arithmetic, however, the omission of certain matters, which "perplex and exhaust the pupil without affording any really valuable mental discipline," was recommended, and more attention was urged to "simple calculation" and "concrete problems." Noting the prevalent belief "that even if the subjects are totally forgotten, a valuable mental discipline is acquired by the efforts made to master them," the committee confirmed its belief that "this discipline has a certain value," in itself, but considered this less valuable than the discipline of "a different class of exercises."[47]

[44] *Report of the Committee of Ten on Secondary School Studies*, 12 f. American Book Company: New York, 1894.
[45] *Ibid.*, 61, 74.
[46] *Ibid.*, 25.
[47] *Ibid.*, 105, 108.

English in secondary schools, it was declared, should "be made the equal of any other study in disciplinary or developing power." "The study of formal grammar is valuable as training in thought."[48] Modern languages, French or German, argued also their contribution to the discipline of mind: Modern language study "will train their [the pupils'] memory and develop their sense of accuracy; it will quicken and strengthen their reasoning powers by offering them, at every step, problems that must be immediately solved by the correct application of the results of their own observation. . . ."[49]

The conference on history, government, and political economy recognized that the "function of history in education is still very imperfectly apprehended," but expressed their belief "in the efficiency of these studies in training the judgment." "The principal end of all education is training. In this respect history has a value different from, but in no way inferior to, that of language, mathematics, and science. The mind is chiefly developed in three ways: by cultivating the powers of discriminating observation; by strengthening the logical faculty of following an argument from point to point; and by improving the process of comparison, that is, the judgment.

"As studies in language and in the natural sciences are best adapted to cultivate the habits of observation; as mathematics are the traditional training of the reasoning faculties: so history and its allied branches are better adapted than any other studies to promote the invaluable mental power which we call the judgment."[50]

In general, the report of the Committee of Ten broadened

48 *Ibid.*, 21, 89.
49 *Ibid.*, 96.
50 *Ibid.*, 28, 168.

the scope of disciplinary claims: "All the main subjects" would be of equal value in getting a youth into college; "they would all be used for training the powers of observation, memory, expression, and reasoning. . . . Every youth who entered college would have spent four years in studying a few subjects thoroughly; and, on the theory that all the subjects are to be considered equivalent in educational rank for the purposes of admission to college, it would make no difference which subjects he had chosen from the programme—he would have had four years of strong and effective mental training."[51] Under the influence of such a report, teachers of studies, old and new, but particularly the new, undoubtedly felt keenly the need to make their specialties the best possible whetstones of the mind. Was it desire for discipline that inspired the following assignment of a teacher of English teachers in a Summer School of the higher learning? "Write a complex sentence, containing a noun clause, adjectival clause, adverbial clause, an adjectival phrase, and an adverbial phrase; use a third person plural pronoun in the objective case and have the verb in the main clause third person plural indicative active past."

Skepticism regarding the soundness of the claims of the regnant general disciplinary conception, always present in some degree, mounted in the last half of the nineteenth century, and, ultimately, all but swept the entire field of education. Chief among the forces which undermined the old theory, and the studies which had long relied upon it for support in their positions of respect in the eyes of the public and of teachers, were: the advancement of science and technology, which profoundly altered man's economy, providing a host of new employments, requiring certain special-

[51] *Ibid.*, 52 *f.*

ized skills—changes of great moment, whether negatively or positively considered; the growth of political democracy, and a dawning, though as yet imperfect, recognition of its educational implications. Two other factors of major import lay in the domain of educational philosophy, rather than in the workaday world of industry, commerce, and politics: the growing acceptance of a naturalistic, utilitarian philosophy, in education as in life, and a consequent proliferation of studies which claimed attention; and a belated, yet long-heralded scientific movement in psychology which, once well underway, inevitably claimed in its province the investigation of many an ancient theory.

Revolt against the formal discipline of faculties as a justification of the pursuit of certain studies was expressed by Horace Greeley, who declared that:

> . . . mind is disciplined best by its own proper work; and not by making this discipline the great end. I would say to the farmer's son, poring over Greek verbs and Hebrew roots and accents; to the damsel of sixteen, wasting her sweetness on algebra and geometry, what do you propose to do with this . . . ? If you propose to turn it to some practical account, very well; but if you only acquire it with an eye to mental discipline, then I protest against it as a waste of time and energy.[52]

He did not doubt but that algebra, trigonometry, and logarithms were valuable for some purposes and some people, but many, he believed, would find other studies more useful and perhaps equally valuable for "mental discipline and growth."[53]

The demands of the vocational world and the enticements

[52] "Education: Its Motives, Methods and Ends." *Pa. Sch. Jour.* (Nov., 1857) VI, 158 *f.*

[53] Beecher, C. E.: *Educational Reminiscences and Suggestions*, 178 *f.* J. B. Ford and Company: New York, 1874.

of a plethora of new studies were evident on all sides. The proliferation of courses in secondary schools was of grand proportions. The Boston Latin School (1789) studied Latin and Greek for four years, with a little English. Between 1814 and 1828 arithmetic, geometry, trigonometry, algebra, geography, declamation, reading, English grammar, English composition, forensic discussion, history and chronology, and constitutions of the United States and of Massachusetts were added.[54] Sharply different were the offerings of high schools a half-century later. Twenty high schools (1860-65) offered fifty-seven subjects. Thirty years later (1896-1900), forty high schools offered a total of seventy-four.[55] The Committee of Ten, facing the problem of multiplicity and variability of offering, gathered figures from forty institutions, and found almost forty subjects were offered in them.[56]

At the college level, inroads of vocationalism and new studies to fit for them were no less evident. Jane Bancroft (1885) pointed to law, journalism, industrial art, architecture, medicine, teaching, and work in various sciences— biology, chemistry, and physics—as professional fields for women.[57] Men's colleges gave way, the elective principle being applied in the choice of curricula at the University of Virginia in 1825, while Harvard made its application to individual studies popular after 1869. Women's colleges followed with considerable reluctance. Thomas of Bryn Mawr, as late as 1908, decried the movement to teach anything in college that is "desirable for a human being to learn" and

---

[54] Inglis, A.: *Principles of Secondary Education*, 164 *f*. Houghton Mifflin Company: Boston, 1918.

[55] Stout, J. E.: *The Development of High-School Curricula in the North Central States from 1860 to 1918*, 62, 67 *f*. University of Chicago: Chicago, 1921.

[56] *Report*, 4 *f*.

[57] "Occupations and Professions for College-Bred Women." *Education* (May, 1885) V, 486 *ff*.

credit it toward the A.B. The elective system rested on the hypothesis that all studies were "equally good for purposes of mental discipline," but no proof had been given to justify the belief. Time, she held, had shown up the fallacy; yet still, she was "astounded to see the efforts which have been made within the past few years, and perhaps never more persistently than during the past year, to persuade, I might almost say to compel, those in charge of women's education to riddle the college curriculum of women with hygiene and sanitary drainage and domestic science and child-study, and all the rest of the so-called practical studies."[58] Sharply opposed to Thomas' outlook, Zook's study of various colleges in Massachusetts (1923) complained of the relative lack of attention to vocational and professional preparation, compared with "extensive facilities" in the "cultural realm," despite the fact that "a large percentage of the graduates of women's colleges in Massachusetts" were entering gainful occupations.[59]

Curricular changes, already in process under the influence of socioeconomic forces, gained fresh impetus from new psychological conceptions. Whether one looks to the Herbartians or later experimentalists and physiological psychologists, the results were much the same, so far as tenability of the general training of mind was concerned. The old faculties and belief in their improvement by certain formal disciplines waned like shadows before a rising sun, disappearing at midday—perhaps to reappear in the afternoon!

Herbart's theory of mind led followers to seek specific

[58] Thomas, M. C.: "Present Tendencies in Women's College and University Education." *Educ. Rev.* (Jan., 1908) XXXV, 76 f.

[59] Woody: *History of Women's Education*, II, 219 f.

discipline rather than general. The bond-forming, condition-
ing school of Pavlov, Cattell, Thorndike, Ladd, Woodworth,
and others, and Dewey's education as problem solving pointed
in a like direction. Said Herbart's disciple, Rein: formal
discipline of the mind is a fiction. "In general, there is no such
education at all." Instead, there are "as many kinds of formal
education as there are essentially different spheres of intellectual employment."[60] Bain wrote (1879): There "is a
discipline that we learn from everything that we have to do;
it is not a prerogative of any one study or occupation, and it
does not necessarily extend itself beyond the special subject."[61] Woodworth concluded: "We act as we have learned
to act, see what we have learned to see, are interested in what
we have learned to be interested in, enjoy what we have
learned to enjoy, and dislike what or whom we have learned
to dislike."[62]

It seemed as though psychologists were saying, with
Thackeray's Pendennis: "Ah, sir, a distinct universe walks
about under your hat and under mine . . . you and I are but
a pair of infinite isolations, with some fellow islands a little
more or less near us." John Adams' summation of the effect
of Herbartianism, equally applicable to other schools of
specificity of learning, put succinctly the shift of emphasis
from *process* to *content:* "Teachers used to have, and ignorant
people still have, a pretty theory that we ought to learn pieces
of poetry in order to cultivate the memory. This venerable,
this ludicrous fallacy has been long exploded. . . . The point

[60] Rein, W.: *Outlines of Pedagogics*, 61. (Trans. by C. C. and I. J. Van Liew)
C. W. Bardeen: Syracuse, 1895.

[61] Bain, A.: *Education as a Science*, 142. D. Appleton and Company: New
York, 1879.

[62] Woodworth, R. S.: *Dynamic Psychology*, 77. Columbia University Press:
New York, 1918.

of view is entirely changed. Pupils learn poetry now not for the sake of the memory, but for the sake of the poetry."[63]

Heavy re-enforcements for the antidisciplinary camp were soon brought up from the laboratories of psychology and educational measurement. James reported (1890) his rather unscientific experiment on transfer and its indeterminate results.[64] A decade later, Thorndike and Woodworth (1901) found slight positive transfer, and some cases of negative.[65] Since then Ossa has been piled on Pelion, with the result that the claims of general disciplinary values have been drastically reduced. Orata mentioned 167 experiments, appearing from 1890 to January, 1935.[66] Recognizing the unevenness of the studies from the scientific standpoint, he classified their findings thus: nearly 30 per cent showed "*considerable* transfer"; almost 50 per cent, "*appreciable* transfer"; less than 10 per cent, "*little* transfer"; less than 4 per cent "*no* transfer." The remainder, under 10 per cent, indicated both transfer and interference. Peter Sandiford summarized his judgment of experimental findings by saying (1941) that "generally speaking, the transfer is usually positive (in about 90 per cent of the cases) and ranges usually between 0 and 20 per cent. *A positive but modest transfer may usually be expected.*" Transfer is higher in those of high intelligence, greater in the "relatively young," and when the training and testing materials have much in common—particularly method and content. In general ". . . it is safer for

[63] *The Herbartian Psychology Applied to Education*, 134. D. C. Heath and Company: Boston, 1897.

[64] James, W.: *The Principles of Psychology*, I, 666. 2 vols. Henry Holt and Company: New York, 1890.

[65] Thorndike, E. L., and Woodworth, R. S.: "The Influence of Improvement in One Mental Function upon the Efficiency of Other Functions." *Psych. Rev.* (1901) VIII, 247-61, 384-95, 553-64.

[66] Orata, P. T.: "Transfer of Training and Educational Pseudo-Science." *Math. Teacher* (May, 1935) XXVIII, 266 *f.*

educators to depend on specific training and practice than to expect results at second hand through transfer of training." But "teaching specifically for transfer . . . in order to lessen the need for training in a multitude of specific items" should not be overlooked.[67]

A number of treatises on the curriculum, by Bobbitt, Bonser, Charters, Meriam, and others, appearing after three decades of verbal and experimental conflict over *training* versus *content* show where the laurel wreaths were hung, emphasis being placed generally, though in varying degree, on the specificity of learning.[68] In an extravagant form—logically enough from the standpoint of specific learning, adaptation to children's everyday life, and an emphasis on the principle of mutation (which the day's events encouraged)— the new tendency culminated in the theory that the curriculum should be made and remade from day to day.

Experimental evidence, if examined, seems to have carried little or no weight in the opposing camp, some of whose defenders attacked the new science itself and set their own "common-sense" and the faith of "educated and practical men" on the other side of the scales. Paul Shorey asserted (1910): "There is no science of psychology, sociology, or pedagogy that can pronounce with any authority on either the aims or the methods of education. . . ." There is no proof "by scientific experiment and ratiocination that mental discipline is a myth . . . and no prospect of it. . . . There is no authentic

[67] Sandiford, P.: "Transfer of Training." *Ency. of Educ. Research*, 1307. (Ed. by W. S. Monroe) Macmillan Company: New York, 1941.

[68] Bobbitt, F.: *The Curriculum*, 42 *ff*. Houghton Mifflin Company: Boston, 1918; *How to Make a Curriculum*, 11-31. Houghton Mifflin Company: Boston, 1924; Bonser, F. G.: *The Elementary School Curriculum*, 150 *ff*. Macmillan Company: New York, 1920; Meriam, J. L.: *Child Life and the Curriculum*, 137, 171, 207, 237, 255, *pass*. World Book Company: Yonkers-on-Hudson, 1920; Charters, W. W.: *Curriculum Construction*, 102, *pass*. Macmillan Company: New York, 1923.

deliverance of science here to oppose to the vast presumption of common-sense and the belief of the majority of educated and practical men."[69]

William Howard Taft, in a signed article in the *Public Ledger* (Philadelphia),[70] compared the critics of monastic abuses in the days of Luther to the new "psychological pedagogues" who "have found in their psychological laboratory analyses that there is no mental discipline gained by these studies [Latin, Greek, algebra, geometry]; indeed, that there is no such thing as formal discipline of the mind, and that the only important thing is 'content.' " He entered a demurrer on behalf of those gathered at Philadelphia under Dr. West:

They deny that there is no formal discipline and training of the mind by the study of one branch of knowledge which will be useful in the pursuit of any other. They insist that the thorough study of Latin and algebra and geometry does help the youthful mind by stimulating close mental attention and by enforcing logical deduction and induction and synthesis and analysis. Such study strengthens mental processes just as well-directed physical exercises strengthen the muscles of the body,[71] and even if in after years the memory of the Latin or mathematics fades, the benefit in the training of the mind remains for use in every necessity for its use. They do not need a prophet from the realm of the new psychology to come and tell them how such studies affect the minds of students, for each one has his own laboratory of research on this subject in his own mental training and experience.

Robert M. Hutchins (1936) found "all the needs of general education in America" satisfied by a curriculum focused

[69] Shorey, P.: "A Symposium on the Value of Humanistic, Particularly Classical, Studies: The Classics and the New Education, III. The Case for the Classics." *Sch. Rev.* (Nov., 1910) XVIII, 598, 607, 608.

[70] July 5, 1921.

[71] Mr. Taft's assurance equaled that of J. P. Wickersham who asserted (1854), "A blacksmith's arm and the mind of a Bacon grew virtually by the same process."—"Educational Aphorisms." *Pa. Sch. Jour.* (Mar., 1854) II, 275.

on reading great classics—a theme which recalls the "great book" theory of Seneca, Milton, and others in ages past— mathematics and metaphysics. Certain arts are necessary for the sake of discipline—a discipline of faculties. To read, one must study grammar, by which one is able to "understand the meaning. . . . Grammar disciplines the mind and develops the logical faculty."[72] To grammar he adds "rhetoric and logic, or the rules of writing, speaking, and reasoning. . . . Logic is a statement in technical form of the conditions under which reasoning is rigorously demonstrative. If the object of general education is to train the mind for intelligent action, logic cannot be missing from it." To this it is necessary "to add a study which exemplifies reasoning in its clearest and most precise form. That study is, of course, mathematics, and of the mathematical studies chiefly those that use the type of exposition that Euclid employed. In such studies the pure operation of reason is made manifest. . . . Correctness in thinking may be more directly and impressively taught through mathematics than in any other way."[73]

With this appeal on behalf of the power of mathematics to teach "correctness in thinking" one may well compare the statement of an eminent mathematician and philosopher, A. N. Whitehead:

I appeal to you, as practical teachers. With good discipline, it is always possible to pump into the minds of a class a certain quantity of inert knowledge. You take a text-book and make them learn it.

---

[72] Hutchins, R. M.: *The Higher Learning in America*, 82, 85. Yale University Press: New Haven, 1936. Among others, Sidney Hook, in "Ballyhoo at St. John's College," *The New Leader* (May 27 and June 3, 1944) XXVII, Nos. 22 and 23, and Harry D. Gideonse, in *Higher Learning in a Democracy*, Farrar & Rinehart, New York, 1937, have given critical attention to the current "Great Books" conception of education. *Cf. Epistle* II. *Seneca: ad Lucilium Epistulae Morales.* (Trans. by R. M. Gummere) 3 vols. William Heinemann: London, 1917-25.

[73] Hutchins: *op. cit.*, 83 *f.*

So far, so good. The child then knows how to solve a quadratic equation. But what is the point of teaching a child to solve a quadratic equation? There is a traditional answer to this question. It runs thus: The mind is an instrument, you first sharpen it, and then use it; the acquisition of the power of solving a quadratic equation is part of the process of sharpening the mind. Now there is just enough truth in this answer to have made it live through the ages. But for all its half-truth, it embodies a radical error which bids fair to stifle the genius of the modern world. I do not know who was first responsible for this analogy of the mind to a dead instrument. For aught I know, it may have been one of the seven wise men of Greece, or a committee of the whole lot of them. Whoever was the originator, there can be no doubt of the authority which it has acquired by the continuous approval bestowed upon it by eminent persons. But whatever its weight of authority, whatever the high approval which it can quote, I have no hesitation in denouncing it as one of the most fatal, erroneous, and dangerous conceptions ever introduced into the theory of education. The mind is never passive; it is a perpetual activity, delicate, receptive, responsive to stimulus. You cannot postpone its life until you have sharpened it.[74]

The disciplinary interlude has ended, so far as representing a ruling conception is concerned. There are in America and elsewhere only vestigial remains.[75] The maximum 20 per cent transfer in optimum cases does not justify teaching a subject for transfer primarily; but teaching for as much transfer as can be gained is sound practice, regardless of the subject. Teachers, generally, have been wiser than Taft; they will hardly follow Hutchins' advice to teach mathematics because it teaches "correctness of thinking." There are sound reasons for teaching mathematics and languages, ancient and

[74] From A. N. Whitehead, *The Aims of Education and Other Essays*, 8 f. Copyright, 1929, by The Macmillan Company, and used with their permission.

[75] For widely divergent views of the question, see *Educ. Yrbk. of the Internat. Inst. of Teachers College*, Columbia University, 1939. (Ed. by I. L. Kandel) Bureau of Publications, Teachers College: New York, 1939.

modern—quite apart from any "formal discipline" that may
or may not be gained.

While disciplinary values of linguistic study were still
pressed strenuously, the significance of Roman life and literature suffered neglect. Tarver, defending the learning of Latin
as a process, a "trainer of intellect," refused to rest the case
for Latin and Greek on their value as literature. He had had,
he said, "no opportunity of measuring the refining influence
of literature," but plenty of opportunity to compare the results of "sound and unsound" teaching and of "testing the
worthlessness" of those who "inform rather than train."[76]

Decline of the disciplinary conception has restored a
former emphasis on language and literature as means to an
understanding of culture. A distinguished Latin scholar remarked recently: "There is no justification for teaching Latin
or Greek to 'discipline the mind.' I teach Latin because it is
the key to a great culture, and in any enlightened age there
will be need of scholarly men and women who can teach it
and interpret Roman life and literature." The Committee on
Classical Studies, reporting to the American Classical League
at Washington (1924) said: "The primary intent of our
recommendations is that Latin should be learned in order to
be read and understood, and that the way should be cleared
for a fuller appreciation of the larger enduring intellectual
and historical values which are derivable from Latin."[77] This
view, emerging after a long interlude of disciplinary effort,
seems like genuine humanism, even like that of Erasmus,
who said: "Knowledge seems to be of two kinds: that of
things and that of words. That of words comes first, that of
things is the most important."

76 *Op. cit.*, xi-xii.
77 Reported in *Sch. and Soc.* (July 19, 1924) XX, 79 *f.*

CHAPTER EIGHT

LIBERAL EDUCATION

FOR

FREE MEN

1

PROBABLY no proposition is less open to dispute than this: We need a liberal education for today. Equally beyond cavil is the fact that, as in Aristotle's time, there is little agreement as to what a liberal education should be.[1] Both theory and practice are confused and contradictory. The range of divergence is great. At one extreme, certain leaders point to the pattern of antiquity as the best and only true education, fit for all epochs, universal; while others urge a return to the medieval mode, and its authoritarian, supernatural sanctions. At the other extreme, history is all but forgot, only the present matters, and a narrow functionalism calls for specific job training, based on as precise an analysis as possible of the skills and information required by everyday life.

Both extremes of theory and practice, and others in between, are sharply criticized: one lacks unity, scatters, leads nowhere; another, too definite, leads into a cul-de-sac. This

---

[1] *Politica*, VIII, 2. *The Works of Aristotle.* (Trans. under the editorship of J. A. Smith and W. D. Ross) 11 vols. Clarendon Press: Oxford, 1908-31.

has no authority, no universal standard; that is completely authoritarian. Here, education cleaves to life; there, it is divorced from it. One is condemned for its lingering inclination toward mental discipline; another, because it offers no mental hazards, cannot strengthen the mind. Preparation for "success" is confessedly the aim of one education; at the intrusion of such mundane matters, the other is displeased, or professes indifference. So it goes ad infinitum. Though variously expressed, and often involving hidden terms, the vast volume of criticism boils down to preoccupation with the question of "liberal" versus "vocational" education.

This is clearly an old battle, indeed a perennial one. Several ages, as has been shown, engaged in it. Each reached a *new* decision, in part similar, partly dissimilar to those that went before and those that came after it. Notwithstanding the excellence, which may be granted, or the seeming finality of one solution or another in its own time, the issue is live today; and good, bad, or indifferent, there will be a decision. The problem is real; it is inevitable. The latest solution but one, no longer suffices. Classical humanism, at its best, rehabilitated the decisions of antiquity which, with slight modifications, served modern class societies as it had those of the past. Since the sixteenth century, however, numerous forces—a religious reformation, the scientific movement and the consequent technological revolution, an expanding world of commerce and industry, the naturalistic philosophy, the rise of political liberalism and the progressive extension of its implications, and the advent of a fuller, more precise knowledge of human capacities—have altered the world radically, both spiritually and materially.

It is beside the point, here, to argue life's improvement or debasement: the crucial fact is that it's basically different.

The net effect of such a profound, many-sided metamorphosis is to throw the old, oft-settled, oft-reopened question of liberal versus vocational education into the lap of modern society. The "disciplinary interlude," sketched above, was one phase of an effort—an abortive, rear-guard action—to meet the impact of social change on education. It may be noted too, *en passant*, that those who are convinced of life's progressive debasement since the sixteenth century, and profess to see its approaching doom, either fly from realities, or prescribe the nostrums of ages past to heal the diseased social body of today.

History, holding a mirror up to life, may function as guidance, providing perspective, orientation, a sense of direction. But one must read inquiringly and with discrimination, not blindly imitate; and keep the mind's eye on present knowledge as well as on the past. So doing, we find some roads excellent to follow; others to avoid. What does the mirror tell us of liberal education at its best in Hellas? It included at Athens letters and music; physical culture, balanced, ideally, with mental; aesthetic and moral training; and preparation for the highest vocation of free men—politics. The city government was nonauthoritarian. The mirror shows neither authoritarian priesthood, sacred book, nor religious lawgiver to impose supernatural sanctions on the mind, nor appeal to pain of punishment to come. These roads, educational and social, seem solid, rather broad, well planned; they are good, judged in terms of what we know of human drives and potentialities. But a good road is good only for those who can reach it. The mirror shows numerous blocks which effectively limited access to, and movement on, the road. The reconstructions of philosophers removed some of them, theoretically; others they seem to have re-enforced.

What were these blocks and hindrances in the practice of liberal education; what was their source? They were rooted in the limitations of society itself: slavery; the subjection of women; the incidence of private wealth, and the resultant discrepancies between rich and poor; a prejudice against most manual labor and gainful occupations. Liberal education was an education for free men, competent to fit them for freedom. The exclusive effect of slavery and subjection is obvious; the bearing of wealth and poverty, less so, is commonly overlooked in eulogies on Athenian education. Yet Plato says plainly that education depended on the family's means, the sons of the rich beginning school earliest and remaining the longest.[2] Some of the poorer sort knew only letters, and that badly; others managed, somehow, to triumph despite poverty of origin.

Bias against *banausic* arts, despite Solon's law, arose naturally in a slaveholding society, and left its impression even in the keenest, most idealistic formulations on education. Agriculture alone was an exception, fit for free men, for gentlemen. Socrates had a good word for the "smell of honest toil," loved by free men.[3] Other "useful arts" were characterized variously: "vulgar," "illiberal," "mean." Plato assigned them to artisans, noncitizens.[4] Aristotle condemned the vulgar arts which deform the body, and "all paid employments" which "absorb and degrade the mind."[5] Clearly, so stigmatized, they could have no part in a liberal education, the education of a leisure class.

[2] *Protagoras*, 326. *The Dialogues of Plato*. (Trans. by B. Jowett) 5 vols. Oxford University Press: New York, 1892.
[3] Xenophon: *Symposium*, II, 4. *Symposium and Apology*. (Trans. by O. J. Todd) (With C. L. Brownson's *Anabasis*) William Heinemann: London, 1922.
[4] *Republic*, VII, 522; *Laws*, I, 644; VIII, 846.
[5] *Politica*, VIII, 2.

Roman society, embodying similar social limitations, accepted the general pattern of Athenian education which had developed, save that Rome demurred at dancing, and scoffed at the Greek gymnasium as a nursery of soldiers. Christianity, although in principle opposed to the most pernicious evils of pagan society, made peace with the world and its inequalities, promising rewards and rest hereafter for the heavy-laden. Although it credited woman with a soul worth saving, it did not emancipate her from subjection, or open the paths to social eminence and power, such as men enjoyed. By taking leave of the world, women might gain an education, such as monasteries afforded men. In Europe of the Middle Ages and of early modern times, the masses of men and women led indeed a servile existence. They had only the "education of life." There was no mass education. Schooling, even when it merited in some degree the term "liberal," was for a very small privileged class, whose cultural opportunities the lower strata shared only occasionally and by dint of good fortune. Grammar—literature in a broad sense—once regarded as first and foremost of the liberal arts, had only a brief moment of popularity at a few schools in the twelfth century, and was then submerged by logic, once banned by Christians but later re-enlisted in the service of theology. Most of the higher education in cathedral schools and universities—being training in theology (the queen of sciences in the Middle Ages), law, medicine, and aiming at professional success and gainful employment—would not qualify as "liberal" by Plato's standard, or by Aristotle's. Strangely enough, some who today eulogize the medieval pattern of life and education, and recommend it as a path of salvation from chaos, demand for our age a liberal education totally divorced from professional and gainful ends.

2

Liberal education of China was similar, yet dissimilar, to that of Hellas. Athenian practice differed from the philosophical reconstructions. Rome's education imitated but, even at its best, did not match Athens'. Despite common elements, the intellectual world of Aristotle and that of the Christian scholastics were poles apart. Classical humanistic education, though it differed sharply from that of Rome and Hellas, had yet more in common with them than with the training of the most liberally educated logicians of the thirteenth century. Similarly, liberal education today necessarily steers a course in some respects new, in channels untraversed and but little explored. It must make use of some old instruments; it must devise and learn how to employ some new ones.

What are the essential features of the new social order in which liberal education must function today? Political liberalism, deeply indebted to Stoic ideas of natural right and reason, set forth the doctrine of man's right to self-rule. Since first adopted as a principle, its implications have been vastly extended. Social changes, the emancipation of slaves and the release of women from subjection, in the nineteenth century, broadened the base of democracy beyond the fondest dreams of antiquity. This revolutionary experiment with mass democracy makes a liberal education universally necessary, on political grounds if on no other. Industrial and technological changes, no less revolutionary, have brought *leisure* to all. Leisure is a primary factor which makes that liberal education possible. These same technological advances that have given man leisure have likewise given him one world. For that world he needs a government. Only by education for one world can he form such a government and fit himself to maintain it. The origin of basic principles involved lies deep in past history; an appreciation of that history should go far in strengthening men and women today for the arduous task of translating ideas into actuality.

Now liberal education in times past was always designed for the free, the socially and politically competent elements of society. These constituted an elite, variously selected. Their education was defined as that fit for free men, fit to make them free. Today the free are the whole mass of the population, men and women, naturally talented or untalented, rich or poor. There is neither acknowledged an elite of blood or of wealth, nor any other special class whose authority transcends that of the whole people. They are the reservoir whence flows all legislative power to make and unmake governments —a right which extends even to revolutionary change, as Jefferson and Lincoln said, if other means fail.[6] There exist, indeed, gross inequalities and injustices, which by no means square with this principle—vestigial remnants of times past that have not been erased. Against them democracy fights, and keeps vigilant watch against new threats of infringement of the heritage of free government.

The instruments of political power are in the hands of the people; their minds, however, have never been fully instructed in, nor have habits been formed adequately for, their use. If they were so, there would be some changes. Plato speculated about the need of kings being philosophers, or philosophers becoming kings. Now the masses have become king—*vox populi suprema lex*. Their primary function is to govern themselves. Their liberal education is, above all else,

[6] *The Writings of Thomas Jefferson*, IV, 370. (Ed. by P. L. Ford) 10 vols. G. P. Putnam's Sons: New York, 1892-99; *Letters and Addresses of Abraham Lincoln*, 197. H. W. Bell: New York, 1903.

to fit them for that function which Aristotle called the "master art"[7]—since it includes and directs all others—the first vocation of free men. For man is political by nature,[8] and only through the state is his "good life" possible.

Aristotle's conception of happiness as an end, good in itself, not a means,[9] is useful. As a principle it is sound, despite limitations of experience and scientific knowledge that led Aristotle, as we think now, into several errors: *e.g.*, that slaves and women, shortchanged by nature, lack rational capacity, and are, therefore, destined to be ruled by others. These we judge serious errors, even were scientific evidence lacking on the point; for we see those once enslaved and women who had neither education nor political rights functioning ably in science, philosophy, politics—or, if not well, at least no worse than men. Happiness, according to Aristotle's thesis, is a state resulting from performance of the functions naturally belonging to anything. Human functions are of three orders, two of them shared with other parts of the living world: nutrition and growth; sensation; and reason, which distinguishes man from animals. Human beings attain happiness when they function fully, but not excessively, in these domains. The lower functions are indispensable to the good life, but they must be ruled by the highest—reason. This principle of happiness, the resultant of proper functioning, Aristotle applied to the state. Its function is to promote and direct all the functions proper to man. A state is happy when it performs well its proper functions. A nonfunctioning, or a malfunctioning state is an unhappy one. It is in danger. Persistent malfunctioning, or nonfunctioning, means disease, decay, and death, as history witnesses.

[7] *Ethica Nicomachea,* I, 2.
[8] *Politica,* I, 2.
[9] *Ethica Nicomachea,* I, 2, 7.

Aristotle was concerned even with the proper functioning of *slaves*—in the master's interest—that they work and be punished as necessary, be well fed and well used, the abler among them to be not without appropriate honor and reward.[10] American democracy cannot be less concerned with the full, normal functioning of *all*, as *free* men and women. "We hold these truths to be self-evident, that all men are created equal, that they are endowed by their Creator with certain unalienable Rights, that among these are Life, Liberty, and the pursuit of Happiness." As yet, however, the United States of America, the richest country in the world, neither houses, feeds, nor clothes her members adequately. For the happiness of the commonwealth, as well as for that of individual citizens, the state must so order affairs that all may be educated in conformity with their capacities and the requirements of their work; may have work suitable to their capacity and education, be well rewarded, and thus enabled to supply the basic elements necessary to physical well being.

But remuneration, directly or indirectly, must go far beyond the supplying of these minimal demands. The good life is more than food and raiment. To be well born, to have health, strength, good stature, athletic ability, beauty, plenty of friends and children, wealth, fame, honor, virtue, good luck besides, and to grow old happily—all were reckoned by Aristotle[11] among the "constituent parts" of man's happiness. Some of these are of nature; most of them are contingent on a wise ordering of the state.

Democracy can neither make all wealthy nor all virtuous. It can provide, however, against extremes of wealth and

10 *Oeconomica*, I, 5.
11 *Rhetorica*, I, 5.

poverty which inevitably defeat the attainment of other elements essential to the happiness of all. Wealth and poverty
have a direct bearing on vice and virtue. If wealthy, surely
one may be liberal and magnanimous; but wealth often invites
intemperance. Poverty cannot support liberality, much less
magnificence; if it discourages some forms of intemperance,
it may fall heir to others.

Of gravest import is the bearing of low pay and poverty on
the wastage of human resources. In low wage groups environment provides little encouragement. The extent of the loss of
talents through failure to discover and develop them is unknown, "but there can be little doubt that the losses of this
kind are enormous."[12] In the United States (1938) 850 of
every thousand entered high school, but only 450 finished; of
these, 150 entered college, or other higher institutions, but
only 70 took the bachelor's degree. A very much smaller percentage of children from lower-class families expect to go to
college.[13] Studies in Indiana, Maryland, and Pennsylvania
show the impact of economic stratification on education.
"Education like other social characteristics," Rosander says,
"is a matter of the income of the family. . . ." Free high
schools fall far short of "equal [educational] opportunity so
long as there is such an uneven distribution of family income
as now exists."[14]

[12] Gemmill, P. F.: *The Economics of American Business*, 434. Harper &
Brothers: New York, 1930; "14 per cent of all families [of two or more persons]
received less than $500 . . . [1935-36]; 42 per cent less than $1000; 65 per
cent less than $1500; 87 per cent less than $2500."—National Resources Committee: *Consumer Incomes in the United States, Their Distribution in 1935-36*,
pp. 2 *f*. Government Printing Office: Washington, 1938.

[13] Warner, W. L., Havighurst, R. J., and Loeb, M. B.: *Who Shall Be Educated?* 51, 66. Harper & Brothers: New York, 1944.

[14] Rosander, A. C.: "The Economic Stratification of Youth and Its Social
Consequences." *Jour. Educ. Research* (Apr., 1939) XXXII, 602 *f*.

3

There has been much talk of balancing the budget in years gone by. Looking at education, it seems equally necessary to balance the curriculum. Long out of balance, both are in a markedly worse condition as a consequence of two wars. That either budget or curriculum, being in a sad state, will be readily brought to a right balance, no one in his senses will suppose. If education, to change the figure, were by happy effort brought to an even keel, ever new forces from the boundless social deep would upset that balance and produce some new list. For though education be, as Plato said, the "first and fairest thing" that men ever have, it takes wrong directions and is ever in need of rectification. Today, the heavy list is toward a specialization and splintering of subject matter, professionalism and commercialism, which leave little time or energy for some matters of gravest importance. On wide watery wastes one needs a compass. Is there no instrument, or set of principles, to guide us amid the wild wastes of over-specialization and kindred tendencies?

Guidance will be found in a genuine humanism, which addresses itself to man, his life today, and the demands that they impose, rather than to subject matter per se, to discipline for the sake of discipline, to a great tradition because it is a great tradition, or to theology or philosophy because someone once thought them a pathway to the stars. All will gain some discipline, perhaps 20 per cent or even more in optimum cases; some will turn to a certain subject for the sheer joy of it; these will revel in great books; those may climb theology's stairway. But what does man and his life today require, that he be free? For happiness, his *body* first requires care and culture. Hand, mind, and tongue are the instruments of *communication,* on which all his enlightenment and civilized enjoyment of life depends. Unfitted to *labor,* he will starve. Unschooled in *politics,* even though he labor, he will die anyway. Were these realms of man's education reduced to order, should we not confidently permit him to be the architect of his freedom?

In what follows, pertaining to these several areas of man's life and education, details of amount of this and that specific subject, books to be read, exercises to engage in, are shunned. These will always admit of some latitude, provided the central principles be clarified, agreed upon, and practiced. Failing of agreement on principles will, of course, leave education confused, as it is today. Likewise, the usual emphasis on the divisions of education in discussions of liberal education, assigning it to college primarily, with now and then a nod toward high schools, and no word of elementary beginnings in school and family, is here avoided. Americans seem to have gone too far in their departmentalizing of educational thinking. The education of man is a continuous affair. Liberal education, properly considered, does not begin at the college level; it may, under favorable conditions, be continued there, and—especially important in this age of technology with its accompanying leisure—into adult life.

If American democracy is intelligently concerned about liberal education—an education fit for free men, fit to make them free—where must it begin, what are the first problems it faces? It must start with physical well-being; without body there is no mind to speak of. That must be a continuing concern from beginning to the end of schooling, and throughout life. Intelligence quotients have been found to rise significantly in improved environments. *Mens sana in corpore sano,* a sound principle of antiquity, was never fully applied, and still is not. The few have adequate nutrition, opportunity and facilities for recreation, physical and mental, and proper provision for sanitation, health, and medical care. The many have not. While a study of the Educational Policies Commission (1940) stated that food consumption per individual in the United States approached what would be termed "gluttony" elsewhere in the world,[15] just shortly before that we were informed that one-third of the nation were "ill fed." And this was termed "an understatement." "Malnutrition affects from one-third to one-half of our population." This and its consequent diseases, "rickets, 'working-class' anemia, and pellagra, and lessened resistance to all diseases," constitute "one of our most urgent problems."[16]

In respect to health, medical science has vastly reduced infant mortality; and the span of life, greatly increased in the past century, now ranges from 59.9 years for the non-white to 67.9 for the white population. Vastly more could be accomplished, but agencies are far from adequate. Said the American Youth Commission, 1939: "The facilities now available to young people are wholly inadequate to ensure that the resources of modern science will be applied to the highest development of their health and physical fitness. These facilities are inadequate for health instruction and physical examination as well as for remedial care."[17]

Health costs money, but it can be bought. The old adage still holds good: an ounce of prevention is worth a pound of cure. People are offered a surfeit of nostrums, too little that would keep them well. Housing is related to health of mind

[15] *Education and Economic Well-Being in American Democracy*, 55. Educ. Policies Commission, Nat. Educ. Assoc.: Washington, 1940. For further reference to bearing of environment on intelligence scores, see *infra*, 274.

[16] Epstein, L.: "One-Third Ill Fed." *Nation* (Aug. 19, 1939) CXLIX, 191 *f*.

[17] American Council on Education, American Youth Commission: *A Program of Action for American Youth*, 11. Washington, 1939.

and body, both of which are needed for individual happiness, and for satisfactory functioning in the world's work. Rich America has fallen far short of human need in this respect. War accentuated the housing shortage; it did not create it. Even in 1939 the United States Housing Authority judged us 6,000,000 housing units short; by 1950 another 10,000,000 would be needed.[18] Sanitary facilities are woefully inadequate in public buildings and private homes. Of 37,325,470 dwellings in the nation, 14,320,519 (about 40 per cent) have neither bathtub nor shower, according to the *Census Housing Report*, 1940. And 1,018,364 (93,221 of them in city areas) have no "toilet or privy."[19]

For many centuries the Western world suffered from a doctrine, held by Christian ascetics, that man should disregard or suppress his natural tendency to play. Games were a devil's snare, set for young and old alike, but most dangerous and pernicious in youth. Puritanism in this country, akin to, but less severe than that which earlier pervaded strict Christian circles, left its stern impression on American education. While certain Colonial communities were less godly, and enjoyed games and merrymakings with considerable abandon, it was not till the early nineteenth century that American schools began gradually to relinquish the old dogma. Play began to be restored to the position which some of the early humanists, following ancient theory and practice, had assigned it. Ultimately, under the influence of naturalistic philosophy, play came fully into its own, being itself

18 The New York Trust Company: "Housing and Homes: Problems of Public and Private Shelter." *Index* (Autumn, 1939) XIX, 41; *Education and Economic Well-Being*, 61; Abrams, C.: *The Future of Housing*. Harper & Brothers: New York, 1946.

19 Cited, *NEA Jour.* (Jan., 1947) XXXVI, 15, from C. M. Olson and N. D. Fletcher, *Learn and Live*.

recognized as education, a means whereby nature promotes growth and nutrition in man, even as she does in lower forms of the living world.

Theoretically this was so. Practice changed slowly. There is yet a long way to go. Many adults, teachers as well as parents, still entertain the view that play is something apart from education—a necessary concession, perhaps, to a perverse nature, if no longer the devil, so that more work may be done. America would do well to recognize that in the earliest years, the happiest development of children is conditioned primarily by proper nutrition, plenty of spontaneous play and rest. Public authorities and educational leaders should exert themselves, first, to provide the means—public and school playgrounds, buildings, pools, and needed equipment for all games and exercises, judged best by the most competent physical education experts; second, to grant liberal time in elementary schools, secondary institutions, and colleges for such a helpful stimulus to mind and body as play alone affords. Liberal education is impossible without plenty of leisure, and suitable employment of that leisure time. One may well reflect on the fact that liberal education in Athens was shared about equally, apparently, between the teaching place and the palaestra.

The very suggestion that American schools fall short in provision for play is apt to be met with the assertion that "too much is already done in that direction; schools have become play places; they ought to be devoted to more serious matters." It is, indeed, true that American communities are play-conscious; their schools, especially higher and secondary institutions, devote much time and money to sports, and have set periods (as a rule, eighty to ninety minutes per

week; often a farce for lack of equipment) for gymnasium
and playground activities. But it is written so large that one
may run and read: KEEP OFF; RESERVED FOR THE
SQUAD. The best interest of the pupils, collectively, is sacrificed to exhibition athletics, the preparation of teams for
interscholastic competition. What is given to five, nine, or
eleven men, and their substitutes, on school and college
teams, in money, time, energy, expert trainers and coaches,
is enormous. At the same time, and partly because of this,
the provisions for others are generally inadequate, often
niggardly.

The choicest places to play, magnificent show grounds, set
aside for public exhibitions, cannot be used between games
by the general student body. In higher institutions, and in
high schools, too, but less so, exhibition athletics have become
a stupendous commercial enterprise, whose pressures, fortunes, and misfortunes often wreck coaches and players. One
recalls Aristotle's judgment that training boys too early and
too strenuously, in order to win crowns at Olympia, made
them unfit in later years.[20] Even if no such injury occurs,
such elaborate training for a commercialized, competitive
exhibition makes what should be part of general education
the most highly professionalized feature of college and university experience. Any youth who really makes good on a
crack college or university team can go into a lucrative job
as a professional. Such professional training, such grueling
labor at a game, suggests a problem in semantics: Why are
collegiate sports called amateur? Of such competitions, whose
rewards are great, and venality not unknown, one might say
with Aristophanes:

20 *Politica*, VIII, 4.

Wealth can see, my boy!
For Wealth is always highly sympathetic
With literary games, and games athletic.[21]

Ultimately, professionalism brought decay to Greek athletics, and effectively defeated the once-prized ideal of harmony and balance of mind and body.[22] Here too, despite the "Gates Plan," the "No Gates Plan," and Carnegie Reports, educational institutions, by condoning professional expertness, help defeat physical culture as a phase of liberal education. There are, happily, signs of improvement in certain directions. Mass sports programs in some colleges and universities are not only soundly conceived but fairly well executed and supported. Elsewhere, however, they are starved.

Individual and social losses accrue from shortcomings in another area. Just as refusal to face squarely the need for play facilities, and to finance them adequately, defeats the efforts of the wisest physical culture experts, so penny-pinching and public apathy have combined to deny children and youth adequate public playgrounds. What a wealth of talent is born to die unknown! Outright death, in appalling figures, is chargeable to the fact that children play in crowded city streets and dirty alleys, simply because they have no playgrounds. Who speaks of liberal education for dead souls? Even if physical life be spared, moral life is adversely affected. Delinquency of youth proceeds undoubtedly from many sources. It is acknowledged, however, that it can be

---

[21] *Plutus*, 1159-63. *Aristophanes*. (Trans. by B. B. Rogers) 3 vols. William Heinemann: London, 1924.

[22] Woody, T.: "Professionalism and the Decay of Greek Athletics." *Sch. and Soc.* (Apr. 23, 1938) XLVII, 521-28. For documentation of proselyting, professionalism, commercialism, and open subsidizing of athletics, and a brief bibliography bearing on efforts to regulate collegiate athletics, see Frederick W. Luehring, "The National Collegiate Athletic Association," *Journal of Health and Physical Education* (Dec. 1947) XVIII, 707-09, 751-53.

reduced by adequate provision for leisure-time activities. Certain crowded cities seem to have found in recreation "the best single delinquency preventive yet evolved." A recent Teen-age Conference pointed out that the "neighborhoods of greatest delinquency have virtually no recreation facilities."[23]

Health of mind and body for adults as well as for children is dependent on recreational activity. Under the conditions of a simpler socioeconomic order, the normal activities of men and women kept the body in better tone. They punched no time clocks, lived more in the open, and their work commonly involved an interplay of mental and physical activity. Besides, they engaged in spontaneous impromptu play. This has been changed, most drastically in the world of labor and business. Industrial and commercial establishments need to recognize this, and to provide for recreation. Some have done so. Part of it should be remedial in character, determined on competent medical advice and that of physical experts. If liberality be a virtue, it would bring its own reward! As Whitehead observes, "To speed up production with unrefreshed workmen is a disastrous economic policy. Temporary success will be at the expense of the nation, which, for long years of their lives, will have to support worn-out artisans—unemployables."[24]

The numbing effect of working long hours, under the pressure of tight organization, has been felt by all so engaged. The best probably feel it most keenly. A. E. once wrote:

23 "Pyramid Club," Philadelphia, Jan. 13, 1945, Magistrate Joseph Rainey presiding. Mimeographed report; cf. Burt, C.: The Young Delinquent, 89 ff. University of London Press: London, 1944; Strang, R., Charters, W. W., et al.: Juvenile Delinquency and the Schools, 115. The Forty-Seventh Yearbook of the Nat. Soc. for the Study of Educ., Pt. I. (Ed. by N. B. Henry) University of Chicago Press: Chicago, 1948.

24 Whitehead, A. N.: The Aims of Education and Other Essays, 90. Macmillan Company: New York, 1929.

"When I was a boy I knew for myself how a great business organisation can draw the soul into itself and dull it to its own inhuman image." "When one works nearly twelve hours a day, hard work, there is not much spirit left for other things. . . ."[25] A. E. rebelled and ran away. Years later he recalled, like a nightmare, the "fierce inhuman activity of body and mind, the exhaustion of energy when the day's work was over." The "twelve hours" may raise a cynical query on the part of employers today: "Working only seven or eight hours, with time off for lunch, what need have you of provision for recreation? Now, when I was a boy. . . ." Nevertheless, eight hours, more or less, of speed-up, as we know it today, brings sooner the need for rest and recreation, and more of it. Not everyone can run away.

Communication is the key to man's enlightenment. Break communications, and the mind begins to grow dark. Throughout millenniums past, several forms of communication, the greatest mental avenues of man—*speech, letters, science, art*—have been perfected. Teach man today to use them well (some, for consumption chiefly; others, creatively as well), and he will be equipped to tread the mental pathways of the past and present, and to deal competently with tomorrow. Each form of communication employs instruments and techniques for the discovery of meaning and its dissemination. *Speech,* to be understood, conforms to laws, and requires a forum; *letters* require writing, books, newspapers, periodicals, libraries; *science* has need of laboratories and books; *art* must have studios, museums, and other means of exhibition. Screen, radio, and television—these are important re-

[25] Fox, R. M.: "A. E.: A Voice of Irish Democracy." *Progress* (Oct., 1946) I, no. 2, p. 41.

cent acquisitions in the realm of means of dissemination, which multiply manifold the potentialities of the basic arts of discovery and communication of meaning. A word of caution is needed: there is a tendency to confuse basic arts with those instruments and techniques which merely extend the range of reception. Who has not experienced the unhappy result: through newspapers, screen, and radio, men and women have gained the whole world for an audience; but many have nothing of importance to say, and can't say it!

Fortunately, there are abler voices, with something to say and skilled in speaking. But they, particularly, are subject to an ever greater danger. The instruments of communication —the forum, the book, the laboratory, the museum, and the rest—are ever liable to seizure, open or covert; and are subject to influences, direct and indirect, which readily make them a means of mental enslavement rather than of enlightenment.

The problem of freedom of communication is age-old. Socrates was put to death. Plato proposed to exercise censorship in his ideal state—for a good end. Always, restriction is allegedly for a good purpose, as some one—an individual, a church, a state, a party—conceives it. Of this we may be sure: when thinking and its expression, whatever the mode may be—literary, scientific, and artistic—are locked in a closet, liberal education becomes a mere name. There is, to be sure, no absolute freedom. In judging the education of any people one must ask: is their liberty of discovery and communication greater or less than it was yesterday; does it give fair promise of becoming greater tomorrow? If freedom of the press, radio, and cinema in America is not to be less tomorrow than yesterday and today, a strenuous fight must be waged to that end.[26]

In the domain of speaking much remains to be desired. It is depressing to reflect that when radio has made speech potentially more important than it was in Cicero's day, oratory, correct speaking, is so uncommon, one is almost tempted to say, a lost art. Who expects eloquence in the House? How seldom one finds it even in the Senate! What a volume of fumbling, incoherent speech gains the air! What do schools make of speaking? Should training in speaking be elective in colleges, or be stressed only for those who go out for debating? Once, teachers required a proper sentence in reply to a question. Now, too often, they accept a half-swallowed word, a phrase, a grunt or groan. It has been observed that speaking maketh a ready man, writing an exact one. One might well recall the relation between the two. Cicero, a master of both, insisted that to speak well one must first write what he intends to say. One does not become a good speaker just by speaking; indeed, by such a process one may become a bad speaker. Writing, he called the best *"teacher of oratory."*[27]

Many now reach high school, even college and graduate school, who cannot yet speak their mother tongue coherently, or write it grammatically. Both are to be gained by practice, by criticism, by doing it over again and again. Anything worth rereading, Horace observed, must be written with the

[26] The Commission on Freedom of the Press: *A Free and Responsible Press.* University of Chicago Press: Chicago, 1947; *The Authoritarian Attempt to Capture Education,* chap. 3. 2d Conference on the Scientific Spirit and Democratic Faith. King's Crown Press: New York, 1945; Hocking, W. E.: *Freedom of the Press, A Framework of Principle.* University of Chicago Press: Chicago, 1947.

[27] *On Oratory,* I, 33; II, 22. *Cicero: On Oratory and Orators; with His Letters to Quintus and Brutus.* (Trans. by J. S. Watson) George Bell and Sons: London, 1891.

blunt end of the stylus.[28] Many an opportunity for expression in writing is lost in schools today. In short-form, so-called objective tests, a check mark takes the place of yes, no, a sentence, or a paragraph. Students ask: "Do we have to write, or will you give us several answers and let us check the right one?" Whatever may be gained in time and in accuracy of measurement, is lost so far as the arts of expression of meaning are concerned.

With the invention of writing began a great metamorphosis of man's mind. Plato represented Ammon, King of Egypt, as condemning Theuth, the inventor of letters, because the new device would weaken memory.[29] A wandering rhapsode could exhibit marvels of memory; but what is written down need not be held ever ready on the tongue. Yet in a profound and more important sense, writing extended man's mind—gave to each a memory of ten thousand years, or as long as time remains. The Hebrews became the People of a Book. In varying degree, others became so. Man's mind in each new generation was potentially richer than before. Still, there was truth in Ammon's words that with written symbols men might indeed hear of more things, yet learn nothing, and, in general, know nothing. As Rousseau said, condemning an education that was wholly bookish, by teaching a child to read one teaches him to say what he does not know. The gain through writing, however, was great, notwithstanding the loss to sheer memory. And if there was danger of bibliolatry and confusion of meaning of the written word, there was, to offset it, a grand prospect of enhancing criticism by meticulous comparison of parallel traditions.

[28] *Satires*, I, 10. *Horace for English Readers*. (Trans. by E. C. Wickham) Clarendon Press: Oxford, 1903.
[29] *Phaedrus*, 274-75.

Letters became, then, an important, though not the sole, means of liberal education. They function *first*, as the instrument of transmission; second, pursued more broadly and critically, they may minister to the cultivation of that "sober sense of honest doubt," which, "keeps human reason hale and stout." We need to read; and we need to read critically. Both are essential to free men who would continue to be so. But unless one reaches first base, he cannot make second. Many do not reach first base: after a hundred years of public and private effort, the United States had (1940) about ten million illiterates; and nearly two million school-age youth were not in school. The usual standard for literacy is very low. By the Army test of World War I—reading and understanding newspapers and writing a letter—a quarter of the draftees were illiterate.

The first step in learning to understand by interpreting artificial symbols is, under any conditions, somewhat baffling. The feat, made needlessly more difficult if complicated by an unfamiliar tongue, is more readily accomplished through the vernacular. There is no sound reason why it should not be. The pillars of the Republic would not fall. Only an old tradition stands in the way: that minorities, if schooled at all, must learn the language of the master-folk. A truly democratic society need not pay tribute to such an imperial mode of thought. The dominant language and literature, that of the state itself, would not suffer, though begun later. In our polyglot society much would be gained, culturally, through preservation of each tongue in purity and the ability to read the great literatures composed therein. Were Italian children to read the *Commedia*, Germans to read *Faust*, Russians *War and Peace*, and other masterpieces in the originals, they would not, therefore, contemn Shakespeare or neglect Emerson. They might fairly be expected to prize them more. Neither would their first sips of science, or of political understanding, suffer from not being drawn through English straws. In fact, those efforts should be more felicitous and effective, unhandicapped by the simultaneous difficulty of learning an unfamiliar tongue. Certainly the children of minority cultures might well prize more a democracy that did not begin by robbing them of their own cultural heritage. There would be an additional, far-reaching benefit. Everyone knows that modern foreign languages have been poorly taught by American teachers who acquired their knowledge and skill rather late and all too hurriedly. Children from Chinese, French, German, Italian, Portuguese, Russian, and Spanish families, who had kept their mother tongues and literatures alive, would be a grand nursery from which to draw foreign language teachers.

Another point bearing on letters as a central line of communication calls for attention: citizens of the United States, whether of English or other origin, need to know foreign languages better and in greater number today than they did yesterday. The frantic effort to gain a smattering of a foreign tongue or two, during the recent war, was amazing, and gratifying; but, at the same time, it is regrettable that it was necessary. We occupy a new world; we have existed in it—one can scarcely say *lived* in it—for some time, but we are only slightly aware of it. The atom bomb is not the key to unlock its gates and make all feel at home. Ennius boasted that he had three souls, Oscan, Latin, and Greek. Cato is said to have feared that Rome's empire would be lost when Romans imbibed Greek letters.[30] It was lost ultimately, but not for that

---

30 Plutarch: *Cato*, 12, 23. *Plutarch's Lives.* (Trans. by B. Perrin) 11 vols. William Heinemann: London, 1914-26; *The Attic Nights of Aulus Gellius*, XI, 8. (Trans. by J. C. Rolfe) 3 vols. William Heinemann: London, 1927-28.

reason. Cato finally gave in and learned Greek in his old age. Today many seem persuaded that the foundations of the Republic are laid in English grammar! Truly, our mother tongue is great and her literature rich. English carries one far, throughout the earth, for aught I know into the bright blue yonder! But the world into which young Americans are thrust today will be infinitely better understood by knowing foreign cultures, particularly those playing a great rôle today and tomorrow.

For some centuries past, for sound historic reasons, first emphasis has been laid on learning the languages of Greece and Rome. Today, many who have laid aside all pleas for learning the ancient languages, still think almost wholly, apparently, in terms of the Graeco-Roman tradition, and emphasize that one must cleave to it because Western Europe is its heir. Certainly no one keenly aware of cultural continuities would slight that study. But it is equally true that that singleness of devotion which was comprehensible and defensible yesterday, falls short of a liberal education for the world of today. Regardless of the mode of their fathers, Western men and women urgently need to pass the cultural barriers which isolate them from China, India, the Arab world, and the Soviet Union. As letters first extended mind backward, giving man a potentially longer range and a better perspective of his own history and culture, and as Greek made the Roman a fitter man for the Mediterranean community he had done so much to form, so now foreign letters inevitably take first place in extending our minds laterally.

Greek and Latin were indispensable to a liberally educated man or woman after the fourteenth century. An army of copyists, editors, and translators were needed to bring the West abreast of a culture long obscured. A smaller proportion is at work today. We need them, and shall need them tomorrow, but not them alone. Another contingent of scholars —not so numerous, but growing—has long been at work making the thought of the Orient accessible in Western translations. There is every reason for taking advantage of their labor, and of supplementing what has already been done, to make possible a liberal education which should be as fitting for our world as that of the ancients was for theirs. It would be a colossal error to think that cultural exchange follows a one-way road. As the Orient has become acquainted with, and has borrowed from us, the West will inevitably know and be influenced by the culture of the East.

Science is language, a means of penetration, interpretation, and communication in realms where English and other letters do not suffice. In antiquity the language of science was but little developed; it was still so at the beginning of the New Life of Western Europe. Consequently, liberal education took little or no thought of it, and that little attention was due to ancient authors who had gathered up what antiquity knew of the world of things. As modern sciences emerged, being newcomers, they were admitted only with difficulty into schools. Long cold-shouldered as no part of liberal education, it is not surprising that when sciences gained a solid footing, not a few of their sponsors affected to believe, or really did believe, that the new language and its learning were the be-all and end-all of a liberal education. The war between scientists and classicists in the nineteenth century must have made a Martian stare, had he been able to drop in on us in that which was after all, compared to ours, a very backward scientific age. "Why," he must have asked, "is not this new scientific language that you are learning to speak concerned with man and all his affairs, quite as much as your other letters?" Today there is no such open warfare. The field is quiet; the warring factions have withdrawn to their respective camps. But the returning visitor, inquiring after our mode of liberal education, might well wonder at the splendid isolation that sets off scientific departments and the "humanities" today. The barriers, raised first by historic necessity, and then fostered by specialists, may seem to serve them well. In any case, they do less injury to them than to those who need, and seek first of all, to grasp their world in its entirety, and may, thereafter, in so far as necessary, become specialists. Truly, as Cicero once said, the "grandeur of the sciences" is reduced by the "distribution and separation of their parts."[31]

The working scientist, worthy of his salt, is bound to be a specialist; though he should be more. Science, as a language—or as languages, for it has as many tongues as Babel cleft the world into—needs, in the first place, however, to be a general study, in so far as a liberal education is concerned; beyond that, a special area will be chosen by those whose life-work will be identified more or less closely with it. Teachers of youth, who teach them science, need, like teachers in other fields of knowledge and investigation, to recall Aristotle's observation: "Every systematic science, the humblest and the noblest alike, seems to admit of two distinct kinds of proficiency; one of which may be properly called scientific knowledge of the subject, while the other is a kind of educational acquaintance with it."[32]

What should one expect this "educational acquaintance" with science to contribute to man's liberal education? Above all things, it seems, one should learn the nature of science,

[31] *On Oratory*, III, 33-34.
[32] *De Partibus Animalium*, I, 1.

what it is, and its relation to our world. Too often, it is viewed from afar off, as though it were something mysterious; and from that it is an easy step to think that it may be evil. The reverse is true. Science is simply a method leading to organized, tested knowledge. Perhaps it would be well if youth learned to look upon science itself as an evolutionary step in man's thinking, a process which Cicero described thus: "For nothing can be reduced into a science, unless he who understands the matters of which he would form a science, has previously gained such knowledge as to enable him to constitute a science out of subjects in which there has never yet been any science."[33]

Society today is more perfectly organized than ever before. This is true, primarily, because more and more of scientific thinking has had its effect in the practical realm of action. Science, organized thought, has produced a better world than yesterday knew; it can produce a better one tomorrow. It is significant that whereas politicians and diplomats give daily evidence of their incapacity to get together and work in friendly coöperation with those of other nations, and are constantly dividing the world into good and bad and other highly unscientific categories, scientists conduct their study and convene their global assemblies in a fraternal, coöperative spirit. Why not persuade some of the ablest of them to serve in Congress, the State Department? Perhaps the time will come when an Einstein or a Shapley may hold the highest office in the land. Through knowledge united with action lies the road to the good life. Liberal education today would be unthinkable without science, man's greatest triumph in organized knowledge. Science, as method, should be applied more extensively and expertly to many fields.

[33] *On Oratory*, I, 41-42.

The results of centuries of scientific development are imposing. One should know many of them; but no education would serve man well which sought to make him a repository of them all. Probably most general of all values that a liberal education should afford is an acquaintance with the scientific method and enough experience of it to be a fair judge of its use in the hands of others. One should be able to read science, as one reads other letters, though he be neither scientist nor literary creator.

Besides acquaintance with the nature of science and its method, a liberal education will indubitably make clear the interrelationship of all sciences, and their human meaning. This calls for emphasis today, as never before, if for no other reason than that humanism and science have been so commonly regarded as opponents. A scientist and a grammarian may both fall short of humanism; but there is no inherent necessity for such a state of affairs in the grammar of science, or in the science of grammar. Interrelatedness of science as an aspect of humanism may perhaps best be realized through the history of science combined with a survey of the present scene. This should not stop short of showing the unfinished work of science: the uneven progress in certain fields of study to date and how necessary it is that the personal and social aspects of life be studied with energy and devotion, even as others have been, so as to rectify the vast unbalance between man's mastery of his material world and his relative incompetence in social science.

There is in some today an unreasoned fear of science, which, fostered by obscurantists, is often translated into hatred and contempt, and the scientist is made to seem a devil. Wars and all kinds of violence are laid at his door. Men, those say, should never have invented science or devised its applications. What is more obvious than that this very view shows the need of more, not less, schooling in scientific thinking, and the application of it in the realm of everyday social affairs. What is sadly needed today is not national support of certain sciences which have already given unwonted mastery over man's material domain, but a unified, coördinated effort, richly supported by public funds. We spend millions every year for research in natural and physical sciences, but we have spent very little on research in the social sciences, to find the solution of pressing problems in that area. Private funds are quite inadequate; and, even if adequate, they are all too likely to back scientific projects that promise profit, rather than be guided by a general view of the commonweal. National support of students of exceptional ability is certainly necessary. It is a commonplace that excellent talent is in many cases allowed to rust in idleness for lack of means to procure an education. To this wastage, that of a short-sighted wartime policy has been added—putting men into uniform who should have been continuing their scientific training.[34] It is a calamity to waste talent in war or in peace. It is no less calamitous to back with all the resources of government those sciences that can be relied on to build more mighty engines, while neglecting those that are sorely needed if that mighty power, already created, is to be governed and used for the well-being of all.

Science as an element of the education to fit men and women for freedom must deal with another broad problem: the destruction of myths. Man, untutored, is a great artificer of myths; as he grows in scientifically tested knowledge he destroys his own fabrication. Whenever science advances it

[34] Bush, V.: *Science the Endless Frontier*, 19. Government Printing Office: Washington, 1945.

negates myths; the best, critically educated men generally have the smallest store of them. "All scientists," Bain says, "are relatively free from both crude and subtle sacred myths."[35] Social scientists cling less to secular myths than do those in the fields of physical and biological science. Clearly, only by conscious, energetic, systematic, coördinated effort can this freedom of mind—which is what destruction of myths means—be brought to those who are themselves not scientists. This is potentially an important contribution of science teaching, so far as liberal education is concerned. If little is accomplished, it is not because it is impossible. Bain hit the nail on the head: "A deliberate attempt to disseminate the scientific habit of mind widely, especially as it pertains to social phenomena, might hasten the decay of secular myths." And this, of course, would be a revolution in politics, and in education which is a branch thereof.

An extraordinary myth, all the more persistent because sedulously propagated, is that certain areas of knowledge are the sources, if not, indeed, the only possible source, of all that man knows of values; and that science stands helpless to deal with those arcana, being itself capable of dealing only with the material world and objective "facts." Some scientists have doubtless concurred in this view; but by no means all. Chauncey D. Leake and other philosophical scientists and scientific philosophers have been concerned with a scientific approach to the question of values.[36] As Julian Huxley once said, it is not a question of the "insufficiency of science" but the need for "more science."

The hierarchy of the sciences, of the order and the amount

35 Bain, R.: "Man, the Myth-maker." Sc. Mo. (July, 1947) LXV, 67 f.
36 "Ethicogenesis." Sc. Mo. (Apr., 1945) LX, 245-53; Cf. Lamont, C.: Humanism as a Philosophy. Philosophical Library: New York, 1949.

of each to be taught, may be left to another occasion, save for a general observation. Traditionally, mathematics—parts thereof—was the beginning, and often the end, of science in schools. Considering the fundamental relationship of the oldest exact science to others, it seems properly to merit the central position today, so far as advanced levels of science teaching are concerned. At the very beginning of education, however, it seems probable that areas of descriptive sciences are more appropriate. Science in general education should give pleasure, as well as the most reliable view of things known. There was a certain aesthetic as well as intellectual value in the astronomy once taught, in that youth learned to enjoy a starry universe that today is often made nameless to them by neglect. From descriptive study, which may be quite non-quantitative, they may come betimes to number, quantity, and space. Even then, the science of how many and how much needs the rein, in the interest of harmony and balance with other aspects of a liberal education. Like the old Romans, Americans have been too much occupied with division of the *as*.

Now nothing is more obvious than that these goods of science are not to be had for young people at the hands of those who have been narrowly, even though excellently, trained as scientific specialists in one or more fields. The most difficult problem in disseminating anything novel is teachers. Teaching of Greek and Latin to ancient Romans often fell short for lack of competent teachers, as one can learn from Cicero, Suetonius, Quintilian, Pliny, and others. Classical humanism failed to deliver its message when, after a time, its instruction fell into the hands of Ciceronian stylists and formal disciplinarians. But failure and difficulty challenge the best in man. The gravest danger to liberal education today is, as has frequently been the case before, that, facing the need of redirection, which Plato knew it was always heir to, we may be led to seek it by reverting to some ancient mode, which is made by able propagandists to appear so fair, rather than face the more difficult and constructive task of charting a new course and going forward.

Art as language—a language of many forms (music, drawing, painting, sculpture, and the constructive arts), a means of discovery, expression, and communication—requires a place with other instruments of human understanding. Many who will never write a word worthy to be read and treasured may discover themselves and live forever as creators in tongues independent of letters. Art is creation and communication: the few will be able to discover and tell something of great moment in one or another artistic medium; the many, competent in smaller measure, will be able to see, hear, and feel. Art in education properly requires a place as creative effort and for consumption. It should begin early and be a continuing element. Like other studies designed for liberal education, art instruction should not overemphasize or hasten on to technical perfection. Raised to professional competence, the liberal end will be sabotaged. As Montaigne said, philosophy itself had been made such a difficult technical matter under the hands of specialists that it was unintelligible and useless. The message of art is naturally felt, experienced, and enjoyed—long before one proceeds to a critical, analytical, technical knowledge of it. Teachers once killed music in public schools by tearing it to pieces and putting it together again, so that one might *know* music! By a similar process great poems and plays, being made the chopping block of linguistic and literary analysis, have been reduced to cabbage, so far as appreciation by students is concerned. Was Horace only pretending when he scoffed at those who longed to see their works made "lesson-books" in schools?[37]

How slight the consideration given to art in institutions that should be homes of liberal education! Why is it so slight? Is it because an authoritative canon of studies reduced art (or elevated it, if one please) to the status of a mental discipline, and that canon, once crystallized and accepted, obscured rather effectively other views regarding the rôle of art in education? Partly, but not wholly so. Whatever the causes—they are doubtless plural—art in American education has been sadly neglected. The true humanist recognizes the importance of opening all the main avenues of human understanding. But there have been too few great humanists among us.

Art played a part, even unconsciously, in man's early labors. He made things useful, serviceable; moreover, he made them, in a measure, beautiful, as primitive pots, pans, and other wares testify. Beyond that, on occasion, he learned to create beautiful things—statues, pictures—serving no such immediately utilitarian end. They were, nevertheless, useful: their beauty pleased and refreshed him. Those unskilled, for one reason and another, in beautiful creation, desiring its benign refreshment, encouraged those who could satisfy their desire and adorn their leisure. Art was encouraged by a class that enjoyed leisure. Americans, having little leisure while they conquered a wilderness, gave but slight encouragement to creative art.

Men labor for the sake of leisure, as Aristotle taught. His view of labor may be in some respects inadequate. One is not "a free man," said Cicero, "who does not sometimes *do noth-*

[37] *Satires,* I, 10.

ing."[38] Both, living in a society ruled by a leisure class, prized art and reckoned its enjoyment among the various forms of leisure activity. Aristotle viewed art as recreation, a medicine for the soul, and judged it part of the liberal education of free men: music for intellectual enjoyment and refreshment; drawing, to make them better judges of beauty —not, as some thought, to keep men from making bad purchases.[39] Moreover, far from considering art as merely dextrous manipulation of materials—as some modern schools, which exalt some of Aristotle's teaching and ignore the rest, apparently do—he saw art as a category of thinking: art is creation, "involving a true course of reasoning."[40]

Now, modern technology has made leisure the possession of all. Art for the leisure enjoyment and refreshment of all is today within reach; but this is not yet fully appreciated. To exploit it, far more is necessary than purchasing collections, housing them, and opening them to the public. Men and women require a right mode of education in art, need to learn its tongues, as they learn the language of letters and science, so that they may understand the message transmitted by those means. A nation today that is fully awakened culturally, if it seeks the good life for all, neither neglects the idiom of art, nor treats it less generously than the language of letters and of science. When America so acts, we shall all, with Whitman, "hear America singing."

Education in America has long been bedeviled by a dispute about vocational *versus* liberal education. In consequence, "liberal" education has been academic; and vocational education has seemed better suited to slaves or

38 *On Oratory*, II, 6.
39 *Politica*, VIII, 3.
40 *Ethica*, VI, 4.

industrial serfs than free men. This academic isolation from life was unfortunate. Cicero—and who could speak to the point more persuasively, seeing that he became for centuries the Western learned world's beau ideal—constantly sought the marriage of the liberal and the practical. Knowledge, he maintained, is barren that is not put to the "service of mankind."[41] Seneca, too, complained: "We learn . . . not for life, but for the lecture-room."[42] To modernists, if Cicero be suspect, let Emerson speak: "Action is with the scholar subordinate, but it is essential. Without it he is not yet man."

It will help clarify the present conflict over vocational versus liberal education if we re-examine the historic sources. The *ancient* conception of leisure as a free-class prerogative has been noted. Liberal education was designed to fit that social pattern. Labor and its training were excluded, for labor was servile and vulgar—save for certain condescending exceptions. Thus agriculture, profiting still from early aristocratic associations, seemed to Socrates, Aristotle, and Cicero worthy of a free man, though they and others of the intellectual circle did not work at it. Cicero also admitted big business, with qualifications. Western European class society, logically enough, accepted this exclusive view of education as an intellectual affair isolated from the labors of the field, the factory, and the counting house. Our institutions today, especially colleges, are descendants of that age of class rule, and reflect its view of studies, although they can no longer live up wholly faithfully to that tradition.

What was the traditional view of liberal studies, more

41 *Offices*, I, 44-45. *Cicero's Three Books of Offices* . . . *On Old Age* . . . *On Friendship; Paradoxes; Scipio's Dream;* [and] . . . *Duties of a Magistrate.* (Trans. by C. R. Edmonds) George Bell and Sons: London, 1887.
42 *Epistle* CVI. *Seneca: ad Lucilium Epistulae Morales.* (Trans. by R. M. Gummere) 3 vols. William Heinemann: London, 1917-25.

precisely? It was, as Aristotle, a well-qualified spokesman, put it, that anything learned for the sake of gain and the vulgar arts tending to "deform the body" could not be reckoned as part of a liberal education.[43] How well did this principle serve? There was no difficulty, if one were entirely independent financially. But law, oratory, the whole training of the lawyer and public man, which embodied at Rome the Greek cycle of liberal studies, posed a difficult question: What of a lawyer's fee? Quintilian's answer—don't take fees, but gifts are another matter; or if one is in need, he may charge a fee, but make it small[44]—scarcely allows him to clear the wire without tearing his toga. Modern humanist educators, mindful of the ancient standard, may well feel misgivings over the salvation of lawyers in the heaven of liberally educated men. By the same token, those who have studied mathematics only to become teachers of mathematics, and so earn a livelihood, can scarcely claim mathematics as liberal education. The same standard would disqualify most masters of Latin and Greek. Even those who pursue logic and theology have their reward.

It seems clear that the advent of modern commerce and industry, and the associated political principle of classlessness (an ideal, not a thoroughgoing reality), have leveled the barriers of class division which antiquity and early Western society knew, and have simultaneously rendered invalid their conception of a liberal education, unsullied by contact with the world of work. For all now labor, save a very few who still have silver spoons at birth. And all now, although they labor, are free men, have leisure, are engaged in the most

[43] *Politica*, VIII, 2.
[44] *The Institutio Oratoria of Quintilian*, XII, 7, 8-12. (Trans. by H. E. Butler) 4 vols. Harvard University Press: Cambridge, 1921-36.

"intellectual" work imaginable, and are apt, nay, almost certain, to be put to work, for which they are paid—though inadequately. Can poverty of pay preserve gentility, even as it was once thought safeguarded if an impecunious Roman kept the fee small? Even if so, probably most men and women would gladly sacrifice gentility—at such a price. Perhaps even the impecunious Roman, not entirely convinced by Quintilian's dubious casuistry, would have sacrificed an uncertain gift for a certain fee!

One by one, certain supports of the ancient dichotomy have crumbled. Recognizing, as one must, that the passing of a leisure class of free men who ruled the state has undermined the old argument that liberal studies are those pursued without gain, or thought of gain, the continuing distinction between studies, classing them as liberal and illiberal on that basis, is a gossamer of self-deception. It has also been shown that another distinction claimed for "liberal" studies—that they are the ones that provide a universal discipline of mind—has been eroded and is reduced to, at best, one-fifth of its former claims, so far as scientific evidence goes. The preëminent value of direct education is scarcely open to dispute. Studies discipline the mind, primarily at least, in their own domains; the appreciable general training that is obtained is dependent on a strict observance of conditions, which schools generally have not met, but which they should strive to satisfy for the sake of the very modest portion of general discipline that may reasonably be expected. We are forced to conclude, apparently, that the liberal character of a study lies, *not* in its generally transferable discipline, and not in its association with, or sponsorship by, a leisure class, but in its *content*, in the contribution that it may fairly be expected to make to man's understanding of himself and of his world, and fit him to carry on happily therein, commensurably with nature's promise.

Now labor, as noted, has become part of the life of all men and women. Inevitably, therefore, the study of that which is inextricably bound up with the life of all, must be reckoned as part of man's preparation for a life of happiness. To eliminate it, to ostracize it, as many schools do, or profess a desire to do, would seem to label themselves less than liberal, for a man cannot in any full sense be free if he be compelled to wander blindly through a large area of his own life without a guide and a staff for his support. As a matter of fact, on this score, educational institutions are commonly not so far afield as their spokesmen sometimes make them appear to be; for, while so speaking, or advised to act contrarily, they actually give their students an education in French, Latin, mathematics, and science, not to mention less traditional studies, and this training is their chief preparation, adequate or inadequate as may be, to earn a living. Besides, colleges, and secondary schools too, offer them quite commonly the services of psychologists, vocational guidance, and the help of offices to secure employment. College youth are apt to think highly of Alma Mater, if her placement service is good enough to discover an opening for them, even as they regard with gratitude the aid of their natural mothers and fathers who do not affect a cold indifference as to whether they survive or perish.

Now what has been sketched out may well appear to many as a description of the degradation of once-noble studies. If to be put to use is to be degraded, then they are debased. Others, however, ridding the mind's eye of conceptions rooted in class societies, may be able to see that by being useful to all, and being understood by more and more men, and more fully, studies are all the more humanized and are therefore ennobled rather than dishonored.

We pass to another consideration. If letters, once a noble study reserved for the exclusive use of the few, have filtered down into the ranks of all men and women, may not the riddance of labor of its one-time slave connections, the many-sided applications of science in its present domains, and the resultant necessity of mingling a vast and profound intellectual content with the physical element, have elevated it to a place of honor on a par with a once exclusive body of knowledge?

Agriculture, despite the advent of slave labor in varying degrees in Greece and Rome, was still esteemed noble, worthy of the free man, as one may gather from Socrates, Aristotle, Cicero, Virgil, and others. Plato scoffed at business men, "stooping as they walk."[45] Cicero, however, admitted business into the charmed circle, as worthy of a free man—provided it were big business, and more particularly if by its gain estates might be acquired![46] Now if modern men of letters, who prize and seek to plumb the wisdom of Aristotle and Cicero, were to survey the present scene of agricultural labor, would they not be compelled to admit candidly that agriculture is a domain fit for free men and, more than that, a liberal study? And if one inclines to believe in trying to get as much discipline from a study as possible, and recognizes, as most do, that overcoming difficulties develops confidence in one's ability to overcome others, is there not difficulty in agriculture, as there is in any other science? In fact, it is a science in which are integrated a host of auxiliary sciences.

45 *Republic,* VIII, 555.
46 *Offices,* I, 42.

Similarly, if one admits Cicero's argument that big business is not unworthy of a free man, who shall say that in the modern world also it is not unworthy of free men and free women, and in a sense higher than Cicero had in mind? For has not business become a science of economics with its host of auxiliaries? If some object that, though difficult as a science and broadening by reason of the many-sidedness of its contacts with the whole wide world, it still is an ignoble one because it seeks a profit, one may recall that Cato, a liberally educated man in his day, seems to have advised buying cheap and selling dear. Or, one may turn business over to the state and so pursue its science in the interest of all, thus escaping the personal stain of studying economics and business law for private gain!

Agriculture, commerce, industry, and a world of sciences great and small, it is said, have no place in a university, for its true function, now "being rapidly obscured" and perhaps soon to be "extinguished,"[47] is to promote an intellectualism, conceived and promoted in antiquity and the Middle Ages. As for what is called "vocational" training, in contradistinction to the older professions, commonly dignified by the term "liberal," American educators are advised by Mr. Hutchins to "forget it." Let industry train its hands; that is no part of the educator's task. What would industry do? In the war, as everybody knows, industry trained men and women at lightning speed.

If the purpose of educating men and women in a free society were solely to make skilled hands, industry could do it. But, as Immanuel Kant well said, man is an end not just

---

[47] Hutchins, R. M.: *The Higher Learning in America*, 36. Yale University Press: New Haven, 1936.

a means to be used by others.[48] When industry merely trains hands so as to make their labor more profitable, it reduces men to means—animated tools, as ancient philosophers called them. Only by making vocational training an integral part of a free person's education, and by keeping that general education broad, while relating it to the problems of his whole existence, can that person be really made fit for freedom.

At present much vocational training in schools is conceived in terms little if any broader than those industry itself, intent on profit, conceives; and men and women are often employed under conditions that actually reduce them to the status of animated tools. A state director of vocational training once advised a vocational highschool principal as follows:

"This school should be run in the interest of industry. . . . English, history and mathematics do more harm than good. . . . What we want you to do is to teach a boy to stand up to a lathe for nine hours a day for a dollar and a half a day and be satisfied. . . ."[49]

That was many years ago. One might hope that the situation would have been improved before now, but E. A. Burtt said (1944): "No one can contemplate vocational education as it now exists . . . without the most serious misgivings. In the presence of the desperate need for the kind of education calculated to produce men and women who can become intelligent citizens in a democratic world order, vocational education as at present practiced is with rare exceptions a

---

[48] Kant, I.: *Fundamental Principles of the Metaphysic of Morals*, 55. In *Kant's Critique of Practical Reason and Other Works on the Theory of Ethics*. (Trans. by T. K. Abbott) Longmans, Green and Co.: London, 1889.

[49] Quoted in W. H. Kilpatrick's *Source Book in the Philosophy of Education*, 150. Macmillan Company: New York, 1924.

terribly narrowing rather than a broadening and liberalizing study. . . ."[50]

The segregation policy, espoused by Mr. Hutchins and others, is designed to isolate "intellectual" from "vocational" training. Were the proposed "reform" successful, we would have industrial serfs, competent to do their jobs, but nothing else, just as serfs and "animated tools" of all ages have been able to do. Emerson, "intellectual" though he was, an able defender and exemplar of scholarship, saw full well, and was happy to greet the dawn that seemed, even then, to be breaking and shedding its benign light upon those who had labored in darkness. "I hear therefore," he said, "with joy whatever is beginning to be said of the dignity and necessity of labor to every citizen. There is virtue yet in the hoe and the spade, for learned as well as for unlearned hands."[51] Without education, he said elsewhere, "Man is . . . metamorphosed into a thing, into many things. The planter, who is Man sent out into the field to gather food, is seldom cheered by any idea of the true dignity of his ministry."[52]

In many quarters, one hears lamentations: man has become "meaningless" with the advent and progress of science in remaking the world.[53] There is fair room for doubt, however, whether man today may not really have vastly more meaning both for himself and others than he had under medieval feudalism, and under clerical guidance which, for all its wealth of theological insight, reckoned most men servile, left

[50] 2d Conference on the Scientific Spirit and Democratic Faith: *The Authoritarian Attempt to Capture Education*, 119.

[51] Emerson, R. W.: "The American Scholar." *Essays for College Men*, 87. 2d ser. (Ed. by N. Foerster, F. A. Manchester, and K. Young) Henry Holt and Company: New York, 1915.

[52] *Ibid.*, 72.

[53] Hocking, W. E.: *What Man Can Make of Man*, 32. Harper & Brothers: New York, 1942.

them without letters—illiteracy being the rule then, not the exception—not to speak of science. Dante, bright spirit of a New Life then dawning, mourned the lot of the multitude that still hungered for intellectual fare; yet they dwelt in his own Italy in the very shadow of the fountain of medieval teaching that had stood there for a thousand years. One fears that were Mr. Hutchins' "reforms" to become general, his truck driver, sans physics, mathematics, chemistry, and sans history, politics, economics, and everything save what concerns his truck, his self-control, his place in his society, and the "meaning and aim of his existence,"[54] might be little better than a medieval serf, and that the "meaning and aim of his existence" would to him be dim or nonexistent.

The situation of vocational training is clearly bad. Its friends say what many know well—that, as practiced, it is generally very narrow. Its opponents do everything possible to persuade educational institutions to close their doors against it, and not permit vocations, by association with profounder studies, to rise to a higher level of competence and understanding. The assumption of the hostile camp appears to be that all those who perform the ordinary tasks of life, and indeed many of those engaged in relatively difficult and intricate tasks which involve much study and a learning of sorts, are not competent to pursue the true higher learning, metaphysical or theological according to differing dispensations. They should not, therefore, clutter the grounds.

That children of proletarian parents can go far, indeed to the very top of learning's scale, need not be seriously argued before an American audience. They have all seen such cases. The American frontier, advancing science and technology, and the liberal politico-educational philosophy went far

[54] "Education for Freedom." *Chr. Cent.* (Nov. 15, 1944) LXI, 1314-16.

during the past one hundred and fifty years to break the class barriers that once denied opportunity to the forbears of those who came here. The Russian revolution burst barriers there, and brought wide opportunities for an education of which peasant and worker had never dared to dream. Whitehead advocates "one foreign language in all education," for he knows "from direct observation" that it is "possible for artisan children."[55] Who has not observed and experienced the same thing, not only in languages but in other, even more difficult studies?

Whitehead's penetrating mind has also seen another matter of great importance: that the "disuse of hand-craft" contributes to "the brain-lethargy of aristocracies." "Great readers, who exclude other activities," he believes, are not great, original thinkers. In judging the "importance of technical education we must rise above the exclusive association of learning with book-learning. Firsthand knowledge is the ultimate basis of intellectual life."[56] As Dewey put it recently, "A truly liberal, and liberating, education would refuse today to isolate vocational training on any of its levels from a continuous education in the social, moral, and scientific contexts within which wisely administered callings and professions must function."[57]

Considered in the large context of modern life and the actualities of American education today, the observations of Dewey and Whitehead mean that "liberal" educational institutions need to come into closer touch with life's *Tun und Streben* to be fully humanized; and, no less, that the so-called vocational and professional schools, shunning narrowness,

---

[55] *Op. cit.*, 91.
[56] *Ibid.*, 78 f.
[57] Dewey, J.: "Challenge to Liberal Thought." *Fortune* (Aug., 1944) XXX, 155 ff.

must relate their various technologies to the whole world of man. Thus might both, notwithstanding past traditions, which no longer suffice, effect that marriage of "liberal" and "practical" which Cicero believed most serviceable to mankind. Speaking of marriage, a distinguished scholar, Howard Mumford Jones, seems ready to perform the ceremony, suggesting that American colleges consider, as a first point in a six-point program, the provision of "professional or vocational training for all."[58]

Lastly, not because it is least important, but because it is the crown, we turn to politics, the major integrating agent in an education fit for free men and designed to fit them to maintain that freedom. It has been called the free man's highest vocation. He learns some calling or profession whereby he earns a living. Politics he learns in order that he may live the good life. Under theocratic rule, theology is the queen of sciences. In a secular state, politics is queen. Aristotle rightly regarded politics as the master art, for it regulates all others. It has always been part of the education of a ruling class. It should be axiomatic that under a "government of the people, by the people, and for the people," politics, far from being the art of a few, should be the possession of all.

Looking back to the founding of the Republic, it is evident that the need of political education, in conformity with the principles of the new government, was not unrecognized. Political leaders and publicists—Jefferson, Washington, Benjamin Rush, Noah Webster, James Sullivan, Nathaniel Chipman, and others—spoke to the point. Education in "political arithmetick" was thought equal in importance to the Revolu-

[58] Jones, H. M.: *Education and World Tragedy*, 91. Harvard University Press: Cambridge, 1946.

tion itself. Webster regretted that whereas the Constitution is republican, education is monarchical. Rush wanted men to be made "republican machines"—which sounds ominous— and to understand that "government, like all other sciences, is of a progressive nature." A detached, skeptical attitude should characterize education; the study of the "ancient re- publics" and the "progress of liberty and tyranny" in Europe, he thought, would help to develop it.[59]

Though political thinkers saw the need of an altered educa- tion, few teachers or schools were competently prepared to produce it on demand. As is so often the case, men called upon education, as though it were a magic wand, to effect some change, but failed to provide direction and means whereby institutions might realize the proposed ends. Politi- cal philosophy was then far ahead of educational practice. As for educational philosophy it was an unknown field, and only fragmentary gains were made in the next hundred years. Without the light of a clear philosophy to guide it, education floundered; but the conditions being relatively easy in the nineteenth century, America muddled through. Having grown up much like Topsy, she senses today, rather belatedly, that an education which was called liberal and disciplinary has neither disciplined minds generally, nor freed them in any acceptable degree; nor has it produced those "republican machines" asked for (though it has others), or reared the staunch political thinkers which the founders ardently de- sired.

Has there then been nothing done to prepare American youth for their political vocation as free men and women? There has been some teaching of civics, history of many

59 Woody, T.: "Retardation in 'Political Arithmetick.' " *Sch. and Soc.* (May 16, 23, 1936) XLIII, 657-63, 693-98.

kinds, geography, economics, political science; in fact, the past two generations, particularly, have seen a vast proliferation of courses in various social sciences. But politics is a practical art—political knowledge joined with action. Have these numerous branches been integrated and reasonably wedded to political action? To some degree, certainly. Yet it is obvious that among a large part of the adult body-politic and the younger generation about to be citizens, politics—political thought in action—is an unknown art. How else explain that somewhat less that 55 per cent of eligibles voted at the national election (1944), and other opportunities for suffrage arouse even less response?

But failure to vote is only one of many evidences of neglect by free men of their highest vocation. From many competent sources come reports of apathy and lack of knowledge in regard to political matters in the armed forces. Stowe relates the judgment of a Scotch captain who was profoundly impressed by the technical knowledge of American men, but found them without *"appreciation of the outside world.* It seems they haven't been educated to make any real effort to understand other people. . . . How are we going to be able to work together after the war?"[60] Was the Britisher pulling our leg? Ask an American "political expert" in the European theater who observed to Mark Van Doren, "Do you know . . . we as a people have never really *thought* about politics. . . ."[61] Owen Lattimore, in his penetrating book, *Solution in Asia,*[62] expressed the judgment that the American army is politically the least literate of all armies in the world. Drew Middleton

[60] Stowe, L.: *While Time Remains*, 291. Alfred A. Knopf: New York, 1947.

[61] "Education and Understanding the Soviet Union." Bulletin of the Committee on Education, National Council of American-Soviet Friendship (Sept.-Oct., 1945), 12.

[62] *Op. cit.*, 82. Little, Brown and Company: Boston, 1945.

found in American soldiers on the African front a shocking indifference and lack of knowledge about ideas and issues pertaining to the war in which they were engaged.[63]

The volume of like judgments is overwhelming. Anyone who takes the trouble to talk with returned soldiers can corroborate the above views, and more. Knowledge and interest were commonly reported as vastly superior in the British forces and in the Red Army. One seeks in vain for consolation in the fact that these are only observations about a few million young men in the armed forces. They were, presumably, a tolerably fair sampling. Confronted with this marked tendency to prefer amusement—comics, sports, and other trivialities—to serious dealing with the most important issues of the day, one may well wonder what proportion of the blame lies on the men and their education (cut short, of course, in many cases), and what on the military authorities and their educational efforts.

There may have been ignorance of politics, but there appears to have been no significant lack of morale on the fighting fronts. Hope kept hopes high in wartime, it is said; but peace requires a morale, courage, and other qualities, which it seems unlikely that amusement can supply, even were it provided as *freely* as it was under the emotional stimuli of war. Many men have conquered large sectors of the world's peoples, yet have been unable to govern them, for lack of the master art—the science of politics. An unlettered Chinese once boasted, "I have conquered the Empire on a horse; what need have I of your Classics?" To which, the Scholar answered, "Sir, you conquered it on horseback, but can you rule it there?" To this query, the rejoinder of the military

<hr />

[63] "What Sort of World Do Our Soldiers Want?" *N. Y. Times Mag.*, May 2, 1943, p. 3.

mind, so bewitched with the efficacy of speed and power, seems to be, "No, of course, not on *this* horse; but give me a bigger and swifter one and I can do it." Beyond a certain point the persistence of myth in the minds of such men endangers the happiness of all. Only in fairyland does one ever have the unilateral fortune to fall into possession of a Little Magic Horse which outruns all others.

As there is no reason to hope for a Little Magic Horse, is there anything more practical to do? The most practical step is to set about rectifying past failures on the political sector of liberal education, so that free youth may be fully prepared to know their rights and perform their duties as free men and women. This is obviously a major task, though scarcely greater than the redirection of thinking and acting, already indicated as necessary in several other phases of liberal education. As in them, here, too, it is desirable to sketch a line of thinking, rather than offer a blueprint of details; for the latter would be useless, and would only add confusion, unless it be possible to come to some understanding as to the general course that should be pursued.

Power has set the stage, but it is no political philosopher; what should be the scope of education that will fit men to play upon it? The interrelation of education and the growth of government on various levels has been outlined elsewhere.[64] In contrast to the little that was done yesterday, which was almost wholly domestic in orientation, today's specifications—laid down by technological advancement, two world wars, and the subsequent efforts to fashion some instrument for rational handling of world affairs—call for political understanding of global dimensions. Willkie put the matter

[64] Woody, T.: "World Integration and Education." *Pol. Sc. Quarterly* (Sept., 1945) LX, 385-411.

well: "There are no distant points in the world any longer. Our thinking in the future must be world wide."

As for extent of time, the political phase of a liberal education needs, like others, to be kept in mind in the elementary school. At that age children's minds are still open to the vision of a larger world than their families have known, or understood, even though they live in it, and have in many cases unconsciously paid toll in blood and tears toward its construction. And habits may then readily be formed compatible therewith. If the fairest moments be not utilized, equal or greater efforts, begun later when children don the dress of adolescence and become absorbed in a host of new preoccupations, may well fail of success. Contrariwise, if the early years are well employed, the education of adolescence and maturity will be a natural continuing process.

If education is to help build a world-order—or even deal competently with domestic issues—it cannot stay with children and adolescents. They alone cannot save the day. A schoolmate cartoonist once depicted a homunculus creeping abashed among the towering stacks of a library, muttering to himself: "How far behind I am in my reading." All adults are so, not just the youngsters who go to college! Beyond the age of formal schooling and assumption of the actual title of citizen, adults will in the future require a constant opportunity and encouragement to keep themselves alert, informed about, and active in matters political. A few efforts have already been made, some of years' standing, to divert a part of adult leisure time to the serious study of the kaleidoscopic political scene, but the scope of forums, study classes, and round tables, is still infinitely small in comparison with what the day demands.

Certain basic conditions handicap the successful functioning of political education for free men and women. Chief among these is the restriction of freedom of teaching and learning which two successful wars, a growing nationalistic fervor, and kindred forces have encouraged. This evil is not irremediable; but its rectification will require sharp attention and energetic application to the task. That freedom of the teacher, as a teacher and as a citizen, is indispensable seems beyond dispute. It is obviously impossible to educate men and women for political freedom, unless freedom of mind be accepted and maintained, *i.e.*, actually provided and defended, as a fundamental condition under which it takes place. Americans commonly accept the condition, in theory; but the breaches of it are startling, of dangerous proportions, and increasing.[65] The most poisonous of all propositions heard today, accepted even by some teachers, is that the preservation of freedom requires the sacrifice of it, that is, so far as their opponents are concerned.

A second handicap lies in the shortage of adequately prepared teachers. The provision of properly qualified teachers carries with it, of course, something that applies equally to all other phases of liberal education: the necessity of pay commensurable with the demands that their life makes upon them, so that the teaching corps may draw from the common reservoir its fair share of high grade natural ability. The

[65] Beale, H. K.: *Are American Teachers Free?* Charles Scribner's Sons: New York, 1936; *cf.* file of the *Bulletin, American Association of University Professors* from its founding to date for carefully documented story of encroachments on the college and university level; *The Gag on Teaching*. Sec. Rev. Ed., 1937. American Civil Liberties Union: New York, 1937; *In Times of Challenge*. American Civil Liberties Union: New York, 1947; *Educational Freedom*. Report to the Commission on Educational Freedom of the Progressive Education Association, New York, n.d.; Woody, T.: "Controversial Subjects: Freedom in Study and Teaching." *Educ. Outlook* (Mar., 1927) I, 102-14; "Retardation in 'Political Arithmetick.'" *Sch. and Soc.*, XLIII, 657-63, 693-98; Stewart, G. R., *et al.*: *Year of the Oath*. Doubleday: New York, 1950.

chosen talent will need an education, broader, profounder, and better integrated than heretofore. Isolated, disparate courses in social sciences will not suffice. So taught, they would be inclined so to teach in most cases. Rather it is necessary that a wide range of particular studies be coördinated and made to focus on the problems of political education.

A query is sometimes raised as to whether ordinary citizens are qualified by natural endowment for the task of self-government. The negative view gained, as the experts in the measurement of intelligence showed the wide spread of ability and its distribution, ranging from genius (above 1.40), 0.25 per cent of the children studied; very superior (1.20-1.40), 6.75 per cent; superior (1.10-1.20), 13.00 per cent; average (.90-1.10), 60.00 per cent; dull (.80-.90), 13.00 per cent; borderline (.70-.80), about 6.00 per cent; and so on down to idiots, not quite as numerous as geniuses. The figures, though variable, "highly" tentative, and even "in some respects misleading," as the authors say,[66] may be taken as an indication of the spread of talent. But do they mean that those of average intelligence cannot play their part in self-government; or even those a little dull by intellectual standards? Is it not something other than lack of intelligence that defeats

[66] Warren, H. C., and Carmichael, L.: *Elements of Human Psychology,* 352 f. Houghton Mifflin Company: Boston, 1930. Moreover, certain studies of the relation between environment and intelligence give ground for a degree of optimism in democracy's household. A "roving I. Q." has supplanted the notion of unalterable fixity. "Superior environments" produce "significant increments of I. Q.," says Barbara S. Burks, commenting on the studies made at Chicago and Stanford. And the earlier the age at which children are placed in better environments, the greater the gains that may be expected.—Frank N. Freeman, *et al.* "The Influence of Environment on the Intelligence, School Achievement, and Conduct of Foster Children." *Twenty-Seventh Yearbook of the National Society for the Study of Education,* Pt. I, 209, 318, *passim; cf.* Beth L. Wellman, "Mental Growth from Preschool to College." *Journal of Experimental Education* (Dec., 1937) VI, 127-38.

self-government? How is interest in it fostered? How is it directed?

Most people know, even dull ones, when a shoe pinches. Politics deals, and should deal, with the pinches. Political knowledge and its correlated action need not be an abstract, technical study. Keep in mind that wise distinction—here as in other phases of a liberal education—between technical proficiency of a science and an "educational acquaintance" with it. Ordinary intelligence, just average horse sense, can function in self-government, if it be shown the relationship of politics to economic problems that are of immediate personal concern; if it be directed to, and instructed in, these and other problems that really matter and which affect vitally the interests of men and women; and if it be correlated with a study of, and participation in, action to secure satisfactory remedies. It is only the strict, technical aspects of politics that lie beyond the grasp of lower levels of intelligence. For those areas, indeed, we need talent of the first water. We should see to it that it is most expertly trained, wherever it may be found, and that men and women who have it be put into all the offices that require it.

Avoiding detail, it may yet be possible to indicate certain essential phases of study and activity that should mark the political education of free youth and future citizens. The interrelation between force and politics should emerge from the study of past and present situations. A clear understanding should be sought of the interrelation of politics and economics. Being heir to a system of self-government, citizens should know well the history of the struggle by which it emerged out of past systems of unfree government, its subsequent development, failures, successes, and present dangers.

This phase of political history might well be part of a comparative study, using selected instances—say, the progress of Roman self-government and its demise under one-man rule; the vicissitudes of democratic rule in Athens; and various authoritarian governments, ecclesiastical and political. The practical operation of American government, local, national, and international, should be emphasized; and attention should be given to frequent observation, contact with, and reporting on, the actual functioning and non-functioning of city, county, and state agencies. Besides study of the history and present status of free government, in conjunction with the various forms and degrees of its negations, the techniques of self-government should be learned by practice, not left simply to books and observation. It is of little value, in this connection to learn ideas alone; there must be a marriage of thought and action. Every school is a potential laboratory of self-government, but little used. If children and youth do not grow up in the actual process of governing themselves, do not form the habits compatible therewith, can one be surprised if nearly half of them do not even vote in major elections, or otherwise take part in government, when they become citizens and have a host of other duties to perform?

In classrooms during the school age, and in public forums and study groups of many kinds, thereafter, there should be an ever-continuing opportunity and encouragement to take part in full and free examination and discussion of social, economic, and political problems—that is, those that really matter, those that are controversial. Political education, in any realistic sense, is impossible, if such discussions are taboo, as they so commonly are. These are, indeed, the very matters that make political education necessary; and they make it interesting. Without them, political study is bookish, dead. Among such controversial areas of the moment are race relations;[67] the conflicts of capital and labor and its social effects; war as an institution, its causes, costs, consequences, and the possible alternatives;[68] freedom of press, radio, screen, and the whole process of the manipulation of news and the manufacture of "public opinion"; tensional relations between states, the actual and alleged reasons for them, and what should be done to reduce them. If these and similar issues were thoroughly faced in a real program of adult political education throughout the country, there might soon emerge some understanding on the part of parents and other citizens as to the necessity of their being a part of their children's education.

As the study of controversial matters is, and always will be, a necessary part of realistic political education—since they are perennial—a word may be said of certain general principles to be kept in mind as a general guide in the process of learning to think about and deal with them. The essentials are simple; they apply to thinking in any area, if one desires to get at truth. Man inclines readily to belief; he needs to learn the value of doubt, and develop the habit of it, not as an end, but as a means to the ascertainment of truth. The first thing one reads or hears, and that which is most commonly accepted, may well be untrue. Children should learn before it is too late that they must compare widely differing sources, examine divergent accounts of the same event. Such comparison will itself be one of the best stimuli to sharpen

67 Consult C. S. Johnson, *Into the Main Stream*, for a valuable treatment of practices in race relations in the South. University of North Carolina Press: Chapel Hill, 1947.

68 Woody, T.: "War and Education." *Bulletin, American Association of University Professors.* (Winter, 1945) XXXI, 587-605.

desire to find out what is really true, or what has the greatest probability. Let them, likewise, learn to look for motives back of statements; the need for discovering any bent or influence that may have distorted reporting; and the relation of editorial bias to the choice of news published. All of this involves, of necessity, the development of an understanding that conclusions must be reached slowly, and should be tentative in nature, open to modification on discovery of fresh information or more reliable sources. Were this done, the hysteria so common today could be reduced to small dimensions. And in thinking and its expression, let every youth learn the import of readiness to hear his or her opponents, and indeed, the necessity of being willing to defend their right to speak; and, very important today, their title to the use of places of assembly and agencies of communication. For if denied these, one is like a voice in the desert, though he dwell among multitudes. Beyond this, it is necessary to seize every opportunity for joining thinking and acting. In politics, thinking without action is sterile; action, without thinking, is a crime against one's self and against one's neighbor.

INDEX

A

Abelard, 133
Academies, 166
Academy (Athens), 33
Accius, 172
Ad Herennium, 160
Ad Uxorem, 92
Adam of Bremen, 141
Adams, John, 215
Adamson, J. W., 126
Adelard of Bath, 141
A.E. (George William Russell), 239, 240
Aemilius Paulus, 68, 74, 85
Aeneas Sylvius, 147, 173, 175, 181
Aeschines, 24, 30
Aeschylus, 29
Aesop, 29, 179, 189
Aesthetics: Aristotle on, 53-54; in Athenian education, 21-22; in Chinese education, 9, 13-14; Christian view of, 107-9; music, 256; neglect of, in U. S., 255; in Plato's educational plan, 42, 43; in present liberal education, 240, 254-56; at the Renaissance, 137-39; in Roman life and education, 64, 68, 86-87
Aetius, 91
Africa, 135
Agricola, 183, 185
Agriculture: Chinese, 5-6; a liberal pursuit, 24, 25, 26, 62-63, 225, 257, 261; in Middle Ages, 128-29; present, and liberal education, 262; Roman, 60, 62-63, 65, 66
Agrippa, 85
Agrippa, humanist, 171
Alaric, 88, 92
Alberti, 139, 167, 170, 173

Albertus Magnus, 142
Alcibiades, 29
Alcman, 29
Alcuin, 115, 117, 123, 125
Aldhelm, 117
Alfred, 124, 125, 130, 132, 156
Alypius, 99
Ambrose, 171
American education: early, 1; institutions of, 165, 201, 202, 203, 208, 211, 213-14, 231, 242
American Youth Commission, 234
Ammon, King of Egypt, 243
Analects, the, 10
Andronicus, 71, 81
Anglo-Saxon Chronicle (Bede), 156
Apollonius of Rhodes, 74
Apostolic Constitutions, 99, 104
Apprenticeship, training, 27 (*see also* Vocations)
Aquinas, 110, 150, 151
Archery: Ascham on, 157, 174, 175; in Chinese liberal education, 9, 10-13, 16
Architecture: favored by Augustine, 108; a liberal art, 75, 116; and "New Life," 139
Aristides, 28
Aristides Quintilianus, 116
Aristophanes, 24, 25, 237
Aristotle, 19, 22, 25, 26, 30, 46, 47, 48, 49, 52, 53, 54, 55, 56, 57, 58, 83, 103, 111, 118, 134, 140, 158, 161, 169, 172, 182, 184, 188, 193, 195, 196, 222, 225, 226, 227, 229, 230, 237, 248, 255, 256, 257, 261
Concerning agriculture, 26, 53; body-soul relation, 51; categories of thinking, 56; cathar-

279

and mortification of the flesh, 95-98; and the Olympic Games, 99; and other-worldliness, 93-111; and pagan arts, 107-8; and letters, 100-107, 114-122; and philosophy, 100, 101-3, 125-26; and physical culture, 94-99, 127; and spectacles, 95, 97, 99; and sports, 97

Chronicon (Cassiodorus), 120

Chrysoloras, 185, 187

Chrysostom, 102, 171, 183

Church: and authoritarian education, 102-7; and the secular order, 109-111; and state, conflict of, since the Renaissance, 149-53; worldly tendency in the, 93, 110

Cicero, 2, 33, 34, 57, 60, 62, 63, 64, 66, 67, 69, 70, 73, 74, 75, 77, 79, 82, 83, 84, 85, 87, 89, 103, 116, 117, 118, 134, 160, 172, 184, 187, 188, 189, 191, 192, 197, 208, 242, 248, 249, 253, 255, 257, 261, 262, 267

    Concerning cosmopolitanism and the Empire, 85; education of an orator, 74-78; Greek culture, 73; leisure, 73; liberal arts, 75; medical profession, 2; five parts of oratory, 76; philosophy, 75, 77-78, 79; philosophy at Athens, 34; physical training, 85, 87; practical end of oratory, 76-78; Roman destiny, 60; science of anything, 249; Stoic virtues, 83; vocations and business, 73; writing and speaking, 76

Ciceronianism, 191-92, 253; parallel of, in China, 17

Cinema, in America, 241

Circus, 98-99

Cities: and modern social problems, 238-39; and the "New Life," 144-149

Citizenship, and liberal education: in Aristotle, 50-56; Athenian, 23, 24, 25, 26, 29-30, 32-33; in Plato's *Republic*, 42-46; in the Renaissance, 162, 163, 164, 172, 175, 176; in Rome, 65-87, 88; today, 228-29, 267-278

City of God, 96

City-state, and Community of Saints, 109

Classes, social: and ancient education, 257-58; Chinese, 6; and Renaissance education, 171, 175, 223

Classical revival, 132-62; and liberal education, 162-92

Classics: in Chinese education, 9-10, 17; Greek and Latin, in Western schools, 184-89, 194, 196, 197, 198, 202, 205, 206, 207, 209, 213, 221, 246; warfare of, and science, 247-48

Classlessness, and mass education, 258-259, 265-78

Claudius Pulcher, 71

Clement of Alexandria, 94, 98, 100, 101, 107, 127

Collège de Guyenne, Bordeaux, 189

Columbanus, 128

Columella, 129

Comenius, 168

Commedia (Dante), 136, 154, 244

Commentari (Ghiberti), 139

Commentaries (Caesar), 189

Commentary on Isaac (Albertus Magnus), 142

Commentary on the Psalms (Cassiodorus), 120

Commercial growth: and present change, 223; and "New Life," 144-148, 149

Commercialism, in sports, 236-38

Committee on Classical Studies, 221

Committee of Ten on Secondary School Studies, Report of, 208, 209, 210, 213

Commonitorium, 92

Communications, arts of: foreign languages and, 244-47; free use of, 241-242; letters, 240-47; and liberal education today, 233, 240-56

Comparetti, D., 159

Conferences (Cassian), 119

Confucianism, 6-18; central place of knowledge in, 8; in Chinese schools, 7; and liberal education, 7-18; reinterpreted, 18; and social order, 7; unprogressive, 7